Southern Celebrations

A Cookbook From The Heart Of A Caterer's Kitchen

Kathleen Howard Rambo

Illustrations
Anne Mullins Rigdon

Cover
Laurie Smith
Kaye Cagle

Photograph
William R. Davis

Wine Suggestions
Frank Ryan

Foreword
Sandra Stephens

Editing
Martha Collins
Scott Penley

Published by
Southern Celebrations
Marietta, Georgia

Southern Celebrations
Published by Southern Celebrations, Marietta, Georgia
Kathleen Howard Rambo

Additional copies can be ordered by sending $27.95 plus $3.50 shipping and handling.
Georgia residents add $1.68 sales tax.
Send order with shipping address to: Southern Celebrations, 3600 Dallas Highway,
Suite 230-115, Marietta, Georgia 30064

Cover Design, Laurie Smith, Copyright © 1998
Cover Photograph, William R. Davis, Copyright © 1998

Illustrations, Anne Mullins Rigdon, Copyright © 1998

ISBN Number
0-9665510-0-1

Library of Congress Catalog Card Number
98-90346

Manufactured in the United States of America
Southern Celebrations

Printed in the United States of America
TOOF COOKBOOK DIVISION

Starr ★ Toof
670 South Cooper Street
Memphis, TN 38104

10 9 8 7 6 5 4 3 2 1

DEDICATIONS

A Celebration of Heritage

It is the method of preparing, cooking and presenting foods that bring about many traditions in our families. Without the teacher in the kitchen, these traditions will be lost forever. My mother was my teacher in her kitchen, and I owe her, in return, to be a teacher in my own kitchen. I owe it to my children to teach them methods of preparing, cooking and presenting foods that have been handed down to me.

That teaching should include not only how to prepare a meal, but how to serve it. Children should be taught about different serving utensils and their purposes. They should know what size plate is appropriate for different foods or courses. We also should pass to our children such timeless traditions as how to steep hot water in a silver service before adding the coffee or how to drain peas of their juices before serving. These things should come naturally to our sons and daughters and shouldn't have to be taught to them by books, as they already will have learned by example.

We are failing our children by not continuing a practice of our ancestors, the traditions of a Southern table such as families working together to plant, harvest, prepare, serve or preserve foods, the tradition of gathering in fellowship to enjoy at table the foods of this harvest and to continue traditions set by the elders in the family.

Heritage is so very important to hold on to in today's world. Traditions will only carry memories of yesterday and create memories of tomorrow for you and your family. Aromas from a kitchen can take a person back to early childhood. Methods of preparing food can bring you closer to the teaching hands of your past. The time, work and love given to presentation of food and table will be appreciated by your family and friends. Your own gratification will be in watching your children's children use the same treasures you once used, and practice the recipes you once prepared, and following the traditions you worked hard to preserve.

Dedicated to my family and my girls

Margaret Nanette,
Frances Marie and
Meredith Louise

FOREWORD

We were having a party to celebrate moving into our new house, and Kathleen had been recommended to cater. She was young and had spent most of her short life as a ballet dancer.

On the day we met to discuss the menu, she floated into our house with feet splayed outward as if in position to rise up on her toes for a pirouette. With pen poised over notebook, she asked, "What colors do you like?" Uh oh. Visions of disaster for my grandiose plans to entertain spurred me to blurt, "Food. We need stuff for people to eat."

"We'll get to that in a minute," she said. "Food is only one part of entertaining." Painstakingly, she grilled me on my preferences for table settings, flowers, and the mood I wanted to create. Finally, we planned a menu.

On the night of the party, she arrived with food and helpers. I said a quick prayer, "She's so young. Please help her pull it off." I soon wondered why I had ever doubted her. Food trays were garnished with fresh flowers tied with ribbons in my favorite colors. The food was fun, different and wonderful. Guests called afterward for her telephone number.

She became the favorite caterer in our area. Having two babies didn't slow her down, but when her third daughter arrived, she retired. I ran into her one day in the grocery store with two children in her cart and a third holding onto her leg.

"I'm writing a cookbook," she told me. I smiled, but thought to myself there was no way she could do that with little ones running around. I should have known better.

When she called to say she had finished the cookbook, I was stunned. She sent me sample pages. As I read them, I noted the subtle blending of the old Southern tradition of gracious entertaining with the new ways of the contemporary South.

Kathleen would have been described by an earlier generation as having been "raised right," but she has the attributes needed by a young woman in today's world --- creativity, focus and determination. Most importantly, she perceives entertaining as more than food and flowers. For Kathleen, entertaining family and friends is the giving of oneself and the sharing of talents.

She has been a dancer and a caterer. Now she's a wife, a mother and a writer. Of course, I always knew she could do anything.

Sandra Stephens
Newspaper Columnist

CONTENTS

Beginning

A Toast to Southern Celebrations 23

A Celebration of Heritage 47

New Seasons of Celebrations 63

Celebrating The Morning Harvest 99

A Garden of Celebrations 117

Hearty Celebrations 137

Sweet Celebrations 189

Index

A Sprinkle of Love
from the Author's Kitchen

Southern families tend to be close-knit and include a large, multigenerational, extended family. By living in the same community as many relatives, I have benefitted much from having the opportunity to know and love many members of mine and my husband's families. From these relatives, I have learned important traditions, and have created new memories to cherish. They have also handed down to me their secrets for successful cooking and entertaining. My great aunt, Margaret Carpenter, became one of the first businesswomen in Cobb County, but still found time to warmly entertain family and friends. She has passed on to me her multiple cooking and entertaining skills. She often tells me stories of her own mother who insisted on having her plate filled with beautiful colors, or of her grandmother who kept pound cakes in the sideboard drawer in her dining room. My favorite stories are of my great great grandmother's lunches she served lavishly from her Roswell home and son's dentist office to patients or to neighbors who gathered to hear a baseball game on the radio. Her feasts would include lunches of two or three meats and countless side dishes, fresh from the garden, and of course, fresh-baked breads.

My mother's mother was born in White County, Georgia, and as a girl, helped her single mother serve breakfast and lunch in their small home on Marble Mill Road in Marietta to the Georgia Marble workers who worked nearby. She had to stand on a box, being only 7 or 8, to make biscuits for the meals. An extraordinary baker of lemon cakes, whole wheat breads, buttermilk pancakes and biscuits herself, she surely gave me my love of baking. She also passed along to me her love of art, flower arranging and gardens. Another gardener, my paternal grandmother, was originally from Texas. She later moved to Atlanta and then to Bells Ferry Road in Cobb County. She gave me a love of fresh-picked berries for cobblers, apple cakes and vegetable gardens. The reputation of my husband's grandmother, as a wonderful cook and inspiring gardener survives her and is reflected in her grandchildren. She gave a love of gardening to my husband, who, in turn, shares it with me through his career as a nurseryman. Although many have touched my life, the time spent with my mother as a little girl in her kitchen and gardens gave me the foundation needed to pursue all my dreams. As I speak of the ones I love and about the homes, kitchens, and gardens they have graciously shared with me, I hope to one day be remembered in such a wonderful way.

My love for cooking and my gift of expressing myself through the presentation of food and tables lead me to send out letters to family and friends to anounce the opening of my catering business. I felt I had a natural ability to pull a meal, along with tables, flowers and serving arrangements, together at the last minute. This, of course, was a great talent to have in a catering business. My love for art helped me focus my abilities on making tables pleasing to the eye. My clients seem to enjoy this special touch.

I catered for 10 years. My business grew by word of mouth. My staff consisted of contract servers and kitchen help during the parties, so my business was able to stay very personal. Since I was often catering in a close community for some of the same wedding parties and repeat clients, my recipes and menus were ever-changing. I found the inspiration to create different menus and recipes. When catering started affecting my time with my family, I started accepting fewer parties and began writing a cookbook. As I tested, revised and improved my recipes and began forming my book, I realized that so many people have forgotten the fundamentals of entertaining. Recipes, although important, will not get a hostess through a party. It was very important to me to teach and inspire beautiful presentation of food to my readers. The side-bars in the book make it easier for me to explain my trade secrets, serving tips and entertaining ideas. Cooking tasty, beautiful dishes is just part of being a good Southern hostess. A message I wanted to convey is that entertaining is not just about food. It is a combination of food mixed with your heritage, traditions, community, family and friends. It is the giving of yourself and of your time.

A melding of past traditions with modern conveniences creates our cuisine of today. However, in this day of fast food restaurants and frozen dinners, it is easy to forget the grace and skill with which our Southern ancestors prepared each meal. It's up to us, now, to preserve the traditions of the past and hand down the lessons learned from our grandmothers to our children. Recipes have been passed from generation to generation for years, and methods of cooking and entertaining have been passed from family to family, heart to heart, home to home, kitchen to kitchen, parent to child, continuing these traditions. Teaching these important skills should be a part of every family and household.

A Celebration of
Southern Entertaining

Anne Mullins Rigdon

A TASTE OF THE SOUTH

Generous Helpings from the American South

The American South projects the pride and respect Southerners feel about their heritage. In most Southern cities, you will experience the taste of tradition in the city's communities, homes, families, hearts, gardens and kitchens. Southern food is the fuel of Southern hospitality. Just as each hostess portrays her individual heritage, she represents her Southern community as well. The South's history and its vast differences in geography, climate and terrain bring many diverse tastes to the South and to a Southerner's table. Early settlers throughout the South brought different tastes to each region. For instance, Florida cuisine and culture reflect the influence of the Spanish explorers in Florida from as early as 1560. Louisiana and Mississippi food and communities show the influence of French settlers as later interpreted by African Americans. The English, vested with land charters, dominated the early history of the Atlantic Coastal regions from Virginia south to my home state of Georgia, and that early history contributes to the modern dining habits of natives of that region.

A Southerner's table will portray the history, geography, climate and terrain of the cook's native region. The recipes and methods of cooking vary between regions and households. Types of baking, family recipes and traditions of each family are passed from generation to generation. In looking at the table fare of the South, you can see its earliest settlers' influence on each state and region. We have wonderful Florida paellas and seafoods originating from that state's Spanish settlers. Louisiana and Mississippi bring us the Creole style with étoufee, jambalayas, gourmet sauces, crawfish, and bourbon pies, all influenced by French and African settlers. Virginia offers up such mouth-watering dishes as shellfish, turkey with cornbread dressing, country ham and apple pies. South Carolina shares with us its Lowcounty style she crab soups, paté, high teas, mint juleps, cheese grits and shrimp boils. North Carolina offers fried okra, black-eyed peas and crab cakes. Alabama favorites include sweet potatoes, beaten biscuits, butter beans and fried chicken. Tennessee takes us home with ribs, barbecue, baked beans and pickles. Georgia puts to table Brunswick stews, corns, chicken and dumplings, peach cobblers and pecan pies. How I love the food of the South!

A Dash of Georgia History

My home state of Georgia is the oldest of the Southern states. It was named for King George II of England. Flat coastal plains extend along the Atlantic Ocean, swamps in south Georgia transition to dense pine forest and low rolling hills in the middle portion of the state, ending in the mountains and lakes of the Blue Ridge Mountains in north Georgia, all of which make Georgia a land of opportunity and possibilities.

In 1732, King George II granted a charter to James Oglethorpe to establish a colony in Georgia. Oglethorpe landed in the coastal city of Savannah in 1733. The city prospered, however, not as Oglethorpe had planned. His visions of an utopia with no slavery and no drunkenness were not fully realized. Even though the city was different than Oglethorpe originally dreamed, Savannah prospered and became a center of export to Europe and the foundation for the beautiful state of Georgia.

The Declaration of Independence was signed by representatives of the 13 original colonies, including Georgia's representatives, in 1775. In 1788, Georgia became the fourth of the 13 original colonies. Georgia seceded from the

Union in 1861 near the beginning of the Civil War. Many native Georgians draw their sense of community and continuity, from this long heritage.

But Georgia is also very much a part of the New South. Modern-time Georgia is best remembered by the world as the host of the Centennial Olympic Games in the state capital, Atlanta. Georgia is also home to such American classics as Coca Cola, Georgia peaches, Vidalia onions, pecans and peanuts. It is the home of America's team, the Atlanta Braves, as well as other major league sports franchises such as the Hawks, Falcons and Thrashers. One of Georgia's most favored native sons is Jimmy Carter, 39th President of the United States. If you are not a Georgian, I hope this book will inspire you to take a little bit of Georgia into your home. Each recipe in the pages that follow is served with a little piece of my community, home, heritage, family, heart, garden and kitchen.

CELEBRATE ENTERTAINING!

Preparations

Remember that entertaining cannot be done effortlessly. An invitation only should be issued when you are able to fulfill it graciously. Getting your home, gardens, guest lists, invitations, and menu together takes time. Shopping, cleaning, cooking, and preparing tables, linens, decorations and flowers is a considerable task, and needs an energetic and gracious host to put it all together. I enjoy entertaining in my home because it gives me a deadline to finish the projects I've needed to get done and gives me time with friends. However, the world doesn't stop revolving just because you will be entertaining. If you anticipate major distractions in advance, you will be pleasantly surprised if they fail to materialize, or you will be prepared to handle them better if they do occur because you have anticipated them. Though entertaining requires work and preparation, it's important to try and have fun with it, too. After expending the time, energy and money to stage a perfect event, remember to enjoy it! Though I'm sure we have all at some point wanted to shut ourselves in a closet as soon as guests arrive, it isn't a recipe for a successful party. Your guests will reflect your mood. If you are enjoying yourself, so will they. If you remain calm and keep your sense of humor during mishaps, so will they. To help you through, I am offering these helpful hints and wish you a wonderful party.

Preparing Your Home and Garden

Be creative when looking at your home, but also be realistic. It's not practical to remodel everything. You are, however, putting on a production, whether large or small. Here is your excuse to overdo it a little. First and foremost, try to decide if you are able to do this all yourself. Be realistic about other demands you will have on your time. Use the help of family and other hostesses when available. If your budget allows, use outside help for cleaning and home preparation. Be sure to contact outside help early to guarantee their availability. It's not a bad idea, even if using your regular help, to have back-up contacts should your scheduled help cancel or fail to show.

Lighting is an important consideration. Always turn on all lamps in your home when entertaining. Be sure outdoor lighting is sufficient and walkways or pathways to cars and home are safely marked. Tiki torches, placed appropriately in planters or hooked to fences, can be a tremendous help with both lighting and repelling bugs. The use of indoor and outdoor candlelight adds a festive touch. Candlelight is proper any time after 1 p.m.

You will need to plan for proper seating arrangements when entertaining. I have found seating concerns to be a source of worry for many of my catering clients. While you can't add or extend rooms in your house for a party, through creative use of the rooms you do have, you can address many seating obstacles. For instance, do not be inhibited from using rooms for other than their customary purpose. A closet becomes a bar area by simply placing a small table across it's opening. What a wonderful way to hide ugly bar items! A study or bedroom can be used for dining by simply placing a table, preferably round, in the room and covering it with fabric and a quilt or fabric topper that coordinates with the room. Add candlelight and flowers or other table arrangement to finish the look. As a great start to four to eight more places to sit your guests, use the wing back chair or stool in the room as seating. How creative and quaint your guests will think you are, not desperate for a bigger home as you might feel. Additionally, each table should seat at least four guests to keep from splitting up a couple or causing awkward seating arrangements.

Outdoor space is ideal for entertaining in good weather. However, outdoor space can vanish with one big rain cloud so always have a rain plan. A garage or basement can be made to look festive with just a little imagination. If the budget for any event permits, tents can be reserved or rented. Tent companies can offer sides, heaters and lighting for their tents to really impress your guests, as well as adding to their comfort. When entertaining outside, wind can be a big obstacle. To avoid the problems a brisk breeze can bring, make sure candlelight is covered with globes, flowers or other arrangements are weighted and tablecloths are pinned to tables (I recommend corsage pins or double-stick tape). Plastic can be purchased at hardware stores and used over tables to protect linens from dampness and falling tree debris until guests arrive. Tiki torches and candles can be set up days ahead and covered with a small plastic or sealable zip bag. Rubber band bags in place. Also, if bugs are a problem, you may want to use foggers, repellents or citronella.

The rules of thumb to remember when seating guests vary for different types of events. For formal dinner parties, everyone needs a seat at a table. For buffet dinner parties, it's preferable for everyone to have a seat at a table, but not imperative. If table seating is not available, make a place for guests to place their drink while getting comfortable on the sofa or living room chair. If a chair of some shape or form is not available for every guest, it is best to cut down your guest list. If you expect to have guests sitting on the ground, you should forewarn them with an appropriate announcement in the invitation, such as an "old fashioned picnic, bring your favorite quilt."

For showers, wedding parties, birthdays or anniversaries where toasts or gift opening will be an important part of the party, see that guests will be comfortable, preferably seated, at the appointed time. Such lengthy events can tire even the sturdiest of guests, so chairs will be greatly appreciated. For cocktail parties, open houses, receptions, teas or coffees, you need not have a place for all of your guests to sit. The general rule of thumb for such events is to have seating for one-third of your guests. This takes care of the older guests and others can take turns sitting to eat. When setting up tables, you will need 10 square feet for a 60-inch round table and chairs (seats eight) or a 16-foot-by-9-foot area for an 8-foot table and chairs (seats eight to 10).

Now that you have found seating, is there a place for guests to gather? Unless the event is held in a large room, such as a church fellowship hall, you will need to make room for guests to congregate. You will need 2 square feet of empty space for each guest. Tables set for eating should be outside of your gathering area. For example, your front hall may look like the perfect place to put your seating tables, but your guests would not be able to get through the front door. Clearing out the living room may appear an ideal choice for the shower, but using it for gift opening may take up your only gathering room. You can use the same space for gathering and eating if you move the tables aside and then pull them front and center 10 minutes before eating. However, you will need help to do this, and it is hard to do even with the best of staff or friends to help. My suggestion is to cut down the size of the party to accommodate your home and lifestyle. You will find yourself entertaining more frequently if you make it easier by only trying to entertain that number of guests your home can accommodate comfortably.

Make initial phone calls to your caterer, consultant, rental company, tent company, decorator, photographer, florist, maids, servers and bartenders, yard help and window washers. Let them know the date and time you will need their services, have them mail you necessary contracts or price lists, and find out about deposits and when you will need to contact them again. If you do use outside services, it still needs to reflect you, your tastes, and your style.

Celebrating Within Your Budget

Set yourself a realistic budget. Try as you plan to save and pinch where you can. Decide what is important to you and place your priorities accordingly. Remember the relationship between you and your guest goes far beyond how much money you spend on a party. You do not need a big pocketbook to throw an extraordinary and memorable party.

Occasions to Celebrate

You don't always have to have an excuse to throw a party. You only need the desire to have one. However, more often than not, we throw a party to celebrate a particular event, such as a wedding, birthday, baby or retirement. In either case, you will need the energy to plan properly for your event.

Gathering Your Guests to Celebrate

Make your guest list. Remember to invite people who get along, who will interest each other, and with whom you or your guest of honor would like to be. The party you are planning should please your guest and particularly your guest of honor. Remember, your home will need to accommodate comfortably all of your guests. If someone other than you is making the guest list, give them a maximum number for the guest list. Let them know you have given them this particular number because that is the number you are able to accommodate comfortably in your home. Most of all, blend your friends so they will complement each other, as you would blend the colors or ingredients in your decor or food.

INVITATIONS

An invitation is a guest's first impression of you and the event, so take time in making this important selection. Invitations can be given by mail or by phone. They can be formal or informal. It is appropriate to hand-write invitations or have them printed. Printed invitations usually are more formal. Either form can be placed on invitation papers or cards or personal stationery. Invitations should be ordered 2 to 4 weeks before you send them. Invitations should be sent, generally, 2 weeks in advance for most dinner parties, cocktail parties, teas, open houses, showers or birthdays. For formal receptions or balls, invitations should be sent 4 weeks in advance. Etiquette books can help with formal wording, however here are a few tips to always include in your written invitation. Let guests know that they are being invited or welcomed. Let them know the date, day and time of the event. As an option, you can include the time when the party will end. The place and address of the party should be included in the invitation. Also, include the name of the host and, if multiple hosts, indicate at which host's home the event is being held, with that host's complete address. Indicate whether guests will be eating dinner or hors d'oeuvres, dessert or cocktails. Tip guests as to how to dress by specifying outdoor, casual, semi-formal, etc. Let them know whether a response to the invitation is required, and, if so, the date by which a response is requested, to whom to respond and the appropriate phone number or address for responding.

Finally, you might want to include a map to the event location for out-of-town guests or guests who might have never been to your home. Be sure when ordering invitations or picking them up that you receive the envelopes in advance if they are not being printed. This will give you time to address them in advance and have one task out of the way. Be sure you ask how long it will take to receive invitations once ordered so that you can make sure you can get them out 2 to 4 weeks before the event. Also, leave ample time for proofreading your invitations, and consider having someone to help you proof.

Invitations by Phone

If extending your invitation by phone, which is a little more casual but still an appropriate way of inviting, you need to remember a few simple rules. Phone invitations work especially well when working on a tight time schedule which doesn't leave you with enough time to issue one by mail. A verbal invitation should be extended with statements rather than questions and should include details such as who is invited, what the invitation is for, date and time of the event, what type of meal, if any, will be served, dress style if applicable, and whether or not a reply is requested.

When expecting an RSVP, you may call guests after the RSVP date if they have not responded to ask if they will be attending. However, based on instinct and an initial count of guests who have responded, a host can make a good guess as to the number of guests to anticipate. Usually between 50 percent and 75 percent of the total guests invited will attend.

TYPES OF CELEBRATIONS

Now that you have determined how many guests your home can accommodate and have a guest list prepared, you can decide what type of party to have. In some cases, the number of guests expected will eliminate certain types of parties. Counting the guest number will let you know if the type of party you choose is a workable idea. Keep in mind, as you decide, the season and time of day, whether your event will be indoors or outdoors, formal, semi-formal, casual, or costume. Consider the type of event. Is it a reception, ball, dinner party, whether seated or buffet, a luncheon or a brunch, whether seated or buffet, a cocktail buffet or cocktail party, a birthday or a shower, open house, tea or coffee, a pot luck or supper club or a meeting, a barbecue, picnic or tailgate. Also, keep in mind whether a meal, finger foods, or dessert will be served. The possibilities for your event are endless, so, making a decision on what type of party to have is sometimes difficult. Recalling such things as your budget, guest number, house style and traffic flow, whether or not help from outside resources or friends is available, staff or service availability, time frame and time of day, will help you narrow the possibilities.

Dinner Parties
A Seated Dinner

A host might find it very difficult to serve more than six or eight guests for a formal seated, coursed dinner. Usually, a formal seated dinner requires staff help and kitchen help. When catering a formal seated function, I plan one kitchen staffer and one server for every five guests. It is not uncommon to have yet another drink or bartender server for every six to eight guests. Casual seated dinner parties for 12 to 16 can be served with the help of family and friends. When planning a menu for a seated dinner, serve food that can be eaten easily. Plan a simple main course with one to two different, lavish courses to add flair. Check etiquette books for seating arrangements and appropriate serving techniques.

A Seated Buffet Dinner or Semi Buffet

This is my favorite way to entertain. It requires being able to seat your guests at tables after they have gone through a buffet line. It is a way to entertain with little or no kitchen or serving help. Having one to two servers for 35 to 50 guests is sufficient for orchestrating a perfectly smooth event. Provide seated tables which can, at the hostess' option, be set with flatware and glasses. Set up a buffet for the main meal from which guests can serve themselves. Then, while guests are seated, serve their beverage and wine, pass or serve hot bread, clear dinner plates and serve dessert and coffee.

A Buffet Dinner

This is a very comfortable and casual way to entertain. All food is set up in the dining room or on a main serving table. Plates, flatware, napkins, glassware filled with beverages, wine glasses with wines to choose from, and breads are served off the main table, and dessert and coffee from a table or sideboard. Guests simply go through the line, serve their food and beverage and find a place to eat. It works particularly well with a main course, salad, two to three side dishes, and bread when only a dinner plate, fork and napkin are needed. Finger desserts can be passed or served, which cuts down on the need for additional serving or for another plate which will have to be washed. Tables or furniture can be used around the house for seating. However, as I've noted, you should provide a chair of some type for every guest.

Suggestions for Buffets

Keep in mind the number of items your guests are going to be required to carry. You do not want a guest to have to come back to the main table to grab a fork or glass. Coming back for coffee and dessert, of course, is only natural. You may serve your guests or have someone serve them any items that require more than two hands. Keep the food in bite-size pieces or easily sliceable with a fork unless sturdy tables and full flatware are provided for each guest. Buffets can be arranged with two lines containing the same food with serving down either side of the table, or with one line going around the table. At the appropriate time, a host might find it beneficial to direct guests on which way to enter the dining room and where they are invited to sit. Remember, plan your menu so that no more than 10 to 15 minutes of your time during the party is required for food preparation.

Cocktail Parties

A cocktail party is different from a cocktail buffet. A cocktail party is for cocktails with a few hors d'oeuvres and usually is hosted earlier in the day, usually between 4 - 8, for before dinner drinks. A cocktail buffet connotes heavier finger foods that could substitute for dinner. Expect your guests to drop in and out of a cocktail party, especially during the holiday season. I have found from catering experience serving buffets that guests will not gather around a table to eat until at least one hour after their arrival. Keep this in mind when planning hot appetizers. Passing appetizers sometimes helps during this gathering time. Drinks can be served at a bar or by a server or host. Having both is nice. Women prefer not to go to a bar, and it's always best to offer and serve the first drink to your guest unless a large reception makes it impractical.

Birthdays, Showers and Special Occasion Celebrations

Traditionally, birthdays, showers, and most anniversaries should be given for someone other than yourself or a family member. If given by one family member for another, customarily only family should be invited. Entertaining today allows large groups of hostesses to stray from this rule when giving a party for their honoree and gives the family the freedom to help friends who are graciously giving the party. The option of style, time and formality for such events is your own. Provide good seating for toasting or present opening. Always have a token or corsage for the guest of honor. Providing a pen and paper for gift recording is always a plus. Remember to provide your home and menu graciously. Guests have been asked to shower your guest of honor with gifts and best wishes. A lovely meal or buffet, colorful flowers or decorations will be appreciated by all.

Picnics and Tailgates

Keep in mind the items which you will have to carry to and from the picnic site. They should not be too heavy or bulky. Coolers should be provided for any meat dish, or dish or dressing containing eggs. Failure to refrigerate these types of food could cause them to grow bacteria or even cause food poisoning. Serve foods that can be served at room temperature, that are easily picked up or served, and that require little to no preparation. Some common items forgotten for picnics include: a trash bag, wraps or baggies for leftovers, knives, wipes or towelettes, wine cork or bottle openers, serving utensils and bug repellents. If it is a gathering of friends and pot luck style, see page 15. Your picnic does not necessarily have to be beautiful when it's being carried. Having it beautiful when it's set up is what counts.

Brunches and Lunches

Brunches are a wonderful and relaxing way to entertain. They also allow great freedom with menu and serving options. Brunches work beautifully served buffet style. At a brunch, it is common to serve the meal with sweet rolls or coffee cakes being served as a dessert item. Brunches work well for close family and friends. They are commonly given for wedding partiesand showers. Lunches in the South are particularly for ladies and can be a wonderful time to serve all that fun "girl food." Lunches work well with fixed plate seating and usually can be prepared in advance, depending on the menu. A host probably could handle 12 to 16 cold fixed plates on her own without kitchen or serving help. Buffet style serving is also very popular for lunches, especially for an event which includes couples or mixed ages. Business luncheons have become increasingly popular and should concentrate on simple menus and efficient serving. A luncheon is a wonderful excuse for bringing out a hostess' beautiful china and crystal. Crystal, linens and flowers go hand in hand with luncheons.

Open Houses, Teas and Coffees

This is a wonderful option for guest lists that are a little too big for your home. You can even list separate times on the invitations for an easier flow. Foods that do not require a utensil and can easily be placed on a small plate or saucer are best. Finger sandwiches, small canapés, tiny desserts or cakes, punch, hot teas and coffees are a few of the more traditional ideas. This is a wonderfully old-fashioned way to entertain. Most of these celebrations will be held in the mid-morning or mid-afternoon hours. A host can handle this type of event with little or no kitchen or serving help. Usually, good friends or family can help serve without giving them too much work and responsibility during your event. It is traditional to have someone serving the coffee, tea or punch, which is commonly set at either end of the serving table.

Pot Luck, Meetings, Fund-raisers or Community Dinners

A wonderful way to entertain for busy families and a practical way to entertain when working with a large group is a pot luck supper. It has been a way to celebrate since pioneer days, and has brought families and friends together for generations to celebrate harvests, holy holidays, births, comings of age, marriages and to offer comfort following a death. For the at-home dinner, the host is usually the one responsible for the main dish, drinks, plates, glasses, centerpiece and providing her home, hall, or picnic area. The hostess also is responsible for organizing which dishes guests should bring (vegetable, fruit, salad, starch, bread, dessert). It is a very practical way to entertain with busy schedules and strict budgets. If organizing a function for meetings, clubs or fund-raisers, be sure you have volunteers who are both willing and interested in participating. Have supervisors for each phase of the event: planning, preparation, shopping, cooking, serving and cleanup.

When you have been invited to a pot luck dinner of this sort, remember these numbered tips:
1- make the dish and remember to take the dish.
2- prepare the dish for serving by heating, slicing or tossing.
3- serve the dish by providing an appropriate platter for transfer and, most importantly, a utensil for serving it.
4- if held in the home, remove the leftovers and place in the hostess' refrigerator. Take your platter, utensil and carrier home with you.

Receptions and Balls

Formal receptions and balls need to be planned months, and in some cases, years, in advance. Pay particularly good attention to the time of day or night the event is being held. Functions after 6 p.m. will require more food as well as events held during lunchtime hours. Early morning or afternoon events such as an open house or tea involve lighter, simpler food. Refer to your favorite etiquette books to help you along. Research local resources and hire services as needed who will help you reflect your own personal ideas and style.

Children's Parties and Playgroups

When planning a children's party, it is most important to remember that you may not be able to count on an exact itinerary of events. Go with the time schedule of the children, be open and flexible with events, have extra events in mind just in case the children finish those you have planned, and have a loving set of hands for every year of the average age of the children who are your guests (3-year-olds need one helper for every three children, 7-year-olds need one chaperone for every seven). Inviting as many children as the child is old is usually about the perfect number of guests for the little guest of honor.

Playgroups are popular in neighborhoods today. When hosting a playgroup, the hostess should plan on serving a simple refreshment and snack for children and parents. Leave time for creative play and plan activities only if desired by your little guests. Put up your child's favorite toys so he or she does not have to worry about sharing the unshareable and store toys with small pieces for safety and quicker cleanup. Morning hours are usually the best time for a play group, but not always. It's up to hostesses to share household rules with guests, or to set a time for ending the party. Hosting children's events does not have to be done in your home, but is always appreciated when it's bravely done.

Theme Parties

Inspiring yourself with a theme from a particular region or culture can be a great way to generate ideas for a party. A theme can help bring together dress, decorations, menu and invitations. It might help you free your imagination and creativity. It can also help educate you about a different area and cuisine of which you might not otherwise be aware. A simple spice or ingredient may spark your and your guests' interest. The average entertainer might only think of themes for children's parties, bridal and baby showers or the typical Hawaiian Luau or Mexican Fiesta. However, with a little research and an open mind, any part of the country or world can be the inspiration for a perfectly original party.

Theme Party Inspirations

A Children's Book Party for book exchanging and punch with cookies.
Dinner and a Movie with bottled Cokes, popcorn and peanuts.
A 1960's Backyard Grill and Pool Party.
A Walk Through a Vineyard, wine and cheese tasting.
A Formal French Ladies Luncheon.
An English Mother-Daughter Tea Party.

A Harvest Party, serving vegetables and giving seeds away as a favor.
A Fourth of July Bike Parade and Picnic.
Sunday Afternoon Ice Cream Party.
A Coke Social.
An English Garden Party with croquet and white dress attire.
A Western Ho Down with line dancing and catered barbecue.

MENUS

When planning a menu for any event, it's imperative that you keep several rules in mind. First, you need to plan a menu that you will feel comfortable in preparing and serving. You also need to prepare food that your guests will enjoy eating. Keeping it simple is another key rule in helping plan a successful menu.

Think of the season in which your event will be held when making menu selections. If it's winter, consider holiday dishes and foods to warm chilled bones. In spring, you will need to select fresh, cool dishes. Summer menus invite lighter foods, while autumn brings an opportunity for hostesses to select wonderful combinations of comforting food.

Also, keep in mind the time of day your party will be held. Early breakfasts or brunches allow considerable freedom in selecting a menu, while lunches and afternoon events call for lighter proportions of food. Dinners or evening cocktail events require more filling dishes. For receptions or buffets, the time of day the event is held will set the type and quantity of food you should serve.

Menu Selections

Think about who you are feeding. Ladies eat differently from men. You will need heavier food and more abundant proportions for male guests than for females. The food preferences of younger or elderly party-goers should also be considered. Teen-agers will either pick at their plates or consume everything in sight, even the garnishes. For an event catering to younger people, I recommend simple, popular fad foods which can be made with little or no effort. Older generations, on the other hand, are better served if proportions are smaller, already fixed on a plate and involve little cutting. Some groups will be more satisfied with popular, identifiable food while others might like the new, trendy or gourmet styles. A hostess should know her guests and be reasonable when thinking of the menu best suited for them. It should be the responsibility of the hostess to be mindful of and accommodate any restrictions of her guests such as allergies, diabetes or disabilities.

Are you going to have any help? Last-minute preparation can be a big challenge when you are taking coats or greeting guests at the door, serving drinks, showing your home and visiting with guests. If you do not have help in your kitchen or in your home, cut down your last-minute preparation time to no more than 15 minutes. Having platters garnished and filled beforehand and having no more than two hot dishes will help cut preparation time. Keep in mind that preparing fixed plates for more than 12 guests without kitchen help will be extremely difficult.

Some other things to think about in planning your menu include: What style will you use for serving? How formal or informal is the function?. Will it be a seated affair or a buffet? Will you have bite-size finger foods your guests can eat while standing or will they be eating from their laps? Will tables be too crowded or not steady enough for cutting? Do you have enough room for seating if you serve off of the dining room or kitchen table?

The colors and textures of the food you will serve also are very important. You do not want to have all of your foods smooth or puréed, nor do you want to them to be all of the same colors. Keep your four basic food groups in mind to help with planning complementary colors and textures. Try to have at least three colors on your plate and at least two different textures. This will get you off to a good start. Considering texture and color is, likewise, an important consideration when serving buffet style, whether for a meal or finger foods. Imagine what your food selections will look like on your guests' plates as they serve themselves from the buffet. Is it still appetizing? Food that looks beautiful when combined on a plate will be enjoyed all the more. Use your artistry and creativity to blend your meal as you do your guests or home decor.

Select foods with a variety of ingredients. Ingredients should not be repeated in dishes served at the same meal, or, when doing so, the ingredient should be used as a subordinate ingredient in at least one of the dishes. This is particularly true with condiments and spices. For example, too much dill, cream based or cream sauce on more than one dish or nuts or breading on more than one dish will not be appealing. However, having strawberries in a fruit salad and then strawberry sauce on a dessert will work because while the same ingredient, strawberries, is used in both, it is not the primary ingredient in either and the dishes are served in two different courses.

When presenting your prepared dishes, remember it is impossible to keep your food hot, even with a chafing dish. Chafing dishes are beautiful, but may not perform to your liking. Commercial chafing dishes do work better, but can be costly and bulky on a regular table. Presentation of food should be beautiful. When choosing a menu and its dishes, it's best to pick foods that do not have a precise serving time. This will give you the time to arrange your food for presentation and visit with your guests, allowing you the freedom to serve your meal when your guests are ready instead of when the food is ready. Your serving pieces and serving utensils are just as important as what is in them. They should be compatible with your dish, menu and home. They should reflect the style, season and formality you have chosen for your party and food. Prepare your food in a kitchen filled with love and present your food with that same love. Your effort will be noticed and your outcome admired. It is your imagination and talents that transform a meal into a special and memorable occasion.

PRESENTATIONS

Presentation is a very important part of entertaining. You need to see your table as an artist would see his canvas. Use ideas from magazines and cookbooks to inspire your own ideas so that your table will reflect your own style and complement you and your home. If you think it is beautiful, so will your guests, and they will share your pride in your table.

For Buffet Serving

Think of the size of serving pieces you will need. It is nice to put out as much food as possible at the start of your party so that, if you do not have help in the kitchen, you can have time out of the kitchen. However, when putting food out, keep in mind any food that might get stale, that might lose its flavor or warmth after a certain amount of time or that might spoil, melt or get runny.

Also consider the heights of your various serving pieces and table arrangements when planning a buffet. All should flow together and enhance one another. See page 21 for methods of achieving different heights with various serving pieces. As a general rule, have at least three to five different heights on a regular size table, such as flowers, a regular tray, a cake stand and a punch bowl.

Think of how to replenish food easily and practically. Have two or three trays or serving pieces per dish if frequent replenishing is going to take place. This will give you time to pre-prepare trays and exchange them for empty trays easily. This works well especially with tiny finger foods or hot breads. Replenish one tray with another rather than trying to fill it at the table or have to take a tray away, leaving an empty space at your table. Always keep extra garnishes on hand for this purpose so that you can make every substituted tray look as beautiful as the one originally presented on the table.

Do not overfill serving pieces with sauces and dips. Fill these compotes or dishes 3/4 of the way full rather than to the top to prevent unnecessary messes. Additionally, placing food unevenly on trays will be easier than a symmetrical presentation in most cases.

Green leafy lettuce is a wonderful way to garnish for lining platters or to use under salads for fixed plates. Have lots of it on hand. Also, fresh fruits and vegetables placed in the corners of platters or plates will help give color to trays. Fresh herbs will bring aroma and intricate detail to any dish. Edible flowers are usually available or easily ordered from local markets to float in beverages or place on platters, especially desserts, for instant color and panache.

For Family Serving

Family style serving has been part of the South's table and America's table for many, many generations. Placing all the food on serving platters on the table and passing among each other is a wonderful way to enjoy fellowship with family and friends. It is very important to remember details when serving this way. Are all the serving pieces small enough to fit on the table? Are they small enough and light enough to pass between guests easily? Do you have adequate protection for the table so that hot platters do not leave a hot mark? Is there a holder or hot pad to pass from guest to guest? If platters are too large or too hot, have the host or head of the table serve the main meat or entree or a particular dish onto plates and then pass clockwise to guests or family members. Appetizers can be offered before any meal. They should only wet your guests appetite and should be passed or displayed for easy self-service. Dessert and coffee can be served at the tables or in another room with any style serving. Remember, with all presentations, when food looks beautiful on its' platter, it will taste better too.

ORGANIZATION

Making a list is gaining control of a party. Being prepared in advance makes an event go well. You cannot prepare too much or too far in advance. Your guests will know that you were ready and it will help ease the flow of the party.

Have a folder or computer file in which you can keep every idea, receipt and list. I recommend manila folders. Keeping your market lists, things-to-do lists, receipts, pictures, menus and recipes together will help you maintain control of your event, as well as giving you a record to refer back to when entertaining again.

In planning ahead, do not hesitate to think months in advance. It is common for formal receptions to be planned years in advance. Planning for semi-formal functions can be started as much as 3 months in advance, while casual entertaining can be planned 3 weeks to 6 weeks in advance. Reserving outside staff and services, ordering invitations, planning menus and preparing your home are all time consuming because of your regular lifestyle and schedule. A host who thinks ahead will stay ahead.

Grocery lists can be made in four separate sections, a pre-grocery list, a wholesale grocery or bulk grocery list, a fresh market list and a final, regular grocery list. The final grocery list sometimes can be eliminated. The first grocery list should include pantry and freezer items that you will need for the party. It should be done with your regular shopping to avoid having to make an extra trip to the grocery store. Bulky items such as beverages are the type of items you can purchase with your regular groceries because they are heavy to load and unload. This first trip to stock up on items should be done 2 weeks before the party or in the week prior to the week of the party. The wholesale or bulk grocery list would include items from special stores or membership groceries. Make this shopping trip when you can plan for frequent stops and loading heavy items. The fresh market shopping should be done 1 to 2 days prior to the event and will include all fresh produce, seafood and meats that you might need. Also, fresh flowers can be purchased at this time for home and table arrangements. Keep an ongoing list of grocery items or party items that you have forgotten or missed in prior shopping trips. This can be used as your final grocery list. Always include your ice and garnishes in this list. Completing this last-minute shopping is a wonderful task to pass on to an eager helper or family member and can be done easily by someone else the day of the party when you have kept a list.

Items that might be forgotten as you're making your lists include:
Candles, leafy lettuce for trays, garnishes for trays, full beverage lists (tonic and juices), odd bar items such as olives or stirrers, ice, matches, napkins and toothpicks.

If it helps you to stay organized, consider making a project, housework and gardening list for personal organizational purposes. Combine a general cooking list with your shopping list. The combined list should help you organize your time so that you have sufficient time for all of your shopping, cooking, cleaning, gardening and errand running. The next page shows an example of a list I might compile:

Pre-party

order invitations
proofread invitations
address envelopes
pick up stamps

Friday
mail invitations

Saturday
Sunday
complete at-home and garden projects

Monday
plan menu
gather recipes for folder
compile shopping lists

Tuesday
grocery day, take party list and regular
grocery list
complete indoor projects

Wednesday
shop for paper and plasticware needed
liquor store, take list
carpool day for kids a.m. and p.m.
add other beverage items for bulk
grocery pick-up

Thursday
bulk grocery trip at membership grocery
store, take list

Friday
bake and freeze bread
bake and freeze dessert

Saturday
hardware store
plant nursery for outdoor plants
gardening, outdoor projects and
spruce up

Sunday afternoon
finish outdoor and indoor projects
review to do lists for the week ahead

Monday
call guests who have not RSVP'd
pick out serving pieces and
serving utensils
gather items borrowed from friends
and family
gather and iron linens
make sure linens fit and match tables
bank
drop off dry cleaning, don't forget party
dress and tablecloths

Tuesday
plan indoor flowers, gather containers
change candles, light bulbs
polish silver
wash crystal
check flatware, dinnerware
fill salt and pepper shakers
prepare lists for servers or outside
service or other help

Wednesday
pick up dry-cleaning
gather greenery for floral arrangements
and soak
do heavy home cleaning
check in with outside services or help,
have list for discussing with them
call other hostess
go over market list and revise as needed

Thursday
market, take fresh produce list and
flower list
pick up rented items from rental
company
prepare flower arrangements
yard work
Tiki candles out and cover with baggies
prepare sauces and dressings
clean bathrooms and bedrooms
mark serving pieces with Post-it notes
check notes for things I might forget
(I keep a notepad & pen by the bed for
thoughts that occur during the night)

Friday
complete home cleaning, grass mowing
and trimming
take phone off the hook
cook main dish
cook side dishes
take freezer items out of freezer
last-minute grocery shopping
polish furniture
sweep and blow off porches and
driveways
water plants and flower arrangements
refrigerate beverages or place in cooler
ready to ice
set tables up, gather table linens indoors
go out to dinner or order take out

Saturday
make salads
slice meats
slice condiments
set up serving table
set seated tables
set up bar
put food in serving containers
spruce up house
wipe down outdoor tables and furniture
tie ribbon on mailbox
send children to sitter or dogs to pens
bath (2 hours before)
check guest bathroom
ice down beverages
turn ovens on
turn lights on, in and out
place flowers outside
put bar items out
put appetizers out
put food in oven
finish last-minute platter garnishing
tuck lists and Post-it notes away
unlock doors
light candles

Sunday
Monday
return rental items
return borrowed items with plant or
flower arrangement
from the party as a thank you.

NOTE: After making this list, I like to add my personal appointments, duties
and errands to it so that I only have to refer to one schedule
during such a hectic time.

FINAL TOUCHES

When hiring outside services, you need to be sure you line them up as soon as you have planned your party. It's important to keep them informed and to reserve from their inventory anything that you might need. Remember, they are in business to serve you, so informing them of your priorities and concerns will only make it easier for them to do a better job. Inform rental companies and linen companies of what you will need so that they will have it for you when you are ready. To help you stay organized as things grow more hectic, keep lists on hand to which you can refer for caterers, servers, florists, photographers and the parking valet. As a caterer, it was helpful to me to know any particulars my client needed or wanted in advance. For example, if a client wanted my staff to be extremely quiet during cleanup or to take coats from arriving guests, or if drinks were to be served directly to guests or from a bar, or if leftovers were to be packaged for other hostesses or all stored in the hostess' refrigerator, I needed to know in advance. Of course, most experienced services have already taken most questions into consideration, however, letting them know what is important to you will keep your party running smoothly.

Plan serving pieces and serving utensils in advance. When selecting pieces for holding and presenting food, you must decide what type of serving piece will be appropriate for your house style and the formality of party. Silver, cut crystal and fine china are the most formal choices and almost always appropriate, but with the popularity of pewter and handcrafted pottery, a formal table can be set just as well with unique collectibles. Baskets, weaves, glass, pewter and pottery are wonderful settings for outdoor events. Brass and porcelains are beautiful also, however, some of these items are not meant for serving food and precautions should be made to protect these pieces with inserts or platters if this is the case.

Before the event, place the serving pieces you have chosen in their places and make sure their size and shapes are adequate for your serving area. Keep in mind where plates, glasses, flatware and napkins will go and allow sufficient room for these items.

The use of different heights when presenting food and table arrangements can add drama and make your table setting all the more impressive. Use different heights of serving pieces. Having three or five different heights on a regular size serving table makes an unique table setting. Use cake stands and footed compotes to bring height to dishes. If these are not adequate serving pieces or not in your serving collection, start from the table up. Books, boxes, or styrofoam can be placed under linens and cloths to give height to a table and flowers without a footed or fancy stemmed bowl in sight. If you choose this approach, more than one linen or cloth will be needed to cover uneven areas that you might create with your ideas. Most importantly, keep in mind your centerpiece and its height. Your food and its presentation should accent and enhance your table centerpiece.

Before the last minute, make sure you have adequate serving utensils for each dish. Utensils should be easy to handle. Test your utensil by using it yourself and see if you can politely move food from platter to plate. Also, with sauces, dips and the like, make sure the utensil is long enough not to fall into the bowl or provide a plate or small platter on which it can rest between uses. If possible, watch the first few guests going through the serving line to see if they need an extra knife here or spoon there. Have extra utensils easily available for such needs. Remember, food that needs two hands for cutting needs to be sliced beforehand or sliced at the table for guests by a server.

Make sure you feel confident with your surroundings, menu and table. Remember to have a sense of humor if something does not go quite right, and be flexible with the party agenda. Most of all, have fun! It's a celebration.

WINE TIPS

Don't be intimidated when purchasing wine! Here's how to approach the task at hand. First decide a few details about what you want - red or white, sparkling or blush, etc. ... Next decide how much money you want to spend. Most knowledgeable wine merchants can easily find what you want if you can convey this information up front. If you are pairing food and wine, ask for suggestions. After taking home particular wine selections, write down the brand name and a few details about what you liked or didn't like about your purchase. The next time you're in a wine store, tell the salesperson these details so that they can steer you toward something that suits your palate. Don't be afraid to be assertive because most salespeople play a guessing game with customers.

Wine publications can be useful sources of information and education, but they can also be sources of frustration because many of their wine recommendations can not be found in most markets. Many industry people such as myself know about these recommended wines months before they appear in wine publications. By the time you read about these touted brands, they often have disappeared from store shelves. People in the trade are tasted on many wines before they are purchased and brought into stores. The savvy shopper is one that develops a relationship with someone such as myself and is not afraid to ask about what wines are new and great bargains. There are many times when highly allocated wines such as Silver Oak, Opus One, Spottweood, etc. never reach the shelf and are pre-sold to customers who are informed ahead of time that they will be available. That is why it is important to develop a relationship with your local wine merchant.

A few thoughts on serving wine

Most Americans drink their white wines too cold and their red wines too warm. I cringe when I see an ice bucket being brought to a restaurant table with a bottle of Chardonnay. Ice cold white wine buries all the pleasurable fruit nuances and flavors. It is best to open chilled white wine and let it sit for about 20 minutes and then watch it open up and develop over the next hour. Red wine that is served at room temperature, especially during the Southern summer, shows all the wine's faults. When at home or in a restaurant that doesn't have a temperature controlled wine cellar, ask that the red wine be put in the refrigerator for 30 minutes so the wine can be consumed as close to 58 degrees as possible. Drinking wine at the correct temperature will increase the taste and pleasure you will derive from your bottle of wine.

Drink in good health.

Frank Ryan
Wine Specialist

A Toast To
Southern Celebrations
Beverages and Appetizers

Anne Mullins Rigdon

◆

LEMON MINT TEA

2 cups sugar
1 gallon water
1/2 cup lemon juice
1 tablespoon lemon peel, strips or twists
2 one-half gallon tea bags
3 mint leaves

Boil sugar, water, lemon juice and lemon peel for 5 minutes in a medium saucepan. Remove from heat. Add tea bags and steep until tea is at room temperature. Remove bags and lemon strips. Add mint leaves and serve over ice with a large slice of lemon. Chill to store up to 2 days. Makes 1 gallon of tea.

ORANGE SPICED TEA

4 cups water
1 1/4 cups sugar
2 tablespoons cloves
3 sticks cinnamon
2 one-half gallon tea bags
1/2 cup frozen orange juice concentrate, undiluted, no pulp
2 oranges, sliced

Boil water, sugar, cloves and cinnamon for 5 minutes in a medium saucepan. Remove from heat, add tea bags and steep for 5 minutes. Remove tea bags, add orange juice and enough water to make 1 gallon of tea. Orange juice can be omitted if a less punch-type tea is desired. Serve with large slices of oranges over ice. For an almond flavor, add 1/2 teaspoon almond extract to tea. Chill to store up to 2 days. Makes 1 gallon of tea.

◆

APRICOT TEA PUNCH

8 cups water
1 cup sugar
1 one-half gallon tea bag
1/8 cup lemon juice
1 (46-ounce) can pineapple juice
1 (12-ounce) can apricot nectar
2 liters ginger ale soda

Boil water on stove in a medium saucepan, add sugar and simmer for 5 minutes, stirring occasionally. Remove from heat and add tea bags. Steep for 5 minutes and remove bags. Add lemon juice, pineapple juice and apricot nectar. Chill to store up to 2 days. Before serving, add ginger ale. Serve over ice. Makes 1 3/4 gallons of punch.

WINTER TEA

1 quart water
2 family size tea bags, one-half gallon size
1 teaspoon whole cloves
2 sticks cinnamon
1 teaspoon whole allspice
1 1/2 cup brown sugar
4 cups cranberry juice
1 cup lemon juice
2 cups ginger ale

Place water in pot on stove and bring to a simmer. Remove from heat and add tea bags, cloves, cinnamon and allspice to pot and steep for 5 to 10 minutes. Remove tea bags, cloves and allspice. Add brown sugar, stirring until dissolved. Cool and add cranberry juice and lemon juice and store sealed in refrigerator for up to 2 days. To serve, add ginger ale and pour over ice. Garnish with cinnamon sticks and fresh cranberries, if desired. Can be served warm without ginger ale.

Tip of the Trade:

*To determine right amounts, keep in mind the ounce size of the glass you will be using, how long your guests will be there, the weather outside and time of day.
A general rule of thumb is 2.5 drinks per guest in a 3-hour party.*

One gallon of tea is needed for every 12 guests.

Tip of the Trade:

If serving one of the specialty teas or punches in a punch bowl, have a hostess or server ladle the beverage into the appropriate glasses. A guest server at a ball or reception should be honored with a corsage for her time and effort.

It works well to have a pitcher of water with sliced lemons and mint to the side of a punch or specialty drink as an alternative.

◆

RUSSIAN TEA

A Christmas recipe collection of the late Mrs. Lou Mullins. A tradition now carried on by her children.
Serve this fragrant tea with Sausage Rolls during the holidays.

> 3 1/2 quarts water, divided
> 1 1/2 cups sugar
> 5 cinnamon sticks
> 4 teaspoons whole cloves
> 4 tea bags
> 6 oranges, juice squeezed
> 4 lemons, juice squeezed
> 1 (46-ounce) can pineapple juice

Combine 1 1/2 quarts water with sugar, cinnamon sticks and cloves and bring to a simmer over medium low heat for 20 minutes. Meanwhile, in a large saucepan, bring 1 quart water to a boil and add tea bags and set off heat. Remove cinnamon sticks and cloves from saucepan and add spiced, sugar water to tea bag water. Replace on stove and bring water to a high steam but not boiling. Add remaining quart water. Squeeze juice from oranges and lemons and add to tea with pineapple juice. Serve warm. Makes 24 servings.

LEMONY BLOODY MARYS

A recipe inspired by my client and friend, Mrs. Madeline Hodges Knox

> 1 (46-ounce) can tomato juice
> 1 cup lemon juice
> 2 teaspoons salt
> 4 tablespoons Worcestershire
> 2 teaspoons black pepper
> 1 cup vodka

Combine all ingredients, excluding the vodka. Store in an air tight container in refrigerator for up to 4 days. Vodka can be added per glass or pitcher. Serve with rock salted rimmed glasses and large celery stalks.

A tradition of Russian Tea at Christmas has been carried on with the Mullins family. Carry on traditions you remember for your family to cherish or simply start your own for future generations to follow.

Tip of the Trade:

When hiring an outside bartender or when caterer provides a bartender service, ask if they will be bringing their own cork screw, opener, scoops, and pourers needed or if you are responsible for these. Always have a trash can, at least three pitchers and plenty of hand towels available at the bar.

My client always wondered if it were the Bloody Marys or just the Brunch that made guests feel so relaxed at her morning parties. Brunches are a splendid way to enjoy friends and family.

◆

LUNCHEON SANGRIA

1 (750 milliliter) bottle white wine
1 lemon, thinly sliced
1 orange, thinly sliced
1 lime, thinly sliced
1/4 cup fruited brandy
1 (10- to 12-ounce) bottle club soda, chilled
1 (750 milliliter) bottle champagne, chilled
Strawberries

In a large Sangria pitcher or punch bowl, combine wine, lemon, orange, lime and brandy. Marinate fruit in wine for at least 1 hour in refrigerator. Before serving, add club soda and champagne. Serve with strawberry halves. Best served very chilled in large wine glasses. Makes 8 to 10 servings.

Tip of the Trade:

Traditionally, Sangria is served out of large glass pitchers with a wooden spoon. The fruit remains in the pitcher while serving and the spoon is used to keep the fruit in place.

APRICOT CHAMPAGNE PUNCH

1 (6-ounce) can orange juice concentrate, undiluted
3 tablespoons lemon juice
1/8 cup confectioners powdered sugar
1/4 cup apricot brandy
1 (750-milliliter) bottle white wine, chilled
1 (750-milliliter) bottle champagne, chilled
2 (10- to 12-ounce) bottles club soda, chilled

In a punch bowl or pitcher, combine orange juice concentrate, lemon juice, powdered sugar, brandy and wine. Before serving, add champagne and soda. Serve in tulip champagne glasses. Makes 6 to 8 servings.

Tip of the Trade:

Remember to have plenty of glasses washed or rented. It is an extremely inconvenient item to not keep on hand. It is important to have the appropriate glasses needed for each particular beverage served and enough for each guest to have one of each if they so desire.
If serving alcoholic refreshments, always have a beverage without alcohol to also offer to your guests. Water, however an alternative, should not be the only nonalcoholic drink offered.

◆

♦

Overcooking is most frequently the problem when baking. Remember to set the timer and keep in mind that undercooking easily can be remedied by placing back in the same-degree oven. Overcooking in this case leaves no solutions.

RICE CRISPY WAFERS

1 1/2 cups margarine, room temperature
8 ounces New York sharp cheddar cheese, grated
2 cups plain all-purpose flour
1/2 to 3/4 teaspoon red pepper
2 1/4 cups crispy rice cereal

R eal butter does not work as well as margarine in this dish. In a mixer, combine margarine, grated cheese, flour and red pepper. Mix until smooth and cheese colored. Add rice cereal and mix through. Do not over mix. Roll into quarter size balls and place on a greased cookie sheet. Press balls flat with a fork. Bake at 350 degrees for 10 to 14 minutes. This wafer will crisp after cooling. Do not fear undercooking. Freezes well. Add another 1/2 teaspoon red pepper to recipe, if desired. Makes 8 dozen wafers.

Use the dough in Cheese Wafers without the pepper jelly as cheese straw dough as well. By placing small amounts of this dough in the microwave for 1 minute, it easily can be put through the cookie press fitted with a star tube to make the cheese straws. In fact, if the tube is plastic, it can be filled and then microwaved before pressed. Press out on a greased light-colored or insulated baking sheet and bake in a 350-degree oven for 8 to 10 minutes. Cut into 2-inch pieces while still hot.

CHEESE WAFERS WITH PEPPER JELLY

1 pound New York sharp cheddar cheese, grated
1 cup margarine, room temperature
3 cups plain all-purpose flour
1 teaspoon salt
1/2 teaspoon red pepper powder
1/2 cup red or green pepper jelly

B utter does not work as well as margarine in this dish. In a mixer, combine grated cheese, margarine, flour, salt and pepper. Mix until smooth. Roll into 1/2- to 3/4-inch balls and place on a greased baking sheet. Place a thumb print in the center. Fill thumb print with about 1/2 teaspoon pepper jelly. Bake at 350 degrees for 12 to 15 minutes. Use green and red pepper jelly at Christmas. These freeze well and go great with cocktails. Makes 5 dozen.

♦

CURRY CREAM MAYONNAISE

1/3 cup sour cream
1 cup high quality mayonnaise
1/4 cup heavy whipping cream
2 to 3 teaspoons high quality ground curry
3 tablespoons tomato ketchup
1/2 teaspoon Worcestershire
Juice of 1 lemon or 1 tablespoon lemon juice

In a food processor with a metal blade, combine all ingredients and purée. May refrigerate for up to 2 days but needs to be served at room temperature. Serve with steamed or fresh asparagus, snap beans or other favorite raw vegetables. Makes 3/4 cup.

GARLIC FRENCH BREAD WEDGES

1 (24-inch) French baguette or loaf
1/8 cup olive oil
1 clove garlic, crushed
1/2 teaspoon garlic salt

Cut baguette into 1/2-inch wedges and place on a baking sheet. Broil approximately 2 minutes on a low broil. Remove from oven, turn over and brush uncooked side with a mixture of olive oil, garlic and garlic salt. Broil this side for approximately 2 minutes on a low broil. Cool and store in airtight bags. May be frozen or kept in refrigerator for 3 days. Serve with desired spread or dip in the place of crackers. Makes 48 wedges.

Tip of the Trade:

Serving more than one dip with vegetables or crackers works well, especially if one of the dips is Curry Cream Mayonnaise. The Indian spice, curry, is not loved by all.

Tip of the Trade:

Homemade wafers that can be served with dips or spreads will really impress guests. They can be made 1 month in advance and frozen until ready to use. A wonderful item if planning a menu in advance. However, have commercial wafers or crackers on hand. Homemade treats go fast.

Garlic French Bread Wafers can be made into an appetizer after baking by topping with slices of goat cheese, freshly chopped basil and tomato slices and baking or broiling again in oven, or topping before baking second side. They can be topped with any assortment of your favorite cheeses, seafood, vegetables or condiments and baked until warm. This is similar to the way Italian cooks make good use of their leftover bread loaves. They can be served warm or room temperature.

◆

RICOTTA RED PEPPER DIP

3 tablespoons butter or margarine
2 cloves garlic, peeled and crushed
2 small onions, peeled and chopped
2 to 3 red peppers, seeded and chopped
1 (15-ounce) carton ricotta cheese
1/4 cup romano or Parmesan cheese, grated
3 tablespoons sour cream
1/2 teaspoon dry mustard
1/2 teaspoon salt

In a skillet, combine butter, garlic, onions and peppers and cook until tender, about 5 minutes. In a food processor fitted with a metal blade or blender combine ricotta, romano, sour cream, dry mustard and salt. Add sautéed vegetables and purée for 3 to 5 seconds until smooth. Serve chilled or at room temperature with your favorite raw vegetables, wafers or tortilla chips. Makes 3 cups.

CRAB ARTICHOKE DIP

1 (14 1/2-ounce) can artichokes, drained well
1/2 bunch green onions, peeled and chopped, (4 to 5 onions)
1 (8-ounce) package cream cheese, room temperature
2 (6 1/2-ounce) cans white crab meat, drained or
    8 ounces pasteurized white crab meat
2 tablespoons Parmesan cheese
1/4 cup mayonnaise
1/4 cup sour cream
1 teaspoon dried parsley
4 tablespoons sherry or Madeira wine, optional
2 teaspoons paprika or 1/2 cup toasted sliced almonds

◆

Drain artichokes by pressing well in a colander. In a mixer, combine artichokes, onions, cream cheese, crab, Parmesan, mayonnaise, sour cream and parsley. Stir in wine if preferred. May be done 1 day in advance up to this point. Pour into a greased baking/serving dish and bake for 25 to 35 minutes at 375 degrees. Sprinkle with paprika or toasted almonds and serve with thin wheat crackers. Makes 24 servings.

GARLIC BAGEL CRISPS

1 package commercial bagels, unsliced
1 1/2 cup butter or margarine
1/2 teaspoon garlic salt
Parmesan cheese

Slice bagles horizontally into 1/4-inch doughnut rounds. Melt butter in microwave or on the stove and add garlic salt. Brush the rounds on both sides with butter mixture or dip slices in on both sides. Cut rounds into fourths and place on a cookie sheet. Sprinkle with a little Parmesan cheese. Bake at 300 degrees for 8 to 12 minutes. Makes 100 pieces.

HOT BEEF AND WALNUT DIP

1 (8-ounce package) cream cheese, softened
1/8 cup high quality mayonnaise
1/2 cup sour cream
1/4 cup heavy whipping cream
1 (2 1/2-ounce) jar dried beef, chopped or snipped
2 green onions, peeled and chopped
1/3 cup chopped walnuts

Mix all ingredients by hand or by mixer fitted with a metal whip or plastic whip. Serve warm in a chafing dish or a crock. Can be served with baby carrots and vegetables or wafers. Makes 2 to 2 1/2 cups.

Tip of the Trade:

Bagel crisps can be bought in most groceries already prepared if baking your own is too overwhelming. They are great to have on hand in case you run out of homemade crisps.

If using a chafing dish for a party, be sure to test the warmer by igniting in advance. Keep the flame low and use the warmers where water can be placed in the bottom portion for best heating results. Have extra candles, fluid or sterno available, and replace water at least once an hour during the party.

Tip of the Trade:

Dried beef can be snipped with kitchen sheers or scissors to 1/4-inch strips.

◆

CILANTRO CORN DIP

1 (8-ounce package) cream cheese, softened
1/4 cup sour cream
1/4 cup mayonnaise
1/8 teaspoon red pepper
3 green onions, chopped
1 (15-ounce) can whole kernel corn, drained
1/2 tablespoons lime juice
1/4 cup fresh Cilantro
1 (3-ounce) can chopped olives

Combine first four ingredients and mix well. Set aside. In a food processor fitted with a metal blade, combine onions, corn, lime juice and Cilantro and process two to three pulses. Combine corn with sour cream mixture and stir in olives. Can store in refrigerator covered for up to 2 days. Serve warm or cold with tortilla chips and fresh vegetables for dipping. Garnish top with one chopped tomato and cilantro leaves, if desired. Makes 1 1/2 cups dip.

ARTICHOKE BITES

2 tablespoons butter or margarine
1/2 onion, chopped
1 clove garlic, peeled and crushed
2 (14-ounce) cans artichokes, drained
6 eggs
12 ounces Monterey Jack cheese, grated
6 tablespoons cornmeal
2 tablespoons white wine

◆

In a skillet, on medium heat, melt butter and cook onion and garlic for 3 to 5 minutes until tender. In a mixer, combine artichokes that have been well drained by pressing in colander, eggs, cheese, cornmeal and wine. Add onion mixture and mix well. Scoop into greased mini muffin pans until 3/4 full. Bake for 15 to 20 minutes at 375 degrees. Must remove from pans as soon as they are room temperature. Store in a plastic or glass container and freeze for up to a month or refrigerate for up to 2 days, covered well. Artichokes do not store well in metal containers. Reheat on a baking sheet in a warm oven for 10 minutes. Serve warm. Makes 4 dozen.

For items that taste better right out of the oven, like Artichoke Bites or Squash Rounds, try passing to guests as they gather for cocktails on small trays. Have small napkins on hand to offer.

SQUASH ROUNDS

1/3 cup butter or margarine
1 medium onion, peeled and chopped
1 clove garlic, peeled and crushed
2 1/2 cups yellow or summer squash, grated
12 ounces sharp Cheddar cheese, grated
6 eggs
3/4 cup butter cracker crumbs
1/4 cup romano cheese, grated
1/2 teaspoon salt
Sesame seeds, optional

In a large skillet, melt butter and cook onion and garlic for 2 minutes. Add squash and cook for 5 minutes on medium heat. In a mixer, combine cheese, eggs, crumbs, romano and salt. Add squash mixture and mix thoroughly. Scoop into greased muffin tins 3/4 full and bake at 350 degrees for 15 to 25 minutes. Remove from tins and serve warm. May be frozen for up to a month until ready to use or refrigerated for 2 days, covered well. Reheat on a baking sheet for 10 minutes in a warm oven. Makes 4 dozen.

Menu Suggestion:
A Popular Wedding Reception Cocktail Buffet

Cheese Biscuits with Ham and Spinach Puff Pastries,

Rice Crispy Wafers,

Ricotta Cheese Balls with Crackers,

Tiny Croissants Filled with Tangy Chicken Salad,

Sweet and Sour Meatballs,

Cold Crab Mousse with Wafers,

Fresh Vegetables with Hot Beef and Walnut Dip and Cilantro Corn Dip,

Fresh Fruit Displays with Toffee Dessert Dip,

Basket Weave Wedding Cake with Fresh Pink Roses and Ivy Sprigs,

Chocolate Groom Cake with Strawberries and Chocolate Garnishes,

Note: Wedding Cakes can be ordered through local bakeries or grocers.

Tip of the Trade:

Commercially frozen puff pastry is great to keep on hand in the freezer. For best working results, keep chilled until ready to handle. Be imaginative with different fillings and shapes. Ham and Cheese Puffs, page 60, can be assembled the same way as Spinach Pastries as an alternate filling.

Tip of the Trade:

Finger sandwiches are a perfect delicacy from our Southern past. They work well for teas, coffee, open houses, receptions and even cocktail parties. The only drawback is that they need to be prepared at the last minute. Preparations should be within 2 to 3 hours of the first guest arriving. Place single layer on trays, cover with a damp paper towel and plastic wrap and refrigerate until needed.

Add thinly sliced apples to sandwiches for a twist. Soak peeled, sliced apples in pineapple juice, dry a little and lay on top of spread.

SPINACH PASTRIES

1 pound package commercial puff pastry sheets
1 (10-ounce) package frozen chopped spinach
1/2 cup ricotta cheese
2 tablespoons romano or Parmesan cheese, grated
4 ounces cream cheese, room temperature
1 teaspoon salt
1 clove garlic, crushed, optional
1/3 cup toasted pine nuts, optional

Defrost puff pastry sheets, but keep chilled. Defrost spinach and drain well. Combine spinach, ricotta, romano, cream cheese, salt, garlic and nuts in a mixer fitted with a metal whip or food processor fitted with a metal or plastic blade. Spread puff pastry sheets out and cut into 3-inch squares and then into triangles. Spoon 1 1/2 tablespoons spinach mixture into each triangle, fold over into triangle and pierce edges together with a fork. Place on a greased baking sheet and bake at 350 degrees for 15 minutes. Can refrigerate up to 2 days in single layers, being careful not to stack and crush the pastry. These freeze well after baking, then reheat in a warm oven. Makes 36 appetizers.

ROQUEFORT SPREAD

4 ounces Roquefort or bleu cheese
1 (8-ounce) package cream cheese, room temperature
1/2 cup walnuts, chopped
2 tablespoons cognac or brandy

Crumble cheese and mix with cream cheese, chopped walnuts and cognac. Refrigerate for up to 3 days, but return to room temperature before spreading. Spread on sandwich bread, remove crusts and cut into small tea sandwiches. Makes 1 1/2 cups, enough for approximately six sandwiches.

RICOTTA CHEESE BALL

1 cup (4-ounces) medium Cheddar cheese, grated
1 cup (4-ounces) Monterey Jack cheese, grated
3 tablespoons high quality mayonnaise
3 ounces cream cheese, softened
3/4 cup ricotta cheese
1/2 walnuts, chopped
1/4 cup chopped dried parsley

In a food processor fitted with a metal blade, combine cheeses, mayonnaise, cream cheese and ricotta. Pulse five to six times until smooth. Place on waxed paper and refrigerate, if necessary, for 15 to 20 minutes to firm for rolling into a ball. Roll cheese ball in a mixture of walnuts and parsley. Refrigerate until ready to serve with butter crackers. Makes 1 ball.

CRANBERRY CHEESE BALL

1 (8-ounce) package cream cheese
1 cup (4-ounces) medium Cheddar cheese, grated
4 tablespoons cranberry relish or canned whole
   cranberry sauce
1/2 cup chopped pecans

In a food processor fitted with a plastic blade, combine cream cheese, cheddar cheese and cranberry relish. Pulse three to five times until creamy. Leave cranberry chutney chunky. Roll ball in chopped pecans and refrigerate for at least 24 hours. Present with butter crackers on a platter of mint and cranberry garnishes. This freezes well. Makes 1 ball.

Tip of the Trade:

Most cheese balls will freeze great for one month. Keep miniature ones on hand for small, last-minute gatherings.

Placing a cheese platter with assorted cheese balls and specialty cheeses works well on a bar or coffee table. Serve with gourmet crackers and large bunches of seedless grapes.

Menu Suggestion:
Casual Cocktails

Squash Rounds,

Cheese Balls with Crackers and Large Bunches of Green Grapes,

Breaded Chicken Fingers with Apricot Mustard Sauce,

Hot Crab Mexican Dip with Large Corn Chips,

Pork Meatballs with Tangy Peach Sauce,

Steamed Asparagus with Curry Cream Mayonnaise,

Fresh Fruit with Hazlenut Fruit Dip

◆

Tip of the Trade:

Camembert is made in France in the winter months and is smaller and thicker than Brie. The crust should not have any black marks and the cheese should neither have holes nor be runny. Quality Camembert is made from whole, unskimmed milk.

Camembert Pie and Cherry Pie Brie look especially beautiful presented in a silver pie holder. Browse antique shops for unique holders to collect and use on your entertaining tables.

CAMEMBERT PIE

1/8 cup golden raisins
1/4 cup dried apricots, chopped well
1/4 cup chopped dates
1 pear, peeled and chopped
1 apple, peeled and chopped
1/4 cup white or zinfandel wine
1 teaspoon lemon juice
1 (4-ounce) package cream cheese, room temperature
1/4 cup butter or margarine, room temperature
1 cup plain all-purpose flour
1/2 teaspoon salt
1 (4-ounce) round Camembert or Brie cheese
1/4 cup walnuts, chopped fine

Place all fruit in a bowl with wine and lemon juice and marinate until ready to use or overnight. In a food processor fitted with a metal blade, combine cream cheese, butter, flour and salt and process until a dough forms. Remove from processor and place on a lightly floured surface and roll out into a 10-inch circle. Cut Camembert in half horizontally and place first half in a greased 9-inch pie plate. Fill with all fruit allowing fruit to overflow into pie plate. Cover with pastry, fold in edges and scallop along pie plate. Sprinkle pastry with chopped walnuts. Can be refrigerated for up to 2 days covered well at this point. Bake at 350 degrees for 20 to 35 minutes until crust is golden. Serve warm with large wafer or butter crackers. Makes 16 to 20 servings.

Tip of the Trade:

*Brie is considered a dessert cheese. It can be placed on a cocktail or dessert buffet.
Brie can be served elegantly with sweet or sparkling wines as an ending to any reception or cocktail gathering.*

CHERRY PIE BRIE

1 (15-ounce) package commercial pie crust sheets
1 (6-ounce) Brie cheese round or Camembert cheese
1 (14 1/2-ounce) can cherries in syrup, drained well
2 tablespoons brown sugar

◆

Place one sheet of pie crust in a well-greased 9-inch pie plate. Cut Brie in half, making two circles. Place one-half of Brie in the middle with cherry filling on top of cheese. Cherries will fall over cheese and should be left this way. Cover with other half of Brie and other pie crust. Pierce edges with thumb prints or a fork. Sprinkle with brown sugar. Bake for 20 to 25 minutes at 350 degrees and cool slightly before serving. Place in a silver pie plate holder with large wafers and fruit. Makes 24 servings.

One pound of crackers will serve 20 guests.
Place crackers out in small amounts. Place in a small cracker server, small compote or bowl one package at a time.

PESTO CHEESECAKE

1/4 cup bread crumbs
1 tablespoon butter or margarine, softened
3 tablespoons Parmesan cheese
2 (8-ounce) packages cream cheese, room temperature
1 cup ricotta cheese
1/4 teaspoon salt
1/8 teaspoon red pepper
3 eggs
1/2 cup spinach, washed and dried well
1/2 cup fresh parsley
1 tablespoon olive oil
1 tablespoon vegetable oil
2 teaspoons minced fresh or 1 teaspoon dried basil
1 clove garlic, peeled and crushed
1/2 cup Parmesan
1/4 cup pine nuts or almonds toasted

Menu Suggestion:
A Fall or Winter Cocktail Buffet

Crab Artichoke Dip with Thin Wheat Crackers,

Ginger Pork Tenderloins, Rolls, Mayonnaise and Mustards,

Apricot Curried Shrimp and Scallops,

Turkey Crepe Torte,

Marinated Poached Asparagus,

Pesto Cheesecake,

Cherry Pie Brie,

Apples and Fruit Display, Toffee Dessert Dip

Combine bread crumbs, butter and Parmesan and sprinkle in an 8-to 9-inch spring form pan that has been greased on bottom and sides. In a mixer, combine cream cheese, ricotta, salt, pepper and eggs and mix well. In a food processor fitted with a metal blade, combine spinach, parsley, oils, basil and garlic and pulse five to six times, making pesto. Add to mixer along with Parmesan and pine nuts. Mix again and pour into spring form pan. Bake in a 350-degree oven for 45 to 55 minutes. Cool and refrigerate covered for up to 2 days. Unmold and serve at room temperature on a cake platter. Serves 30 to 36 guests.

♦

Tip of the Trade:

When selecting a baking dish for Baked Cheese and Artichoke Loaf, use a new Teflon or non-stick coated loaf pan. Cooling before unmolding and loosening from edges with a knife is important to keep it from breaking apart.

Menu Suggestion:

An Afternoon Tea or Reception

*Tiny Assorted Quiches
and
Cheese Biscuits filled
with Honey Ham,*

Assorted Finger Sandwiches,

*Baked Cheese and Artichoke
Loaf with Crackers,*

*Golden Raisin Scones,
Whipped Butter and
Homemade Jams,*

*Lemon Squares, Shortbread and
Strawberries,*

*Chocolate Mint Decadence with
Raspberry Purée and
Whipped Cream,*

Berry Champagne Punch,

*Teas, Coffees, Creamers, Sugars
and Lemons*

BAKED CHEESE AND ARTICHOKE LOAF

3/4 cup Feta cheese
1 (8-ounce) package cream cheese, room temperature
1 (14 1/2-ounce) can marinated artichokes, drained
1 tablespoon lemon juice
1 egg
2 drops hot sauce

Mix Feta cheese, cream cheese, artichokes, lemon juice, egg and hot sauce together in a mixer fitted with a metal whip or in a food processor fitted with a plastic blade. Pour into a greased 9 x 3 Teflon loaf pan and bake for 45 minutes at 350 degrees. Cool to room temperature and unmold mold onto serving platter or cake stand. Garnish with fresh herbs and serve with wafers or crackers. Makes 12 to 16 servings.

FOUR CHEESE LOAF

1/2 cup Monterey Jack cheese, shredded
1/2 cup medium or mild Cheddar cheese, grated
1/2 cup Gruyere cheese or Swiss cheese, grated
1 (4-ounce) package cream cheese
4 tablespoons sour cream
2 tablespoons ricotta cheese
2 tablespoon mayonnaise
1 teaspoon horseradish sauce
2/3 cup pistachios, chopped
1/3 cup walnuts, chopped

♦

Bring cheeses to room temperature and beat in a mixer fitted with a metal blade with all other ingredients, with the exception of the nuts, until smooth. Line a 5 1/2 x 3 x 2 loaf pan with plastic wrap overlapping edges by 2 inches and then grease. Sprinkle half of the pistachios and half of the walnuts in the pan. Press half of the cheese mixture over nuts. Top with remaining nuts and press with remaining cheese. Chill loaf covered for at least 2 hours and up to 2 days. Unfold on serving tray and remove wrap. Garnish with herbs and serve with wafers. Makes 16 to 24 servings.

An assortment of open-face sandwiches with white and wheat sandwich bread cut with cookie cutter shapes and topped with mayonnaise, peeled and sliced tomatoes and cucumbers is a true Southern treat. Sprinkle the tops with a seasoned salt or paprika, and garnish with a fresh herb for a beautiful presentation. The bread can first be spread with room temperature butter before the mayonnaise to keep it from becoming soggy. For pre-party preparations, the bread can be cut into shapes, spread with room temperature butter, then frozen in an airtight container until ready to assemble right before the party.

Serving Tip:

When presenting tiny finger sandwiches on an entertaining table, have two to three trays. One for presentation and 1 to 2 for replenishing. Being such a dainty treat, garnishing one corner of the tray with a tiny bouquet of flowers tied with ribbon would add the delicate touch needed. Fresh herbs work beautifully on open-face sandwiches. Be artistic and creative with your display.

For assorted fillings for closed finger sandwiches, use:

*Carrot Tea Sandwich Spread,
Tangy Chicken Salad,
Pimento Cheese,
Egg Salad
and Roquefort Spread*

CARROT TEA SANDWICH SPREAD

4 carrots, peeled and grated
1/4 cup chopped dates
1/8 cup walnuts, chopped
1 tablespoon high quality mayonnaise
4 ounces cream cheese, room temperature

Combine carrots, dates, walnuts, mayonnaise and cream cheese in a mixer and mix well. May refrigerate for up to 2 days. Makes 1 cup, enough for approximately four sandwiches.

◆

Menu Suggestion:

A Grand and Elegant Buffet

Cheese Wafers with Pepper Jelly,

*Marinated Beef Tenderloin,
Rolls,
Horseradish Cream,
Stone Ground Mustards,*

*Wine Baked Whole Salmon Fillet
with
Garlic French Bread Wedges and
Dilled Capered Sauce,*

*Crab and Artichoke Dip with
Garlic Bagel Crisps,*

Camembert Pie,

*Brandy Gelatin Mold with
Fresh Fruit and Wafers,*

Tiny Chocolate Éclairs,

Coffee Bar

Tip of the Trade:

*Apricot Mustard Sauce is an
excellent sauce for ham or pork.*

BREADED CHICKEN

1 1/2 pounds chicken strips
2 cups bread crumbs
3/4 cup Parmesan cheese
1 tablespoon paprika
1/4 to 1/2 teaspoon pepper
2 tablespoons chopped dry parsley
1 cup butter or margarine
1/4 cup Worcestershire
1/4 cup buttermilk

Cut chicken strips into 1- to 2-inch pieces. Combine bread crumbs, Parmesan, paprika, pepper and parsley. Bread crumbs may be done 2 days in advance, or weeks in advance and frozen. In a large saucepan, melt butter then add Worcestershire and buttermilk. Do not boil. While very warm, dip chicken breasts in this mixture and then into bread crumb mixture. (If doubling recipe, divide breadcrumbs mixture into smaller portions to keep from becoming soggy.) Place on a greased baking sheet and bake at 375 degrees for 15 to 20 minutes until done. Serve warm or room temperature on a platter of green leaf lettuce with apricot mustard sauce. This dish does not reheat well, but cooks beautifully with large breast filets to be served at dinner parties. Makes 8 servings.

APRICOT MUSTARD SAUCE

1/2 cup deli style mustard or stone ground mustard
1 (12-ounce) jar apricot preserves
1/4 cup mayonnaise
1/2 cup sour cream
1 tablespoon honey
1/4 teaspoon lemon pepper

Mix all ingredients together and store for up to 3 days in refrigerator sealed tightly. Serve with Breaded Chicken Fingers.

◆

PORK MEATBALLS WITH TANGY PEACH SAUCE

2 pounds lean ground pork
1/3 cup dry bread crumbs
1/4 cup milk
1/3 cup chili sauce
1/2 onion, chopped fine
1 egg
1/2 teaspoon salt
1/4 teaspoon pepper
1 (6-ounce) jar peach preserves
1/2 cup cream
1 tablespoon Worcestershire sauce
1 teaspoon Dijon mustard
3 tablespoons chili sauce
1 1/2 tablespoons apple cider vinegar
1/2 teaspoon horseradish

Combine pork, bread crumbs, milk, chili sauce, onion, egg, salt and pepper in a mixer and mix well. Form into 1-inch balls and lay single layer in a greased baking dish. Bake in a 350-degree oven for 25 to 35 minutes until browned. Drain off excess liquids from the pan and set aside. In a food processor fitted with a metal blade or in a bowl using a hand-held blender, combine preserves, cream, Worcestershire, mustard, chili sauce, vinegar and horseradish. Blend well. Pour over meatballs and place covered in oven at 350 degrees for 25 minutes. These can be made in advance and refrigerated for up to 2 days or frozen in sauce until ready to use, then reheated covered in a warm oven. Makes 5 dozen meatballs.

Serving Tip:
Have long and sturdy toothpicks or hors d'oeuvre forks available at the side and have a slotted spoon to serve meatballs to plates.

Tip of the Trade:

Meatballs are best served during winter or fall cocktail buffets. They work especially well for wedding receptions.

For safety purposes and rolling smoothness, keep meat refrigerated and bring out in small portions to roll. Also, choose prime ground meats that are lean and fresh for best results.

Serve meatballs out of a chafing dish that holds water in the bottom portion. Large chafing dishes can be rented for big events. Check the water and fuel at least once during the event.

Plan on 3 to 5 meatballs per person depending on the time of day and menu of the celebration. If serving other meats, 3 per person should be plenty.

◆

Tip of the Trade:

Sweet and Sour Meatballs are very popular. Using a good quality, lean, freshly ground meat will make the difference. The extra cost is well worth it and will keep the sauce from becoming too greasy as well as keeping the meatballs from shrinking too much with the cooking.

Tip of the Trade:

When preparing Shrimp Pâté, use a mold container with a removable lid for easier unmolding. If kitchen inventory has only regular molds, line the bottom with plastic wrap and then grease the wrap before filling with pâté or other desired recipe for an alternative in easy removal of any dish.

Shrimp Pâté is very popular and guests might take more than a usual congealed mold or spread. Try serving as a first course at a seated dinner for a simply elegant start. Individual molds can be used for this.

SWEET AND SOUR MEATBALLS

2 pounds ground sirloin
2 eggs
1/2 cup bread crumbs
1/2 cup milk
1 onion, chopped fine
1 teaspoon salt
1/2 teaspoon pepper
1 (20-ounce) bottle tomato ketchup
1 (12-ounce) bottle grape jelly

Combine ground sirloin, eggs, bread crumbs, milk, onion, salt and pepper. Mix well and roll into 1-inch balls. Place single layer in a greased baking dish. Mix together ketchup and grape jelly. This will be rather lumpy. Pour on meatballs and cover. Bake at 375 degrees for 30 minutes. Remove from oven and gently scoop and stir to smooth out sauce. This can be done easily with a large slotted spoon scooping from underneath and from sides of pan. Return to oven for 20 minutes. Drain excess sauce and serve warm in a chafing dish with picks or forks. Meatballs can be frozen well-covered until ready to use, or refrigerated for up to 1 day. Defrost if necessary and reheat in a warm oven, covered. Makes 4 dozen.

SHRIMP PÂTÉ MOLD

1 1/2 pounds shrimp
1/2 cup butter or margarine, melted
1/3 cup mayonnaise
1 tablespoon lemon juice
1/4 to 1/2 teaspoon salt to taste

◆

Cook, peel and clean shrimp. In a food processor, combine shrimp with butter, mayonnaise and lemon juice. Process 5 to 6 seconds. Add salt as needed. Place in a greased 4-cup mold. Chill for 8 hours and unmold on green leaf lettuce. Serve with crackers and cucumber slices with sides of cocktail or tartar sauces. Makes 16 to 20 servings.

Serving Suggestion:

Remember to use height when planning serving platters for a buffet table. Compotes, footed trays or cake stands can give a start to my suggested three to five heights for a regular sized eight to twelve seated size serving table. Plan ahead by placing platters on the table pre-party and using an artful eye to adjust where needed. Mark the platters with a note to remind you which one you had chosen for each dish.

Serving Tip:

A congealed cocktail mold can be served any time of year and with any type of party. It can be as formal or informal as needed. Serve with a side of butter crackers or wafers. Small butter knives or spreaders can be used for easy guest serving.

COLD CRAB MOUSSE

1 (8-ounce) package cream cheese
3/4 cup undiluted canned tomato soup
1 1/2 packages unflavored gelatin, measuring 3 teaspoons
1/8 cup cold water
3/4 cup mayonnaise
3/4 cup sour cream
2 tablespoons lemon juice
2 green onions, peeled and chopped
3/4 cup celery, chopped fine
1 (8-ounce) package pasteurized white crab or
    2 (6-ounce) canned white crab
1 teaspoon horseradish
1/2 to 1 tablespoon minced fresh basil, optional

Tip of the Trade:

If using canned shellfish, it can be made better tasting by removing from can and soaking in salty water in the refrigerator for 1 hour. Drain shellfish well by pressing in a colander. This will remove the canned taste, if so desired.

In a medium saucepan combine cream cheese and soup and heat on medium heat for 3 minutes. Dissolve gelatin in cold water and then add to soup mixture and heat through. Remove from stove and add remaining ingredients. Pour into a greased 4-cup mold and chill for 8 to 24 hours. Unmold and serve with cucumber slices and butter crackers. Makes 16 to 24 servings.

♦

MEXICAN CRAB DIP

1/4 cup butter or margarine
2 tablespoons plain all purpose flour
1 (12-ounce) can diced tomatoes and green chilis
1 (8-ounce) package cream cheese
8 ounces Monterey Jack cheese, grated
1 pound pasteurized crab or 4 (6-ounce) cans white crab
8 ounces sharp Cheddar cheese, grated

In a medium skillet over medium heat, melt butter and add flour. Stir until smooth to make a paste or roux. Add diced tomatoes and green chilis with their juice. Simmer for 5 minutes. Add cream cheese and Monterey cheese and heat until melted. Add crab. If artificial crab is used, place crab in food processor to chop fine before adding to dish. Place in a 9 x 13 greased dish or a greased glass chafing dish. Sprinkle with Cheddar cheese. Can be stored covered in refrigerator for up to 1 day at this point. Bake in a 350-degree oven for 20 to 30 minutes. Serve warm in a chafing dish or holder with large corn chips. Makes 24 servings.

CRAB FILLED MUSHROOMS

1 pound small ripe button mushrooms
1 (8-ounce) package cream cheese, softened
2 (6-ounce) cans white crab meat, drained well

Remove stems from mushrooms and peel outer skin off of each mushroom. Mushrooms must be well ripened to do this. If skin does not remove, wipe clean and remove stem. Place on an ungreased baking dish with sides. Mix together cream cheese and crab meat. Fill each mushroom well. Crab mixture will not overflow during cooking so you may overfill if you wish. Broil on low broil for 10 minutes. Best if heated in small batches just before serving warm. Makes 12 to 16 servings.

♦

BRANDY GELATIN MOLD

12 ounces cream cheese, softened
1/4 cup butter or margarine, softened
1/2 cup sour cream
1/2 cup sugar
1 envelope unflavored gelatin to equal 2 teaspoons
1/4 cup brandy, any flavor or brand
1 cup almonds, sliced

In a mixer with a whip or processor with a metal blade, combine cream cheese, butter, sour cream and sugar and mix well. Soften gelatin in brandy and then heat on high for 1 minute in a microwave or on stove. Add gelatin and brandy mixture to cream cheese mixture and mix through. Using a 1-quart greased mold, sprinkle almonds on bottom. Pour in filling and refrigerate for 3 to 5 hours. Unmold and serve with strawberries, apple and pear slices and kiwi with sweet graham wafers or ginger snaps. Makes 24 servings.

HAZELNUT FRUIT DIP

1 (8-ounce) can crushed pineapple, drained well
1 (8-ounce) package cream cheese, room temperature
1/2 cup sour cream
1/4 cup hazelnuts, chopped and toasted, or almonds
1 tablespoon honey
2 teaspoons hazelnut liqueur
1 carrot, grated

Combine pineapple, cream cheese, sour cream, nuts, honey, liqueur and carrot in a mixer and mix well. This may be prepared 2 days in advance. Serve room temperature with sliced fruit. Makes 12 servings.

Tip of the Trade:

In most cases, cocktail buffets do not require rich desserts. Brandy Gelatin Mold is a wonderful alternative for a dessert served with Fresh Fruit Displays and Sweet Crackers

Present molds on cake platters and footed cake stands. Garnish with a bouquet of fresh herbs or flowers on one side. Remember, flowers, greenery or herbs are great for hiding flaws or breaks that might occur.

The Brandy Gelatin Mold, Shrimp Pâté and Cold Crab Mousse work better in a small, solid round mold without a hole in the middle.

Serving Tip:

Fruit trays for a party can be assembled up to 12 hours in advance. Berries and kiwi fruit need to be prepared at the last minute.

Dips look beautiful in a footed compote placed beside or on the corner of the tray. Fill dips 3/4 full in the dish for the best look. Garnish the dip with a slice of fruit so that guests will know the sweet dip is for the fruit.

◆

Strawberry Trees are beautiful for any event and take only a little while to prepare, however, they do require day-of-the-party assembly, so plan ahead to give ample time. A Styrofoam cone will need to be purchased from a craft, floral or party supply store, and floral pins could be handy but not a necessity. Have ready toothpicks, green leafy lettuce and fresh strawberries. Place cone on serving platter and secure green leafy lettuce to cone with floral pins or toothpicks. This keeps guests from seeing cone when removing a strawberry. Push the toothpicks into the cone by themselves. Have strawberries washed and dried with greens attached and place green side down on the toothpick. The first toothpicks might need to be pushed further in to the cone for a good start, whereas additional toothpicks can be left a little longer after the first group of strawberries have been placed. Keeping the Strawberry Tree centered and uniform might be a difficult task. Keep in mind the beauty of the different shapes and sizes. Keep refrigerated until serving time. Best to be put together no more than 6 hours before the event with very fresh strawberries. Washing strawberries too far in advance will cause rotting, so wash just before assembly. Serve with any of the dessert dips or simply on a fruit display.

MOCHA DIP

12 ounces chocolate or chocolate flavored bars
1/2 cup whipping cream
4 tablespoons mocha liqueur

In a microwave-safe dish, combine chocolate and whipping cream. Heat for 5 minutes on medium high in microwave. Remove and stir. Heat in 3-minute intervals until smooth and add liqueur. Serve room temperature with strawberries and other favorite fruits. If preparing this dish in advance and refrigerating, heating in microwave again before serving might be necessary. Makes 12 to 16 servings.

Serving Tip:

Serve dessert dips out of crystal or silver compotes or small bowls. Fill the bowls 3/4 full with dip. Laying the bowl on the corner of the platter of fruit looks beautiful.

TOFFEE DESSERT DIP

6 ounces white flavored baking bars or white chocolate
1 (8-ounce) package cream cheese
1/4 cup whipping cream
1/2 cup sour cream
1 (6-ounce) package toffee bits

In a microwave-safe dish, combine white baking bars or white chocolate, cream cheese and whipping cream. Heat for 5 minutes on high and stir. Heat for 4-minute intervals and stir with a whisk until smooth. Add sour cream and beat until smooth. Stir in toffee bits and serve with sliced apples and pears. Makes 12 to 16 servings.

◆

A Celebration of Heritage
Breads

Anne Mullins Rigdon

♦

Tip of the Trade:
Cinnamon Rolls

If making cinnamon rolls out of dough or leftover dough, roll out to 1/8-inch thickness into a rectangle 6 x 12 inches. Fillings should not cover the outer 1/2-inch of dough. For each rectangle, brush with 3 tablespoons melted butter (leaving 1/2-inch from side.) Sprinkle with 3 tablespoons brown sugar, and sprinkle with 1/2 teaspoon cinnamon. Crushed nuts can be added if desired. Roll dough up carefully, slice into 1/2-inch pinwheel rounds and place on a greased baking sheet to rise for at least 1 hour. Bake at 350 degrees for 15 to 20 minutes. Brush the tops of rolls with an icing made of 1/2 cup powdered sugar and 1 tablespoon milk or lemon juice or brush with apricot jam while hot. These can be stored, frozen, and reheated just like dinner rolls.

For Storing:

If storing rolls or biscuits in the freezer, cool completely to room temperature after baking before placing in freezer bags or desired containers. Laying in container with waxed paper between layers of two to three deep gives great results. Make sure container is sealed well and even wrapped for extended freezer time.

DINNER ROLLS

1 cup butter-flavored shortening
1/2 cup sugar
1 1/2 teaspoons salt
1 cup boiling water
2 eggs
2 packages yeast, regular or rapid rise
1 cup lukewarm buttermilk
6 cups plain all-purpose flour
2 sticks butter or margarine, melted

In a mixer fitted with a pastry blade, combine butter, sugar and salt. Pour in boiling water and beat well. Add eggs one at a time while beating. Dissolve yeast in warm buttermilk that has been heated in a microwave or on the stove. Add yeast mixture into mixer and then add flour. Knead well in two parts on a lightly floured surface. Roll to 1/2-inch thick, cut into rounds, dip half of roll into butter and fold overlapping onto a greased baking sheet. Let rise for 1 hour. Bake at 350 degrees for 20 minutes. Brush tops with butter and serve warm. These freeze well-cooked, then reheat in a 350 degree oven for 5 to 10 minutes. Makes 5 dozen rolls. Extra dough can be used for cinnamon rolls.

CHEESE BISCUITS

2 1/2 cups self-rising flour
1 1/2 cups extra sharp Cheddar cheese, grated
1 cup butter-flavored shortening
1 cup buttermilk

♦

In a mixer fitted with a pastry blade, combine self-rising flour and cheese. Cut in shortening and mix slightly. While mixing, add buttermilk. Cream together, but do not overmix. Knead on a lightly floured surface four to six times. Roll out to 1/2- to 3/4-inch thick and cut with a 3/4-inch cutter. Bake on a greased baking sheet at 350 degrees for 12 to 15 minutes. Bottom of biscuit should be slightly brown when done. These freeze beautifully. Serve warm, filled with shaved honey ham or with whipped butter. Makes 3 dozen biscuits.

> *Angel Biscuits have a little yeast making them a cross between a biscuit and a roll. They are easy to make because they only need to rise once, right before cooking. Cooking thm 3/4 of the way in advance and finishing them right before serving works very well. Simply mouth watering.*

ANGEL BISCUITS

5 cups plain all-purpose flour
1/4 cup sugar
1 teaspoon baking soda
3 teaspoons baking powder
1 cup shortening
2 packages yeast
1/8 cup luke warm water
2 cups buttermilk
1/2 cup butter, melted

In a mixer fitted with a pastry blade, combine flour, sugar, soda and baking powder. Cut in shortening, mixing slightly. Dissolve yeast in warm water. Add yeast mixture and buttermilk to mixer and mix through. Keep dough covered in refrigerator until ready to use. Knead dough on a floured surface and roll out to 3/4-inch thickness. Cut with a 3/4- to 1-inch biscuit cutter and brush with butter. Let rise for 1 hour and bake at 375 degrees for 15 minutes. Serve warm with whipped butter. Makes 4 dozen.

Tip of the Trade:

Each region of the South has its own form of biscuits and each family has its own method of preparing and baking. Take time to form your own recipe and method of preparing this authentic Southern bread. My mother's friend and maid Beulah, taught her how to make biscuits. She in turn taught me, teaching me from the heart of her kitchen.

The **Buttermilk Biscuit** *that was handed down to me follows the Cheese Biscuit recipe without the cheese. Adding 1 teaspoon baking powder to the recipe will make a light and fluffy biscuit. Follow the recipe directions as given in Cheese Biscuits and sneak one as they come right out of the oven.* **Ham Biscuits** *that Southerners often speak of are regular biscuits that have been cooked, sliced and filled with ham. The biscuit filled with ham are reheated in a 350-degree oven for 10 minutes and served hot. Sliced country ham, regular ham or even deli ham can be used.*

Tip of the Trade:

Buttermilk can be substituted with equal amounts of plain yogurt, or by adding 1 tablespoon vinegar or lemon juice, to each 1 cup of regular milk.

♦

PECAN CHEESE SCONES

2 cups plain all-purpose flour
1/4 teaspoon salt
1/4 teaspoon red pepper
1 1/2 teaspoons baking powder
2 1/2 cups sharp Cheddar cheese, grated
2/3 cup butter, room temperature
2/3 cup milk
1 egg
1 1/2 cups pecans, chopped fine

In a mixer fitted with a pastry blade, combine flour, salt, red pepper, baking powder and cheese. Cut in butter and mix slightly. Add milk and egg and mix until dough forms. Chill dough for 30 minutes. Roll onto a floured surface into 1/2-inch thickness and cut with a 3/4- to 1-inch cutter. Place pecans in a shallow dish and press tops of scones with pecan pieces or chopped pecans. Bake on greased baking sheets for 12 to 20 minutes at 350 degrees. Serve at room temperature or warm with honey and butter and a cup of tea, coffee or a glass of dry sherry. Makes 5 dozen.

GOLDEN RAISIN SCONES

3 cups plain all-purpose flour
1/3 cup sugar
1 1/2 teaspoons baking powder
1/2 teaspoon baking soda
1/4 teaspoon salt
6 tablespoons butter or margarine, room temperature
2/3 cup buttermilk
2 eggs
1 teaspoon vanilla
1/2 cup golden raisins
1/2 cup butter or margarine, melted
1/2 cup sugar
1 tablespoon cinnamon

♦

In a mixer fitted with a pastry blade, combine flour, 1/3 cup sugar, baking powder, baking soda and salt. Cut in 6 tablespoons butter, and while mixing, add buttermilk, eggs, vanilla and raisins. Knead four to five times and roll out to 1/2-inch thickness. Cut with a small biscuit cutter and place on a greased baking sheet. Brush with melted butter. Sprinkle with a mixture of 1/2 cup sugar and 1 tablespoon cinnamon either before or after you bake. Bake at 350 degrees for 15 to 25 minutes. Serve with lemon curd, butters and hot tea. Makes 24 scones.

Serving Tip:

Breads should be served hot unless specified otherwise. Serve by passing in small batches. Linens can be used in bread containers to help retain heat by placing the linen in the server, filling with hot bread and covering with linen corners. Bread linens are made especially for this purpose. Ceramic warmers can be purchased and used by heating with the bread in oven, then placing in server under linens to keep warm.

CHEESE SOUR CREAM MUFFIN BREAD

2 cups self-rising flour
1 cup butter, softened
1 cup sour cream
1 tablespoon sugar
1 1/2 cups Cheddar cheese, grated

In a mixer fitted with a pastry blade, combine all ingredients. Mix on medium speed just until smooth, or mix by hand in bowl. Fill greased muffin tin 3/4 full and bake at 450 degrees for 15 minutes. Serve warm as a dinner muffin. Makes 2 dozen.

Tip of the Trade:

Self-rising flour can be made by using 1 cup plain all-purpose flour with 1/2 teaspoon salt and 1/2 tablespoon baking powder, if a substitution is needed due to low pantry inventory.

For Storing:

Flour can be kept in the freezer tightly sealed in freezer bags or containers to keep freshness for months at a time.

Tip of the Trade:

Two dozen bread pieces will make 8 dinner servings or 14 to 18 cocktail or tea servings.

♦

CORNBREAD

Believed to be a recipe from a collection of my husband's great aunt, Mrs. Billie Flanagan, Greenwood, Mississippi

1 cup cornmeal
1 cup plain all-purpose flour
2 tablespoons brown sugar
3/4 teaspoon baking soda
1 teaspoon baking powder
1 teaspoon salt
2 eggs, beaten
1 1/2 cup sour milk (or buttermilk)
1/4 cup bacon fat or shortening, melted
1/2 onion, peeled and grated

Sift together cornmeal, flour, brown sugar, baking soda, baking powder and salt. Place in a medium mixing bowl or a mixer fitted with a metal whip. Combine separately the eggs, sour milk and melted shortening. Add to dry ingredients and mix well. Grease or oil desired iron skillet, 10-inch cake pan or 12 muffin tins. If oiled, place in a 350-degree oven for 5 to 8 minutes to heat oil. Pour batter in pan and bake in a 350-degree oven for 15 to 35 minutes depending on size of pan. Bread should be golden brown on top and slightly removed from edges. Makes 8 to 10 servings.

CRÊPES

1 cup plain all-purpose flour
3 eggs
1 1/2 cup milk
1/2 teaspoon salt
1 tablespoon butter or margarine, melted
Vegetable cooking spray

♦

In a food processor fitted with a metal blade, combine all ingredients and process 5 to 6 seconds. Spray a small nonstick skillet with cooking spray or use 1/2 to 1 teaspoon butter or oil in pan and place over medium heat. Pour 1/4 cup batter into pan and tilt back and forth to cover evenly. Cook 1 minute to a minute and a half on one side, flip and cook 30 seconds on the other. Keep waxed paper pieces between crêpes for easy storing or freezing for crêpe dishes. Delicious served hot off the stove with butter and syrups or used with crêpe dishes or desserts. Makes 12 to 16 crêpes.

Tip of the Trade:

If crêpe, pancake or waffle batter is too thick, add milk by tablespoonfuls for desired consistency. In most cases, batter will thicken while sitting just a few minutes.

Serving Tip:

Be creative when serving waffles. Peel and slice apples or bananas and cook in a little butter and brown sugar in a skillet. Add pecans, if desired. Top with sliced peaches, maple syrup and toasted almonds. Fresh berries sprinkled with a little powdered sugar will add color and taste.

QUICK WAFFLES

A recipe from the collection of my grandmother, Mary Jo Carpenter

2 cups plain all-purpose flour
1 teaspoon salt
4 teaspoons baking powder
2 tablespoons sugar
1 1/4 cups milk
2 eggs
1/2 cup vegetable oil

In a mixer fitted with a whip, a blender or food processor fitted with a metal or plastic blade, combine all ingredients and mix well. Place 1/2 cup into a double waffle iron and cook according to appliance directions. Spraying iron with vegetable cooking spray will keep waffles from sticking. Makes 4 servings.

Tip of the Trade:

Heating syrup or honey in the microwave on medium high heat just until warm will remove any crystallization that has occurred during storage.

Variations for Pancakes:

*Add 3/4 cup fresh blueberries or
raspberries before cooking by
flouring berries with
1 tablespoon regular flour and
stirring in with a wooden spoon.
Add 1/4 cup finely chopped or
ground nuts to batter before
cooking. Toasted hazelnuts
are a real treat.
Add 1/2 teaspoon nut-flavored
extract to 1 cup maple syrup to
serve with pancakes, or add
3 tablespoons favorite liqueur to
syrup and heat before serving.*

*If a griddle is not part of your
kitchen inventory, a small square
griddle that fits right on the stove
can be puchased at cooking or
discount stores for extremely
reasonable prices. (Electric
griddles are also available.)
It makes pancake cooking
twice as easy.*

Tip of the Trade:

*Sour Cream Coffee Cake is
made much like a pound cake.
One of my most useful sweet
bread recipes.*

BUTTERMILK PANCAKES

2 cups plain all-purpose flour
2 teaspoons baking powder
1 teaspoon baking soda
1/2 teaspoon salt
3 tablespoons sugar
2 eggs or 4 egg whites
3 cups buttermilk
4 tablespoons oil

Combine all ingredients and mix by hand just until mixed through. Let sit for 10 minutes. Pour 3-inch pancakes on a medium hot griddle that has been well preheated and sprayed with vegetable oil cooking spray. Cook until browned on first side about 1 to 2 minutes and flip. Second side takes 1/2 the time to cook as first side. Spread with butter and serve with maple syrup. Can keep warm covered in a 150-degree oven for up to 30 minutes. If wanting to use less buttermilk, use bread flour rather than plain flour and substitute 1 1/2 cups whole milk plus 1 cup buttermilk for 3 cups buttermilk. As easy as pancake mix, but twice as good. Makes 14 to 16 pancakes.

SOUR CREAM COFFEE CAKE

1/2 teaspoon baking soda
1 cup sour cream
1 cup butter or margarine, room temperature
1 cup sugar
2 eggs
1 1/2 cups plain all-purpose flour
1 teaspoon vanilla extract or other favorite extract
1/2 cup brown sugar
1/2 cup walnuts or pecans, chopped

Place soda in sour cream, mix in and set aside. In a mixer fitted with a metal whip, combine butter and 1 cup sugar and cream until smooth. Add eggs one at a time, beating well. Lower speed of mixer and add flour and sour cream alternately. Add vanilla and mix well. Prepare two (9-inch) cake pans or one small Bundt pan with grease and flour. Place one half batter, dividing evenly between chosen pans. Sprinkle the top with a mixture of 1/2 brown sugar and 1/2 walnuts. Place remaining batter and sprinkle with remaining brown sugar and walnuts. Bake in a 350-degree oven for 25 to 45 minutes. Knife inserted in middle should come out clean. Freezes and travels remarkably well. Makes 12 to 16 servings.

ZUCCHINI BLUEBERRY MUFFINS

2 cups grated zucchini
1 cup oil
3 eggs
2 cups sugar
3 cups plain all-purpose flour
1 teaspoon salt
1/2 teaspoon baking powder
1 teaspoon baking soda
2 teaspoons ground cinnamon
1 cup walnuts, chopped
1 1/2 cups blueberries

In a mixer fitted with the wire whisk, combine grated zucchini, oil, eggs and sugar and mix well. Measure flour and add salt, baking powder, baking soda and cinnamon. While mixing slowly, add flour mixture to egg mixture. Add walnuts and mix through. Pour batter into desired greased muffin tins or greased and floured bread loaf pans. Drop blueberries on top, push into batter a little and bake at 350 degrees. Bake 36 mini muffins for 10 to 15 minutes, 12 large muffins for 20 to 25 minutes, and two small loaf pans for 35 to 40 minutes.

Tip of the Trade:

Brunches and breakfasts usually do not require a dessert. Having a sweet roll, doughnut, sticky bun, coffee cake or Danish will work well as a sweet with any morning event. Any of these pastries can be purchased through a specialty or grocer bakery.
If baking at home, try this Sour Cream Coffee Cake. It freezes perfectly. I suggest making more than one.
Serve the cake on any breakfast or brunch buffet or as a breakfast appetizer along with coffee before the meal.

Tip of the Trade:

The unique Zucchini and Blueberry Muffin was created one summer by my mother when the zucchini plants and blueberry bushes were abundant. The combination is quite tasty, and it makes buying the ingredients worthwhile.

Tip of the Trade:
The Celebrations of Giving

Baked breads have been a Southern treat shared from family to family throughout our past. Sharing a gift from your kitchen is sharing with someone your gift of nourishment and of your time. It is a ritual that has been part of our history for centuries. It can be a gift to congratulate, to comfort or to assist a friend or loved one. A gift of food is your gift of love.

Give Fruited Muffins to a friend. For a special presentation, individually wrap each one with plastic wrap. Lay the top portion of the muffin in the middle of the plastic wrap and fold the edges along the bottom. Place in a basket, a pretty bag or a pretty planter or bowl. Include a jar of jam or special butter, teas or coffees, collection of garden seeds or bouquet of flowers.

Loaf breads can be wrapped in plastic wrap also. Colored wraps are now available for the festive look. Tie them with ribbons, raffia or tool. Start collecting beautiful satin or specialty ribbons rather than the ordinary package ribbons. Tiny ornaments or flowers can be added to the middle of the bow as an extra gift and loving touch.

FRUITED MUFFINS

1 egg
1/2 cup sugar
1/2 cup butter or margarine, melted
2 tablespoons oil
2 cups plain all-purpose flour
2 teaspoons baking powder
1/2 teaspoon salt
3/4 cup milk
1 cup fruit (blueberries, raspberries, cranberries, strawberries, peaches)

In a mixer or by hand, combine egg with sugar, butter and oil. Add flour, baking powder and salt. Pour in milk and mix well. Add fruit and stir gently by hand and pour batter into 12 large muffin tins or 24 greased small muffin tins 3/4 full. Bake 15 to 25 minutes, depending on size of muffin, at 350 degrees.

APRICOT CAKE

A recipe from the collection of Spud Dobbs, Marietta

1 cup vegetable oil
3 eggs
2 (4-ounce) cans apricot baby food, (prunes or plums)
2 cups sugar
2 cups self-rising flour
1 teaspoon ground cinnamon
1 teaspoon ground cloves
1 cup chopped pecans, floured
3 tablespoons grated lemon rind
1/2 cup lemon juice
1 cup confectioners powdered sugar

In a mixer fitted with a metal whip, combine oil, eggs, baby food, sugar, flour, cinnamon, and cloves Mix well and fold in pecans. Pour into two greased and floured 9 x 3 x 5 loaf pans. Bake at 300 degrees for 50 to 60 minutes. Let bread cool for 5 to 8 minutes and turn out of pan onto foil. Raise sides of foil slightly around bread. Combine lemon rind, lemon juice and powdered sugar and pour over hot bread. This bread ages wonderfully in a freezer. A delicious travel or gift bread. Makes one loaf.

SOUTHERN LOAF BREAD

A recipe from the collection of my husband's grandmother,
Mrs. Marie Barnes Rambo

1 yeast cake, 1 package active dry yeast
1 cup warm milk
1/2 cup butter, room temperature, or margarine
1/3 cup sugar
3 eggs, beaten
1 quart plain all-purpose flour, (4 cups)

This is a very traditional Southern loaf bread. Recipes will vary from family to family. Place yeast cake or package of yeast in warm milk and set aside. Cream together, in a mixer fitted with the pastry whip, butter and sugar. Sift flour and add to mixer alternately with yeast milk and eggs. Pour into one well greased tube pan and let rise 2 to 3 hours. Bake in a moderate oven, 350 degrees, for approximately 1 hour.

Serving Tip:

Treat your family and friends, especially the children in your kitchen, to bread straight out of the oven. Make sure you have the butter in arm's reach.

Tip of the Trade:

Southern Loaf Bread is extremely easy to make, however, the time to rise needs to be allowed in your baking time. This is a very traditional Southern bread. The recipes will vary from family to household. This one is a treasured recipe from a wonderful cook.

Tip of the Trade:

So many new cooks are afraid of yeast. The temperature of the liquid should be warm to the touch and the yeast should always be added to some type of warm liquid before adding to the dough. After adding the yeast to the warm liquid, it should completely dissolve. Sometimes it will even bubble or rise a little during or after dissolving, giving you great indication that it has been done properly. Follow the expiration dates on the yeast packets carefully. Do not let a failed experience discourage you from trying again.

GRUYERE LOAF

2 cups plain all-purpose flour
1 tablespoon sugar
3/4 teaspoon salt
3/4 cup buttermilk
1 package active dry yeast
1 egg
1/2 cup Gruyere cheese, grated
1 tablespoon butter or margarine, melted
2 tablespoons almonds

In a mixer fitted with a pastry whip, combine 1 cup of flour, sugar and salt. Measure out buttermilk and heat on stove or in microwave until warm to the touch. Dissolve yeast in buttermilk. Add yeast to mixer and mix well. Add egg and grated cheese to mixer and then add remaining flour to make dough. Grease a 1-quart loaf pan generously. Scoop batter into prepared pan. Cover with plastic wrap and refrigerate for 2 to 24 hours. Let bread stand at room temperature for 20 minutes uncovered before baking. Brush with melted butter and sprinkle with almonds. Bake in a 350-degree oven for 30 to 35 minutes. Serve with butter. Makes one loaf.

CHEESE STUFFED ROLLS

12 commercial (2-inch) dinner rolls
1/2 cup butter or margarine, room temperature
1/2 cup mayonnaise
1/4 cup Parmesan cheese
1/4 teaspoon parsley flakes

Tip of the Trade:

Substitute other favorite cheeses for Gruyere Loaf, if desired.

This loaf bread is wonderful because it does not have to be kneaded. Preparation must be done in advance due to refirgeration time but the actual time preparing is short and easy.

Tip of the Trade:

The Cheese Stuff Roll recipe is a really good secret. It fits into any schedule and gives the taste of a hot homemade bread. It can be used with any type bread or roll. Try as an English muffin or bagel topper and place under a broiler until bubbly.

Cut rolls horizontally 3/4 of the way, leaving outer 1/4 attached to keep from messy splitting. In a mixer fitted with a metal whip or by hand, combine butter, mayonnaise, Parmesan and parsley and mix well. Spread a shy tablespoon into each roll and place on a baking sheet and cover with aluminum foil. Before serving, heat rolls for 10 to 15 minutes in a 350-degree oven. For large dinner parties, these may be done a week in advance and frozen well sealed before thawing and cooking. Makes 6 to 8 servings.

Tip of the Trade:

Add two garlic cloves, peeled and crushed or minced to Cheese Stuffed Rolls, as desired.

When cooking the Cheese Stuffed Rolls, the aluminum foil cover can be taken off the last 5 minutes of cooking to crisp the roll, if desired. Use your best judgement.

Serving Tip:

Always try to garnish the Pâte a Choux Puffs when using as an unsweet appetizer. A tiny sprig of parsley or dill really adds to the bland color.

PÂTE A CHOUX PUFFS

1 cup water
1/2 cup butter or margarine
1/2 teaspoon salt
1 teaspoon sugar
1 cup plain all-purpose flour
4 eggs

In a medium saucepan, combine water, butter, salt and sugar. Over medium high heat, bring to a boil. While stirring with a whisk, add the flour and stir for 2 to 3 minutes over heat. A thin coating will start to form on bottom of the pan, indicating that the flour is cooked. Remove dough from heat and cool slightly. Place dough into a mixer or have a hand mixer available. Add eggs one at a time while beating. Fill a 1/2- to 3/4-inch pastry tube or cookie press with dough. Press dough through on greased, light colored baking sheet or greased waxed or parchment paper into desired puff shape. One-inch diameter rounds work nicely for most dishes. Bake in a 400-degree oven for 15 to 20 minutes. Cool and refrigerate or freeze in a closed container. Makes 36 puffs.

Tip of the Trade:

Use these pastries for Tiny Chocolate Éclairs. They also can be used for an appetizer shell for chicken, ham, shrimp, crab or lobster salads. The middle of the puff is hollow. Simply remove the top or break open the top leaving 1/3 attached to the pastry to make a shell for desired filling. Fill no earlier than 2 hours pre-party for best results. They tend to get soggy if they sit too long.

◆

Tip of the Trade:

*Spinach and Ricotta French Bread
is presented better in a whole loaf
with a serving knife. A cake knife
can be used for easy transferring
from table to plate. Place on a
large cutting board or pewter
platter and have guests slice their
own. An outstanding buffet bread.*

*Spinach Ricotta French Bread can
be served with a simple pasta
tossed with butter or Meatless
Bolognese, page 186, for a simple,
every day meal. Fresh Fruit to the
side or for dessert will balance it
off nicely.*

SPINACH AND RICOTTA FRENCH BREAD

A recipe from the collection of my friend, Melda Pressley Collins

1 frozen French bread dough round
3/4 cup ricotta cheese
3 tablespoons Parmesan cheese
1/2 cup grated mozzarella cheese
1 cup fresh spinach leaves, chopped
1 tomato, sliced thin
4 fresh basil leaves, chopped

Roll out bread dough on a lightly floured 2-foot piece of foil or waxed paper to 1 1/2 feet by 5 to 6 inches. Divide into two rectangle portions . It is important to roll dough before dividing. Dividing ingredients between the two dough portions, spread ricotta cheese evenly around dough leaving 1/2-inch from edges. Sprinkle Parmesan and mozzarella evenly over ricotta. Cover with spinach and fresh, chopped basil leaves. Roll each up separately cinnamon roll fashion and pinch the ends together. With hands, stretch cylinders as long as baking pan will allow. Place on a greased baking sheet and bake uncovered at 350 degrees for 15 to 25 minutes. Let cool 5 minutes before slicing. Makes 12 to 16 servings.

Tip of the Trade:

*Ham and Cheese Puffs can be made
into tiny bite-size pastries by
following the instructions on
Spinach Puff Pastries, page 34.
This recipe works well at room
temperature, as well as a hot bread.*

HAM AND CHEESE PUFF

1 (16-ounce) package commercial puff pastry dough
1/2 pound shaved honey maple ham
1/2 pound Swiss cheese, sliced thin or grated
4 tablespoons Dijon mustard

◆

Defrost commercial puff pastry dough in refrigerator. Dough will be in two pieces. With one piece of dough laying on a greased baking sheet, place half of ham and cheese along one side, keeping 1-inch from sides. Spread half mustard on other half and fold over. Pierce edges together with fork. Repeat with other half. Bake for 20 minutes in a 350-degree oven. Individual puffs can be made by dividing dough into smaller portions. Cool 10 minutes before slicing. Makes 8 to 12 servings.

Tip of the Trade:

Puff Pastry is best to work with when chilled. It thaws best in refrigerator, but keeps fresh frozen. Move from freezer to refrigerator the night before preparing.

ARTICHOKE BREAD

2 (12-inch) French bread loaves
1 1/2 cup Monterey Jack cheese, grated
3/4 cup Cheddar cheese, grated
3/4 cup sour cream
1 (14 1/2-ounce) can artichokes, drained
1/4 cup butter or margarine
2 garlic cloves, peeled and crushed
3 green onions, peeled and chopped or
    1/8 cup sweet onion, chopped
1/2 teaspoon dried parsley or 1 tablespoon fresh, snipped

Tip of the Trade:

For best results, cool the Artichoke Bread 5 to 10 minutes before trying to slice. A bread server or cake server can be used to transfer easier from platter. This works best as a buffet bread. If individual servings are wanted, use rolls instead of loaf bread. Sour dough bread works too.

The artichoke filling could be divided between 3 (12-inch) bread loaves, if desired. This would work particularly well for large crowds.

Cut a boat out in each loaf, leaving the top in one piece. Gut out bottom loaves, leaving a 1/2-inch shell of crust on bottom and sides. By hand or in a mixer, combine cheeses, sour cream and well-drained artichokes and mix well. In a small skillet or in a microwave safe dish, combine butter, crushed garlic, green onion and parsley. Microwave covered on high for 1 1/2 to 2 minutes, or heat over medium heat in a small skillet for 3 minutes. Add garlic mixture to artichokes and mix through. Fill each bread loaf with artichoke mixture. Place top back on and wrap tightly in aluminum foil and place on a baking sheet. Bread can be refrigerated for up to 24 hours at this point. Bake at 350 degrees for 15 to 20 minutes and bake uncovered for an additional 5 to 10 minutes. Makes 12 to 18 servings.

♦

Bread Spreads:
Olive Sunflower Spread

2 1/2 tablespoons olive oil
1 (3-ounce) can black olives
1 clove garlic, crushed
2 tablespoons sunflower seeds
1/4 teaspoon salt

Place all ingredients in a food processor fitted with a metal blade and pulse several times. Serve room temperature with French or Italian loaf breads.

Garlic Cheese Butter Spread

8 ounces cream cheese, softened
1/2 cup butter, softened
1 clove garlic, crushed
2 green onions, chopped fine
1/4 teaspoon oregano
1/4 teaspoon basil
1/2 teaspoon parsley

Cream together in a mixer and serve with rolls or Italian bread.

Olive Oil with Garlic and Cracked Peppercorns

1/4 cup olive oil
1 clove garlic, peeled and crushed
1/2 teaspoon black peppercorns

Place olive oil in a lipped platter and swirl crushed garlic through. Crush and spinkle peppercorns over and have guests dip own bread bites. Try with roasted garlic too.

STUFFED PIZZA BREAD

1 (6-ounce) tube commercial can pizza dough
1 tomato, seeded and sliced thin
1 cup mozzarella cheese, grated
1/4 cup romano, asiago, or Parmesan cheese grated
1/4 cup mayonnaise
2 cloves garlic, peeled and crushed
1/4 cup chopped fresh basil
Olive oil
1/2 teaspoon dried chopped parsley

Prepare a 1 1/2-foot piece of waxed paper or aluminum foil by sprinkling with a little flour. Lay dough flat on floured foil and stretch into a 6-inch wide rectangle. Chop or slice tomatoes and lay on a paper towel to drain a little. Lay evenly over dough, leaving 1/2-inch from all sides. In a food processor fitted with a metal blade, combine mozzarella, romano, mayonnaise, garlic and basil. Pulse several times until basil is chopped. Dollop and spread over tomatoes. Roll pizza dough up cinnamon roll style. Press ends together to keep cheese from coming out and lay on a greased baking sheet. Brush roll with olive oil and sprinkle with parsley. Bake in a 325-degree oven for 20 to 25 minutes, uncovered. Cool 5 to 10 minutes before serving. Makes 4 to 6 servings.

Celebrating Your Heritage

Find a family bread recipe to use in your own kitchen. Take time to learn from the cooks of your past. If possible, join these teaching hands in their kitchens to learn their secrets and techniques. Write down these treasures and share them with your children or young family members one day.

♦

New Seasons of Celebrations
Soups and Salads

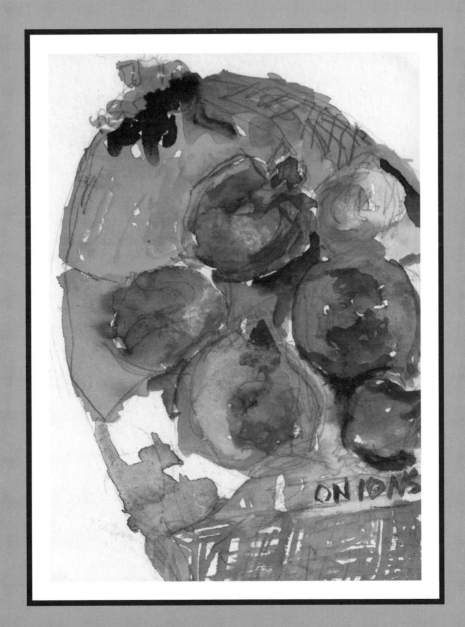

ONIONS

Anne Mullins Rigdon

◆

Tip of the Trade:

Garnish soups with herbs or fresh chopped complementary vegetables. Formally in seated dining, soups are served as a course after the appetizer and before the salad.

The Chilled Avocado and Cucumber Soup can be topped with Roma tomatoes for color, if desired. During preparation, peel the cucumber with a potato peeler and remember to gut out seeds before slicing.

CHILLED AVOCADO AND CUCUMBER SOUP

4 small cucumbers, peeled with seeds removed
1 (14 1/2-ounce) can chicken broth
3 green onions, peeled and chopped
2 (10 3/4-ounce) cans cream of potato soup
2 avocados, peeled and seeded
1 teaspoon lemon juice
3/4 to 1 cup buttermilk
1/2 cup whipping cream (or plain yogurt)

In a blender or food processor fitted with a metal blade, combine the cucumbers, chicken broth, onions and one can of soup. Blend until smooth and remove from container. Without rinsing the blender or food processor, combine the second can of soup, avocado, lemon juice, buttermilk and whipping cream. Blend until smooth and combine both mixtures. Chill until ready to serve, up to 2 days. Makes 4 to 6 servings.

CHEESE SOUP

6 tablespoons butter or margarine
6 tablespoons self-rising flour
1 (14 1/2-ounce) can chicken broth
2 cups milk
4 slices American cheese
1 cup Colby or Monterey Jack cheese, grated
4 tablespoons sour cream
2 Roma tomatoes, seeded and chopped

Tip of the Trade:

Add crumbled cooked bacon, chopped chives or green onions to Cheese Soup for variety and beautiful presentation.

Use Cheese Soup with 1/4 teaspoon ground curry as a sauce to your favorite Chicken Divan recipe.

In a medium saucepan or soup pot on medium heat, melt butter and add flour to make a roux or paste. Add chicken broth and heat until mixture becomes thick, stirring occasionally. Add milk and cheeses and heat until soup is smooth. Serve warm or cold with a dollop of sour cream and sprinkled with Roma tomatoes. Makes 4 to 6 servings.

◆

BUTTERNUT SQUASH SOUP

2 1/2 pound butternut squash
2 cups water
1/2 cup onion, peeled and chopped
1 clove garlic, peeled and crushed
2 tablespoons olive oil or vegetable oil
1 1/2 cups chicken broth
1 cup orange juice
4 ounces soft goat cheese or cream cheese
1/4 teaspoon ground ginger
1/4 teaspoon ground curry powder
1/4 teaspoon ground dry mustard

With a strong serrated knife or small saw, cut the butternut squash in half. Gut out seeds and place face down in a microwave-safe dish. (If the squash is too hard for cutting, place whole squash in microwave in 3 to 5 minute intervals until knife or saw can be inserted into easily.) Add water to sliced butternut dish and cover with plastic wrap. Heat squash on high for 5 to 7 minute intervals until cooked and soft. Scoop squash from skin and set aside. In a medium soup pot or sauce pan, combine onion, garlic and oil and cook on medium heat for 3 minutes until tender. Add squash, chicken broth and orange juice and simmer on low to medium heat for 10 minutes. Purée soup mixture with a hand blender or transfer to a blender or food proessor to purée and return back to pot. Add goat cheese or cream cheese and stir until mixture is smooth. Add spices and serve warm. If making in advance and reheating, spices may need to be freshened and thickening or thinning can be done as necessary. Garnish with apple slices. Substitute with canned or fresh pumpkin, if desired. Makes 4 to 6 servings.

Serving Tip:

Serve Butternut Squash Soup in a gutted out pumpkin in the autumn months for a small dinner or luncheon.

Tip of the Trade:

Potato flakes or potato pearls can be added to soups to thicken. Both are great emergency pantry items to keep on hand. Additional milk, broth or cream can be added to thin soups. Measure 1- to 2-tablespoons portions.

Additional roux or paste can be made to thicken soups or sauces. Equal parts of melted butter and flour can be mixed and added to soup. It must be then heated again, to near boiling temperatures, to thicken.

Tip of the Trade:

If a soup or broth is too greasy, place in refrigerator and fat will solidify on top when chilled. It then can be skimmed off easily with a spoon.

♦

CHILLED PEACH SOUP

1 (15-ounce) can peaches with syrup
2 tablespoons powdered sugar
1 tablespoon corn starch
1/2 cup white or blush wine
1/2 cup peach nectar, orange juice or other juice
1 tablespoon cider vinegar
1 cup sour cream or plain yogurt
Dash of salt
1/2 cup heavy cream, optional
Fresh-sliced strawberries and peaches

In a blender or food processor fitted with a metal blade, place peaches with juice and powdered sugar. Process until fruit is smooth. Dissolve cornstarch in wine and place in a medium pot. Add juice to pot and heat over medium heat until thickened, whisking occasionally. Add puréed peaches and vinegar and remove from heat. When room temperature, add sour cream and salt. Chill in a sealed container for up to 2 days until ready to serve. Place soup in small chilled soup bowl. Add a little cream and swirl with a skewer or thin utensil or mix in completely before placing in bowls. Additional cream might be needed for desired consistency. Serve chilled with sliced strawberries or whole raspberries and fresh sliced peaches. Strawberries or raspberries can be substituted in recipe, if desired. Garnish with a sprig of mint. Makes 4 to 6 servings.

Serving Tip:

If formal china soup bowls are not available in your serving inventory, start collecting pottery or glass soup bowls or cups to use. Remember, every one of the place settings does not have to match, but needs to be complementary to each other.

♦

TOMATO AND ROASTED RED PEPPER SOUP

2 red bell peppers
3 cloves garlic, peeled and crushed
1 large onion, peeled and chopped
2 tablespoons olive oil or vegetable oil
4 cups chicken broth
1 (14-ounce) can tomato paste
1 cup white wine
2 1/2 cups milk or cream
1/4 cup butter or margarine
1/3 cup self-rising flour
1 1/2 teaspoons salt
1 teaspoon sweet pepper blend or seasoned pepper

Place peppers on a baking sheet 5 inches from heat on low broil and cook 5 minutes, turn over and cook an additional 5 minutes. The skin of the peppers should start to turn splotchy brownish black. Remove from oven and while very hot, immediately place peppers into a plastic bag and seal tightly for 10 minutes. This will help during peeling. Remove peppers from bag and peel as much skin off as possible. Remove stem by pulling and gut out seeds. Chop peppers and place in a soup pot or large saucepan. Add garlic, onion and oil to peppers and cook for 5 minutes. Add chicken broth to pepper mixture and cook with vegetables for 5 minutes. With a hand blender, regular blender, or food processor fitted with a metal blade, purée pepper mixture until smooth. Return to pot and add tomato paste, white wine, and milk, simmering on low heat for 2 to 3 minutes. In a separate saucepan or in microwave, melt butter and mix with flour and salt, making a roux or paste. Add to soup mixture and heat soup until thickens, 5 minutes. Add sweet pepper blend and serve warm. This soup can be chilled and served with celery or cucumber slices in the summer season. Makes 8 to 10 servings.

Tip of the Trade:

If budget allows, additional red peppers can be added to Tomato and Roasted Red Pepper Soup for a stronger bell pepper taste.

As an alternative to roasting, peppers can be cooked fully in oil in skillet with onions and garlic, if desired.

The peeling of a raw, whole bell pepper can be done with a potato peeler, if roasting is not desired. Peeling of a pepper sometimes helps remove the bitter taste that some people dislike and which sometimes causes a sour stomach. Peeling can be done easily before the pepper is cut and cooked by shaving with a good quality potato peeler. It will be impossible to peel all the skin, so do not become frustrated with the pepper crevices.

Serving Tip:

Your guests will not stop talking about this soup! It is a spectacular accompaniment to any meal.

♦

Tip of the Trade:

If a soup is too salty, add a peeled and quartered white potato to it during cooking. It will absorb some of the salt. Additional ingredients can be added if this trick does not remove what is needed.

Vegetable soup is a wonderful way to use up leftover or unused fresh vegetables in your refrigerator. If making Soup and Salad, use fresh or leftover vegetables in the place of frozen vegetables listed in the recipe.
For a real Southern treat, top soup with a few fried okra pieces.

If making in advance, the bacon can easily be made crispy again by placing in the microwave for 1 minute on medium high heat.

Menu Suggestion:
Casual Committee Lunch

Ricotta Cheese Ball with Butter Crackers,

Cornbread Muffins or Turkey Sandwiches,

Iced Tea and Coffee,

Almond and Brandy Tart with Fresh Fruit

SOUP AND SALAD

4 ounces bacon, uncooked and chopped
1 yellow onion, peeled and chopped
2 garlic cloves, peeled and crushed
1 (14 1/2-ounce) can chopped or diced tomatoes
1 (6-ounce) can tomato juice
1/2 pound frozen chopped soup vegetables
**   or mixed vegetables**
1/2 cup water
1 (15-ounce) can tomato sauce
1 teaspoon chopped or dried basil
1 teaspoon chopped or dried oregano
1/2 teaspoon salt
Iceberg lettuce, chopped thin

In a soup pot, fry bacon on medium heat until crunchy. Remove bacon from pan, reserving bacon grease. Cook onion and garlic in bacon grease until tender, about 2 to 3 minutes. Add chopped tomatoes, tomato juice, frozen vegetables and water to pot and simmer for 10 to 15, minutes covered. Add tomato sauce, basil, oregano and salt and simmer for 5 minutes. In the bottom of a soup bowl, place 1/4 cup thinly chopped iceberg lettuce sprinkled with 1 to 2 tablespoons bacon pieces. Ladle hot soup over lettuce and serve immediately. Makes 4 to 6 servings.

Serving Tip:

Serve Soup and Salad from the stove just to have the chance to watch your guests' faces as you scoop the soup over the lettuce. If making in advance, keep the bacon and lettuce separate until ready to serve.

♦

◆

Chowder came from the traditions of French fisherman. Originally, the fishermen would throw their catch from the day into a large community soup pot to share with everyone. Today, a chowder can contain any fish or vegetable and is usually chunkier than soup. Add shirmp to the Chicken and Corn Chowder for an authentic touch.

CHICKEN AND CORN CHOWDER

4 large chicken breasts with bones, skin and rib meat
6 cups water
1 1/2 teaspoons salt
1 1/4 sticks butter or margarine
1 cup self-rising flour
5 cups chicken broth
3 cups 2 % or whole milk
2 (15-ounce) cans creamed corn
2 to 4 dashes hot sauce

In a large pot, place chicken breasts with water and salt and simmer for 30 to 45 minutes over medium heat, covered. Remove chicken breasts and reserve broth. In a medium pot or soup pot, place butter over medium low heat and melt. Add flour to butter to make a roux or paste. Measure out 5 cups broth and add to roux in pot. Heat over medium heat until thickened, stirring with a whisk occasionally. Remove chicken from bone and dice. Add chicken and milk to soup and stir in creamed corn. If using whole milk you might need to thin soup a little by adding 1/8 cup more milk or broth. Add hot sauce to taste. Serve warm. Makes 8 to 10 servings.

Menu Suggestion:
A Fireside Dinner for Four

Sunflower Salad,

Spinach and Ricotta French Bread,

Fresh Fruit,

Famous Chocolate Pie

Tip of the Trade:

Chicken and Corn Chowder has become a favorite recipe among my circle of close friends. I demonstrated how to make this soup at a garden club meeting and friends claim they make it often when they boil chicken for salads or dishes. It is the perfect gift to take to friends in need of a good, soothing meal.

◆

A Monterey Jack cheese, a pepper jack cheese or even a processed cheese could work well in Chicken Enchilada Soup as a substitution, if desired. If the soup is cooked with the Cheddar cheese, the cheese will become grainy if cooked too hot. For this reason, the cheese is added just before serving.

CHICKEN ENCHILADA SOUP

A recipe from the collection of my friend, Angela DuPre

4 chicken breasts, about 2 1/2 to 3 cups chopped chicken
1 onion, peeled and chopped
1 garlic clove, peeled and crushed
1 tablespoon oil, any kind
1 (14 1/2-ounce) can chicken broth or reserved chicken stock
1 (14 1/2-ounce) can beef broth
1 (10 3/4-ounce) can cream of chicken soup
1 3/4 cup water
1 (4-ounce) can green chilis
1 teaspoon chili powder
1 teaspoon ground cumin
3 cups Cheddar cheese, grated
10 corn tortillas, cut into 1/2-inch strips

Cook chicken by boiling or baking covered until done, approximately 35 to 45 minutes. (Reserve stock in place of broth, if desired.) Dice chicken into bite size pieces, removing any skin and bones. In a medium to large pot, cook onion and garlic in oil for 3 to 5 minutes. Add diced chicken, chicken and beef broth, chicken soup, water, drained green chilis, chili powder and cumin. Place on medium low heat and bring to a simmer and cook for 45 to 60 minutes, stirring occasionally. Ten minutes before serving, add cheese and corn tortillas. For topping, extra flour tortillas cut into julienne strips can be fried in a little butter and sprinkled on soup with diced tomatoes and a little dried parsley. Makes 4 to 6 servings.

When making soups, spices should be added at the end of cooking to give more flavor. When reheating soups after refrigeration, spices might again have to be added. In most cases, thinning of the soup will need to be made after storage. Thin with broth or cream in amounts of 1 to 2 tablespoons so not to overthin.

Serving Tip:

When serving soup to a seated guest, have a service plate provided on the table on which to place the soup bowl. Then the service plate and soup are removed for the salad or main course. A soup spoon should be placed to the far right of the flatware service.

◆

Menu Suggestion:
A Bridge Luncheon

Luncheon Sangria,

Rice Crispy Biscuits,

Turkey Crêpe Torte,

Spinach and Orange Salad,

Vegetable Pasta Salad,

Strawberry Napoleons,

Coffee

Serving Tip:

Serve soups in pottery bowls or small gutted out bread loaves that have been baked in a 200-degree oven for 35 minutes until crispy. Guests can even eat the dishes.

SHRIMP AND ARTICHOKE CREAM SOUP WITH FETA

1/2 pound shrimp, cooked and peeled
2 (14 1/2-ounce) cans artichokes, drained well by pressing
1/2 cup butter or margarine
1 onion, peeled and chopped
1/2 cup celery, trimmed and chopped
1 garlic clove, peeled and crushed
1/4 cup plain all-purpose flour
4 cups chicken broth or fish stock
2 cups milk
1/2 cup white wine
1/2 teaspoon white pepper
1/2 cup crumbled Feta cheese

Tip of the Trade:

This soup is not too heavy or creamy. A perfect first course to a dinner or luncheon celebration.

Place drained artichokes and shrimp in a food processor and pulse three to four times to chop, but do not purée or chop by hand until diced well. In a large pot or soup pot, place butter over medium low heat and melt. Add onion, celery and garlic and cook for 3 minutes. Add flour to pot and mix well to form a roux or paste. Add broth and milk and cook on medium heat to a simmer, until thickened. Add diced shrimp, artichokes and wine and stir well. Simmer soup over medium low heat for 10 minutes. Add spices and serve warm. Salt may be needed in this recipe if canned chicken broth is not used. Can make 1 day in advance and reheat. Makes 6 to 8 servings.

Tip of the Trade:

Dissolved arrowroot in water, cornstarch dissolved in water, potato flakes or potato pearls or whisked egg yolks can be used to thicken soups or sauces.

◆

Tip of the Trade:

The safest way to buy crab is to purchase it from a government licensed seafood retailer. Pasteurized crab is very safe and is of good quality. Whether buying canned, fresh or pasteurized, feel through for excess shells before adding to soups and dishes.

UNCLE RYLAND'S CREAM OF CRAB SOUP

A family recipe from the collection of my friend, Eleanor Knox

1/4 cup butter or margarine
1/3 cup plain all-purpose flour
1 cup chicken broth
1/4 teaspoon pepper
5 cups milk
1 pound backfin crab meat
Dash salt
Dash hot sauce
1 teaspoon Worcestershire sauce

Melt butter in a 3-quart pan on medium heat on stove. Blend in flour and stir until smooth. Slowly stir in broth and pepper and simmer for 2 minutes. Add milk, cooking slowly, stirring constantly until mixture thickens. Do not boil. Add crab meat, salt, hot sauce and Worcestershire sauce. Serve warm. Makes 4 to 6 servings.

Tip of the Trade:

Although water chestnuts are not a traditional gazpacho ingredient, they add a flavor and crunch that is very pleasing. This is a good low-fat, healthy dish that can be used as a light and cool first course or as an entree for a luncheon or light dinner.
The onion and garlic taste is very strong. Cooking these in a little oil will give a subtle flavor, if desired.

CRUNCHY GAZPACHO

4 cups tomatoes, chopped
1/2 cup onion, peeled and chopped
2 cloves garlic, peeled and diced
2 stalks celery, trimmed and chopped
2 carrots, peeled and chopped
1 (6-ounce) can water chestnuts, drained
1/2 teaspoon salt
2 teaspoons sugar
2 (11.5-ounce) cans tomato juice
2 tablespoons vodka
Hot sauce, to taste

◆

Prepare all vegetables. Place all ingredients except 1 1/2 cups of chopped tomatoes into a food processor fitted with a metal blade. Pulse several times but do not purée vegetables. Add remaining tomatoes on the last pulse. Chill before serving and store for up to 2 days sealed in refrigerator. Serve with homemade croutons. Makes 6 to 8 servings.

MIXED GREENS WITH ARTICHOKE FETA DRESSING

3/4 pound Feta cheese, crumbled
4 green onions, peeled and chopped
1 clove garlic, peeled and crushed
2 tablespoons lemon juice
1/2 cup olive oil
1/4 cup white wine
1 tablespoon parsley, chopped fresh or
   1/2 teaspoon dried
2 (6-ounce) jars marinated artichokes, drained and chopped
1/4 cup mayonnaise
1 head green leaf lettuce
2 heads red leaf lettuce
2 tomatoes, seeded and chopped
2 cucumbers, peeled and chopped

In a mixing bowl, combine crumbled and drained Feta cheese, green onion, garlic, lemon juice, olive oil, wine, parsley, finely chopped artichokes and mayonnaise. Mix well by hand, a hand mixer or mixer. You may make up to 2 days in advance and store in refrigerator in a quart Mason jar.
For Salad: Wash lettuce and place to drain. Chop or tear lettuces and lay in serving bowl on large pieces of paper towels. Top with a paper towel and cover loosely with plastic wrap. Lay chopped tomatoes and cucumbers on top of plastic wrap and cover. This may be done up to 6 hours in advance. Before serving, remove plastic wraps and paper towels and toss with dressing. Makes 12 to 14 servings.

Tip of the Trade:

Salad comes from the Latin word Salata, *meaning salted greens. It can be a part of any meal. Guests love a good salad, so take the time to make it really special.*

Tip of the Trade:

Grow an assortment of lettuces in early spring or fall in a container or raised garden outdoors so that you can easily pick enough for your salad bowl.

♦

Serving Tip:

Green salads are beautiful served out of crystal bowls. For large crowds, a crystal or cut-glass punch bowl works nicely. Tongs work great as the serving utensil, especially the ones you can use with one hand. Try out the utensil first to make sure it can be worked easily and efficiently.

Tip of the Trade:

I love keeping the dressing for Sunflower Salad on hand for everyday meals. It stores great tightly sealed in a quart jar for up to 2 weeks in the refrigerator. Using low-fat mayonnaise, yogurt and buttermilk cuts down the calories and fat content making it practical for healthier living

Tip of the Trade:

Tossing of the salad would be the next to last chore done before calling your guests to table or the buffet.
The removal of hot bread from the oven is the last kitchen task done.

SUNFLOWER SALAD

2 heads green or red leafy lettuce, (not iceberg)
1 to 2 cartons sunflower sprouts
1 or 2 tomatoes, seeded and chopped
1 cucumber, peeled and chopped
DRESSING:
3/4 cup mayonnaise
1/4 cup plain low-fat yogurt or sour cream
3/4 cup buttermilk
2 tablespoons white wine vinegar
1/8 cup white wine
2 tablespoons prepared Dijon or stone ground mustard
2 tablespoons sunflower or vegetable oil
3/4 teaspoon lemon pepper or pepper blend
1/4 teaspoon salt
1/2 teaspoon dried parsley flakes
1/8 cup sunflower seeds

Wash lettuce. Tear paper towels two to three at a time and lay two layers inside serving bowl. Tear and lay lettuce in bowl. Top with paper towel and layer sunflower sprouts. Cover this loosely with plastic wrap making the wrap as a bowl for vegetables. Prepare tomatoes and cucumber and lay on top of plastic wrap. Cover again tightly with plastic wrap, and refrigerate for up to 6 hours.

For Dressing: In a bowl, mixer or blender, combine mayonnaise, yogurt, buttermilk, vinegar, wine, mustard, oil and spices. Blend well. This dressing can be made up to 1 week in advance. Store in a jar or tightly sealed container in refrigerator until ready to use. Ten minutes before serving, remove all towels and plastic from serving bowl. Pour dressing over salad and toss well. Sprinkle with sunflower seeds and serve cold with large tongs. Dressing makes a little more than 1/2 quart. Makes 4 to 6 servings.

♦

HAZELNUT AND GOAT CHEESE GREEN SALAD

4 to 5 ounces firm goat cheese
1/4 cup oil
1/4 cup hazelnut, chopped fine into crumbs, or other nut
1/3 cup bread crumbs
1/3 cup vegetable or olive oil
3 tablespoons champagne vinegar
1/2 teaspoon lemon pepper
2 tablespoons white wine
1/4 teaspoon dried parsley
1/4 teaspoon thyme, fresh chopped
1 leek, chopped or green onion, chopped
5 cups torn bibb, radichio, Boston and/or leafy lettuce
2 tomatoes, seeded and quartered
1 (6-ounce) jar marinated artichokes, drained
Italian vegetables, prepared, optional

Cut goat cheese into four to six pieces and place in a dish. Sprinkle with olive oil and marinate 30 minutes in refrigerator. Mix together hazelnut crumbs and bread crumbs. Roll goat cheese into this mixture and place on a greased baking sheet. When ready to serve, bake in a 350-degree oven for 10 to 12 minutes until golden brown. **For Dressing**: In a mixing bowl, combine oil, champagne vinegar, lemon pepper, wine, parsley, thyme and finely chopped leek. Mix well and store in a closed airtight jar or container until serving time. Both the dressing and the unbaked goat cheese can be prepared 1 day in advance. **For Salad:** In a serving salad bowl, place lettuce on paper towels and top with a paper towel. Cover lettuce with plastic wrap and place chopped tomatoes and artichokes on wrap. Cover bowl tightly and store in refrigerator until ready to serve. Lettuce and vegetables can be prepared 6 hours in advance. Other Italian vegetables can be added to salad as wanted. Chopped peppers, olives, mushrooms, onions, can be added with the artichokes and tomatoes as needed. While cooking goat cheese, toss green salad with dressing or fix on individual plates decoratively with dressing on top. Place warm goat cheese balls on salad as you would croutons and serve. Makes 4 to 6 servings.

Tip of the Trade:

The goat cheese balls can be coated with their breading and kept covered in refrigerator until ready to cook for up to 8 hours, if desired. They are truly delicious.

For busy lives, substitute your favorite Italian dressing for the Hazlenut and Goat Cheese Green Salad.

Tip of the Trade:

Soggy green salads are due to adding salt or a spice with salt to greens before serving time. Include spices in the dressing rather than the salad for best results. Tossing with the dressing should be done right before serving or the dressing can be offered to the side.

Toasted Pecan Salad looks beautiful on a fixed plate. Use fruit in your centerpiece to complement this dish

TOASTED PECAN SALAD & CHEVRE DRESSING

1 large head green leafy lettuce, chopped
1 to 1 1/2 cup pecan halves
1 tablespoon oil
1 tablespoon butter or margarine
5 to 6 ounces goat cheese
1/2 cup vegetable oil
2 tablespoons apple cider or white wine vinegar
3/4 cup sour cream
1/4 teaspoon salt
1 (6-ounce) can pineapple juice, divided
Seasonal Fruit

Prepare leaf lettuce for salad by washing, drying and placing in a storage bag with paper towels until ready to serve. This may be done 8 hours in advance. Place pecan halves in a bowl. Toss with 1 tablespoon oil and melted butter. Sprinkle with 1/4 teaspoon salt. Lay in a single layer on a baking sheet in a 350-degree oven for 10 to 12 minutes. Remove from oven and cool. **For Dressing:** In a blender or with a hand blender or food processor, blend goat cheese, oil, vinegar, sour cream, salt and 1/3 cup pineapple juice. (Reserve remaining juice.) Blend well and store in an airtight container. Dressing can be made and stored for 2 to 3 days. **For Salad:** Slice fruit and toss peaches, apples, or pears with remaining pineapple juice. Using plums, cherries and berries are wonderful. To serve, arrange lettuce in salad server or bowls, place fruit along edges, drizzle with dressing and top with toasted pecans. Using field greens would be a wonderful alternative to green leaf. Makes 6 servings.

SPINACH AND ORANGE SALAD

3 tablespoons honey
1/2 cup vegetable or nut oil
1/4 cup white zinfandel wine
1 teaspoon Dijon mustard
1 1/2 tablespoons grated onion

1 pound fresh chopped spinach, washed and dried
1 cup mushrooms, peeled and sliced
1/4 red onion, chopped or 3 green onions, chopped
1 (11-ounce) can mandarin oranges
1 cup mushrooms, peeled and chopped
6 slices bacon, cooked and crumbled, optional
1/3 cup sunflower seeds
1/8 cup slivered almonds

Mix together honey, oil, wine, mustard and onion and store in a sealed jar or airtight container in refrigerator for up to 1 week. Salad can be prepared 6 hours in advance by chopping, tearing and completely drying spinach and placing in desired serving bowl. Prepare other ingredients and store separately. All salad and prepared ingredients should be kept sealed in refrigerator until ready to serve. Five to 10 minutes before serving, combine all ingredients and toss. Makes 10 to 12 servings.

Serving Tip:

Salads can be served formally right before the main course.
Appetizers and soups come before the salad course.
Plates can be chilled to help keep the salad crisp and cold.

Tip of the Trade:

Spinach and Orange Salad is one of the best recipes. For convenience, spinach leaves can now be easily purchased in packages from grocers and markets, already washed and dried. Usually trimming of the stems and tearing will be the only preparations needed. If you ever have washed spinach leaves yourself, you know what a real treat this is. Also, mushrooms can now be bought already sliced and bacon in packages ready to cook in microwave for just a few minutes. Of course, it is more economical to prepare the items yourself, but less time consuming to have some of the ingredients partially prepared for you. Either way, this salad is worth the trouble. The zinfandel wine gives a beautiful color to the dressing, but any wine can be substituted.

Tip of the Trade:

Save a few of the salad vegetables, fruits or condiments to sprinkle on the top of a green salad after tossing with dressing. This will make a beautiful presentation on buffet tables or fixed plates.

FRUITED GREEN SALAD WITH ORANGE MADEIRA DRESSING

1/4 cup apple cider vinegar
1/4 cup Madeira wine
1/4 cup olive oil
1/4 cup vegetable oil
1 1/2 tablespoons honey
2 tablespoons orange juice concentrate
1 1/2 teaspoons lemon pepper

1 head bibb lettuce
1 head red leaf lettuce
2 granny smith apple, peeled and copped
2 hard pears, peeled and chopped
3 tablespoons pineapple juice
1/2 cup red grapes, halved
1/2 cup sliced strawberries
1/3 cup walnuts, chopped

In a 1-quart Mason jar or closed container combine vinegar, wine, oils, honey, orange juice and lemon pepper. Dressing gets betters as it ages. Can be made 1 week in advance. **For Salad:** Six hours before serving, wash, dry and tear bibb and red leaf lettuce and place on paper towel lined serving bowl, cover and refrigerate. In a separate bowl combine chopped apples, chopped pears and pineapple juice. Toss gently and drain. Before serving, toss lettuce, apple, pear, grapes, strawberries and dressing. Top with walnuts and serve chilled. Makes 6 to 8 servings.

> *Serve salads out of crystal or glass bowls for formal entertaining and wooden for casual entertaining. Pewter and most pottery can go either way.*

LIME VINAIGRETTE

1/4 cup sugar
1/8 cup lime juice (or lemon juice)
1/8 cup white wine vinegar
1/4 cup olive or vegetable oil
1 teaspoon white Worcestershire sauce
1 clove garlic, crushed well
2 green onions
1 teaspoon fresh thyme, chopped

In a microwave-safe dish or small saucepan, heat on medium setting sugar, lime juice and vinegar until sugar is dissolved. Cool slightly and add oil, Worcestershire, garlic, green onions and thyme. Shake or mix well. Store up to 3 days in advance in a sealed container or jar in the refrigerator. Serve with spring greens and vegetables. Makes approximately 1 cup.

Tip of the Trade:

Substitute puréed and strained raspberries for the lime juice, or in addition to the lime juice in the Lime Vinaigrette Dressing and omit the garlic for a Raspberry Vinaigrette.

CREAMY PORT DRESSING

1/3 cup olive oil
1/3 cup vegetable oil
1/2 cup sour cream or plain yogurt
1/3 cup apple cider vinegar
1/3 cup port wine (or sweet sherry)
1 tablespoon sugar
3/4 teaspoon lemon pepper or seasoned pepper blend

Mix all ingredients together and store in an airtight container or sealed jar in the refrigerator. Can be made 1 week in advance, shaking before serving. Serve with mixture of bitter greens with or without fruit. Add chicken or shrimp for a light luncheon or summer supper with fresh peach or nectarine garnishes. Makes 1 1/3 cups.

Tip of the Trade:

Port is a Portuguese wine. It is made from grapes which are quite sweet and soft. It's most commonly used in preparing sauces or as an apertif, a before-dinner drink, used to stimulate an appetite.

♦

Tip of the Trade:
Fresh Herbs in Salads

Basil, particularly sweet basil is wonderful in tomato and cheese salads.
Chervil is good with salads containing eggs.
Dill is great with salads accompanied by cucumbers, tomatoes, potatoes or creamy dressings.
Marjoram complements pastas or green salads.
Parsley goes with about anything. Try growing different varieties.
Rosemary can go with potatoes or fruits. I like to use in vinegars with lemon sprigs.
Tarragon is also wonderful placed in vinegars to use all year long.
Thyme is strong but works well with meat and seafood salads.

Serving Tip:

When presenting salads for entertaining, make sure the greens, vegetables or fruits are cut in small bite-size pieces. This makes the salad much easier for guests to eat, especially if serving buffet style.

TOMATO GOAT CHEESE DRESSING

1 (14 1/2-ounce) can diced tomatoes
1/2 cup wine vinegar
1/2 cup oil
2 tablespoons sugar
1 1/2 teaspoons basil
3 tablespoons red wine
6 ounces soft goat cheese
1/2 teaspoon paprika
1/2 teaspoon salt

Combine all ingredients in a blender or food processor fitted with a metal blade and blend well. Store in a 1-quart sealed container or jar in refrigerator. Can make 2 days in advance. Serve with a bitter lettuce mixture of endive, raddichio, mustards and leafy lettuces with roasted new potatoes and quartered tomatoes. Makes approximately 2 cups.

BLEU CHEESE DRESSING

3/4 cup sour cream or plain yogurt
3/4 cup mayonnaise
1/4 cup vegetable oil
1 1/2 tablespoons vinegar
2 tablespoons parsley
1/4 cup buttermilk
2 tablespoons white wine
1/2 cup crumbled bleu cheese
Dash of hot sauce

♦

Whisk all ingredients by hand or in a mixer. Store in a 1-quart jar or container. Can be made 1 week in advance and stored sealed in the refrigerator. Serve with chilled garden salads, using canned drained beets as a garnish. This thick dressing consistency is for serving on the side rather than tossing in salad. Makes approximately 2 cups.

Tip of the Trade:

Most blue mold cheeses are made in France. Blue cheeses all have something in common with the popular Roquefort cheese, which is a very mild and delicate flavored blue mold cheese. (It can be easily substituted in this recipe.) French regions will produce different varieties of blue cheeses, some even being made from cows' milk. Personally, using a very mild flavor is always safe. If the odor from the cheese is very strong through the wrapper, chances are it's rather strong. Most markets have someone that could suggest the type for which you might be looking.

Blue mold cheeses (like most cheeses) can be frozen for up to 1 month sealed tightly. In fact, crumbling is quite easy when bleu cheese is frozen.

Serving Tip:

In my experience, when serving a salad by fixed plate, the dressing works nicely drizzled on top of the salad rather than passing from guest to guest.

CREAMY RUSSIAN DRESSING

2/3 cup oil, any kind
1/2 cup ketchup
1/4 cup honey
3 tablespoons lemon juice
2 tablespoons white Worcestershire sauce
2 tablespoons vinegar, any kind
2 tablespoons white wine
1/2 cup sour cream
1/2 cup mayonnaise
1 tablespoon grated onion or 1 green onion, chopped
3/4 teaspoon dried parsley
1/2 teaspoon paprika
1/2 teaspoon salt

With a hand blender or in a blender or food processor fitted with a metal blade, combine all ingredients and blend well. Store in an airtight container or jar in refrigerator for up to 1 week. Serve with a chilled garden salad with tomatoes, carrots, cabbage, broccoli and radishes. Makes approximately 2 cups.

Tip of the Trade:

One pint (16 ounces), equal to 2 cups of dressing will serve 12 to 16 guests.

◆

PEPPERCORN DRESSING

3/4 teaspoon whole black peppercorns
1/8 cup oil
1/4 cup sour cream
1/4 cup mayonnaise
1 tablespoon vinegar, regular, wine or cider
1/4 teaspoon salt

Place whole peppercorns in a small plastic bag and crack them with a mallet or hammer. Mix all ingredients together, adding cracked peppercorns. Store in a sealed container for up to 1 week. Shake well before serving. Use with favorite mixed greens and vegetable salads. Makes 3/4 cup, 4 to 6 servings.

HONEY MUSTARD

1/4 cup prepared Dijon, stone ground or fancy mustard
1/3 cup vegetable, sunflower or nut oil
1/8 cup vinegar, white wine or cider
2 tablespoons sour cream or plain yogurt
1/8 cup honey
1/2 teaspoon lemon pepper

Mix all ingredients together and store in a sealed airtight container for up to 1 week. Yellow prepared mustard makes the dressing and color too strong. Other types of mustards work well. Serve with mixed greens or as a side sauce with chicken. Makes 4 to 6 servings.

◆

♦

CARROT APPLE AND CRANBERRY SALAD

1 large apple, peeled and chopped fine
2 cups carrot, peeled and shredded
1/4 cup golden raisins
1/4 cup dried cranberries
1 (4-ounce) can pineapple tidbits, drained very well
2 ounces cream cheese, room temperature
1/2 cup mayonnaise
1 teaspoon brown sugar
1/4 cup pecans or walnuts, chopped

Mix together apple, carrot, raisins, cranberries and pineapple in a bowl. In a separate bowl, whisk together cream cheese, mayonnaise and brown sugar. Add to carrot mixture with pecans and store covered in refrigerator. Makes 6 to 10 servings.

Tip of the Trade:

This carrot salad is a wonderful balance of color, texture and flavors. The tangy, chewy cranberries complement the crunch of the carrots and the sweetness of the apples.

BROCCOLI RAMEN SALAD

1 (16-ounce) bag broccoli slaw or
    2 broccoli stems, shredded
2 1/2 to 3 tablespoons oil
3 tablespoons apple cider vinegar
3 tablespoons mayonnaise
1 (6-ounce) can sliced water chestnuts, drained, optional
1/3 cup sunflower seeds
1/4 cup slivered almonds
6 ounces original Ramen noodles, uncooked

In a medium bowl, combine slaw, oil, vinegar, mayonnaise, halved water chestnuts, seeds and almonds and mix well. This can be prepared 1 day in advance. Before serving, mix in crushed, uncooked ramen noodles. Serve chilled. Broccoli flowerets can be used as substitution to slaw if preferred. Makes 10 to 12 servings.

Tip of the Trade:

Broccoli is a very nutritious vegetable that can be used in so many ways. Being able to have a use for the stem is practical and economical. This Broccoli Ramen Salad makes a perfect covered dish salad or wonderful to keep for a side to sandwiches for weekends.
The crunchy noodles make it addictive and different.
The water chestnuts are optional. This salad has plenty of crunch without them.

♦

FRUITED SLAW

1 1/2 pound green cabbage, chopped
1 teaspoon salt
1/8 cup dried cranberries
1 tablespoon honey
4 tablespoons walnut oil
1 to 2 teaspoons lemon juice, to taste
1/2 teaspoon pepper
2 Granny Smith apples
4 tablespoons pineapple juice
1 (11-ounce) can mandarin oranges
1/2 cup walnuts, almonds or cashews
1/2 (3-ounce) package original Ramen noodle, uncooked

Combine chopped cabbage, salt, cranberries, honey, oil, lemon juice and pepper. Store in an airtight container and store in the refrigerator. This can be done 1 to 2 days in advance. Marinating the slaw will improve the taste. Peel and chop apples and soak in 4 tablespoons pineapple juice for 1 minute and drain. Before serving, gently toss in apples, oranges, nuts and crushed ramen noodles. Serve chilled. Makes 6 to 8 servings.

FRESH CORN SALAD

6 ears corn, shucked and cut from cob
Water
1/2 red pepper, chopped
1/2 cup celery, chopped
1/4 cup Vidalia or sweet onion, peeled and chopped
3 tablespoons rice vinegar, or other vinegar
2 tablespoon vegetable oil
1/8 cup chopped fresh cilantro
1/2 teaspoon dried parsley or 1 tablespoon fresh
Salt

Place cut corn in a medium boiling pot and cover with 1/2 cup water. Boil corn over medium heat for 5 minutes. Drain immediately. Combine corn with pepper, celery, onion, vinegar, oil and spices. Toss well. Can be prepared 1 day in advance. Can be used for a relish side dish to chicken, turkey or pork, or as a vegetable side dish. Makes 6 to 8 servings.

Sweet potatoes are native to India, but are available in all warm countries. Lost Mountain, the small mountain that can be overlooked from my family farm in Powder Springs, Georgia and the surrounding land is perfect soil for sweet potato crops.

The best variety are Virginian, which have a yellow flesh, however, any variety of fresh sweet potato will work in this recipe. Absolutely no canned potatoes.

Serving Tip:

Serve Fresh Corn Salad out of a footed compote with a small serving spoon for the perfect look. Using canned corn would take away from this recipe.

SWEET POTATO SALAD

3 pounds fresh sweet potatoes
1 medium sweet onion, chopped fine
1/2 cup almonds, toasted
1/2 cup chopped celery
1/4 cup oil
2 tablespoons wine vinegar
2 teaspoons prepared mustard, deli, stone ground or Dijon
2 tablespoons honey or brown sugar
4 tablespoons sour cream

Serving Tip:

When serving Sweet Potato Salad, guests might not be able to figure the main ingredient. Possibly this is from the potatoes being served cold and in cubes rather than hot and creamed.

Peel and dice sweet potatoes and place in a medium pot. Cover with water and cook over medium heat. Boil potatoes for 6 to 12 minutes and drain immediately. Potatoes should be cooked but still be firm and brightly colored. Mix potatoes with onion, almonds, celery, oil, vinegar, mustard, honey and sour cream. Cover and chill for up to 2 days. Makes 6 to 8 servings.

Tip of the Trade:

Stuffed Celery is a traditional Thanksgiving condiment in my husband's family. The 2-inch celery boat is simply filled with cream cheese in their family recipe. The recipe given is a little fancier. Either way is a delicious and beautiful way to serve this crunchy vegetable.

Wild celery was used by the Romans until cultivated in the 16th century. Some countries use the root, where others use the leaves. Different varieties are grown for each use.

STUFFED CELERY

6 ounces cream cheese, room temperature
1/2 cup grated American cheese
1 tablespoon whipping cream
1 tablespoon mayonnaise
1 tablespoon grated onion or 1 green onion, chopped
1 bunch celery
Paprika

In a food processor fitted with a metal blade, combine cream cheese, American cheese, whipping cream, mayonnaise and onion. Cream together. Cut celery into 1-inch strips, leaving a boat-like filling area. Larger bottoms of celery can be saved for other uses. Stuff celery with cheese mixture and sprinkle with paprika. Chill covered until ready to use, up to 2 days. Makes 10 to 12 servings.

Tip of the Trade:

Broccoli flowerets or tips as we know them are not full grown.

The secret of a beautiful salad is to cut the broccoli and cauliflower very tiny. This will require wasting most of the stems, but they can be used in Broccoli Ramen Salad, page 83.

BROCCOLI SALAD

1 large broccoli head
1 cauliflower head or broccoli head
1/2 cup golden raisins
3 green onions, peeled and chopped
1 1/4 cups mayonnaise
1/4 cup sugar
4 tablespoons vinegar
1/2 cup walnuts, pecans or peanuts
1 carrot, grated
1 (6-ounce) can Mandarin oranges, drained
10 slices bacon, cooked and crumbled

Cut broccoli and cauliflower into tiny flowerets to measure approximately 6 cups and place in a bowl with raisins, onions and mayonnaise. Measure out sugar and vinegar and place in microwave on high for 2 minutes, or place on medium heat on stove to dissolve sugar. Mix well and add to broccoli. Prepare nuts and carrots and place with salad. If making a day in advance, nuts and carrots should be set aside to keep from discoloring cauliflower. Before serving salad, mix prepared ingredients together and layer in bacon and oranges. (Tossing oranges might cause breakage.) Makes 8 to 10 servings.

Tip of the Trade:

If wooden salad bowls are part of your serving inventory, rub the bowl with a piece of crumbled waxed paper after cleaning to seal.

TORTELLINI PASTA SALAD

8 ounces dried pasta
8 ounces dried cheese tortellini pasta
1/4 cup oil
3/4 cup mayonnaise
1/8 cup Parmesan, shredded (or Feta cheese)
1/8 cup vinegar
1/2 cup sour cream
1 tablespoon fresh parsley or 3/4 teaspoon dried
1/2 teaspoon salt
1/2 teaspoon seasoned pepper or course black pepper
1 1/2 cups vegetables or
      chopped chicken or shrimp

Tip of the Trade:

Tortellini pasta is a wonderful cheese or meat-filled pastry. It is highly recommended to use the cheese filled for pasta salads. In my experience, using a pasta that has been dried completely for cold pasta dishes or salads give the best results. Fresh pasta can be rather sticky after cooking.

Different pastas must be cooked separately to avoid overcooking. Penne rigati, twists, salad shells all work well in this dish. Cook pastas according to package directions, taking 1 minute off the lowest cooking time suggested. Drain pasta, rinse with cold water and drain again. Combine pasta, oil, mayonnaise, Parmesan, vinegar and sour cream. Toss well with parsley. This may be done 2 days in advance and stored in the refrigerator until ready to add desired vegetables. Raw broccoli flowerets, olives, black beans, artichokes, seeded cherry tomatoes, hearts of palm, pimento, bell peppers, onions, Feta cheese and/or (chicken, shrimp, or ham) can be used. Vary your vegetables according to taste, seasons and color. Makes 8 to 10 servings.

♦

Tip of the Trade:

*Fruited Pasta Salad tastes
especially good if served very
chilled. A great covered dish and
picnic recipe.*

Tip of the Trade:

*Waldorf Salad is a popular dish
which is not made often by
entertainers. Keep it in mind for
your next menu, especially during
the winter holidays.*

*The secret to a beautiful
presentation is using a variety of
colors of apples and keeping on
their skins. Use a small, sharp,
serrated knife to keep the skin
from tearing and cut lines
straight and clean.*

FRUITED PASTA SALAD

8 ounces dried pasta
2 green onions, chopped
1/2 cup red grapes, halved
1 (8-ounce) can pineapple tidbits, drained
1 tablespoon fresh mint, chopped
1 tablespoon orange juice concentrate
1/3 cup sour cream or plain yogurt
2 tablespoons mayonnaise
2 tablespoons brown sugar
3 tablespoons apple cider vinegar
4 ounces cream cheese, room temperature
4 oranges peeled and sectioned or
   (11-ounce) can Mandarin oranges, drained
2 apples, cored and chopped

Cook pasta according to package directions, taking 1 minute off of the lowest cooking time suggested. Drain pasta, rinse with cold water and drain well. Combine pasta, onions, grapes, pineapple and mint. In a separate bowl or mixer, combine orange juice, sour cream, mayonnaise, brown sugar, vinegar, cream cheese and mix well. Heating cream cheese in the microwave until very warm will help in stirring, if mixing dressing by hand. Add dressing to salad. Toss oranges in gently and add apples and chill. Can be prepared 1 day in advance. Makes 6 to 8 servings.

WALDORF SALAD

8 apples, mixed varieties
1 cup red grapes, halved
1 cup celery, chopped
1 (10-ounce) can pineapple tidbits, or 1/2 cup chopped fresh
1/2 cup golden raisins
1/2 cup walnuts or pecans, chopped large
1/2 cup mayonnaise
1/8 cup sour cream

Chop apples into bite-size pieces, leaving peeling on. Picking out a variety of colors will add to salad presentation. Mix apples, grapes, celery, very well drained pineapple, raisins, walnuts, mayonnaise and sour cream. Toss well and store covered in refrigerator. Can be made 1 day in advance. Serve chilled. Makes 12 to 15 servings.

Serving Tip:

Salads that need to be mixed before serving should be mixed in a separate bowl and neatly transferred to serving bowl.

GINGER FRUIT

3 Granny Smith apples
1 (11-ounce) can Mandarin oranges, drained well
3 cups grapes
1 (20-ounce) can pineapple or 1 fresh pineapple
1 (20-ounce) can grapefruit or 2 grapefruits sectioned
3 cups strawberries
8 ounces cream cheese, softened
4 ounces sour cream
1 1/2 teaspoons brown sugar
3/4 to 1 teaspoon ground ginger
1/4 cup whipping cream, whipped

Peel and chop apples, drain oranges, and half grapes. Reserve any juice from pineapple to toss on apples to keep from browning, and drain or chop pineapple and grapefruit. These fruits may be done 1 day in advance. Strawberries should be sliced as near to serving time as possible. In a separate bowl, mix together cream cheese, sour cream, brown sugar and ginger. In a mixer fitted with a metal whip or with a hand blender, whip whipped cream until stiff. Fold into dressing. Before serving, toss fruit, strawberries and dressing. Cantaloupe and honeydew melons work well, also. Makes 12 to 16 servings.

Tip of the Trade:

Ginger is a condiment that comes from a rootstock of a tropical plant originally grown in Malabar. It can be bought in the whole root form in grocer or markets, but is used easily in cooking through the powder spice or candied form.

Serving Tip:

Ginger Fruit can be used as a fruit salad or a fruit display using the ginger dressing as a dip. To design a beautiful fruit display for a buffet, line a platter with green leafy lettuce. Slice fruit into wedges. Fan out apples, keep melons in their whole form after slicing. Place pineapples and small berries in compotes or small bowls sitting around the trays. A footed compote on one corner and a small shallow bowl in the opposite corner works nicely. Garnish with bunches of grapes and sliced tropical fruit and strawberries. Remember, achieving an unsymmetrical design might be less frustrating than a symmetrical one. Fruit trays can be prepared 4 to 6 hours in advance, wrapped in plastic wrap and refrigerated until ready to use. Make sure the tray fits in the refrigerator before you get started.

◆

Tip of the Trade:

It was my great grandmother who truly believed in a colorful plate. Her Fruit Salad Dressing recipe is very rich and delicious.
In her honor, decorate your fruit with mint sprigs, fresh, whole colorful berries or lemon slices.

NANNIES FRUIT SALAD DRESSING

A recipe from the collection of my great grandmother, Mrs. Lillie Mae Carpenter

1 egg
1 tablespoon vinegar
1/4 teaspoon salt
1 teaspoon sugar
18 large marshmallows
1/2 pint whipping cream, whipped
1/2 cup chopped pecans

Combine egg and vinegar and place in a double boiler over medium heat. Whisk the mixture constantly. Add salt and marshmallows when it starts to thicken, and whisk until marshmallows melt. Cool to room temperature. Fold in whipped cream and nuts. Serve chilled with 6 to 8 cups of your favorite fresh fruit salad or fruited congealed salad.

Tip of the Trade:

Frozen Fruit Salads are well known in the old South. This is perfect for a ladies luncheon. Tea rooms still serve this sweet frozen treat around Atlanta and other parts of the South. Try serving it at your next luncheon to keep the tradition.

FROZEN FRUIT SALAD

4 egg yolks
4 tablespoons sugar
5 tablespoons apple cider vinegar
12 large marshmallows
1/2 pint whipping cream
3 cups mixed fruit, canned or fresh

◆

Tip of the Trade:

When preparing fruit for a fresh fruit salad, use lemon juice or my best trade secret, pineapple juice, on apples, pears and bananas after slicing. Pineapple juice will keep the apples and pears from turning for 24 hours or more. Bananas always should be sliced as near to serving time as possible, but the pineapple juice will keep them as fresh looking as possible.

In a double boiler over medium heat, combine yolks, sugar and vinegar. When heated and starting to thicken, add marshmallows and whisk until melted. Add whipping cream and immediately remove from heat. Cool mixture before adding fruit. Place in a greased 9 x 13 pan, covered tightly, and freeze. Can be made several days in advance if bananas are not used. Using canned fruit cocktail and pineapple with fresh berries is a wonderful combination. To serve, remove from freezer, slice into desired squares, and serve on green leaf lettuce with a dollop of mayonnaise. Recommended for seated luncheons or brunches for the true Southerner at heart. Makes 16 to 20 servings.

SPINACH MOLD

2 envelopes unflavored gelatin
1 (14-ounce) can chicken broth
2 tablespoons lemon juice
1/2 cup mayonnaise
1 (8-ounce) package cream cheese, softened
1 (10-ounce) package frozen chopped spinach, thawed
2 green onions, peeled and chopped
1 (8-ounce) can water chestnuts, drained and chopped
4 hard boiled eggs, chopped
8 ounces bacon, cooked and crumbled

Tip of the Trade:

Vegetable Congealed Molds were in great demand 20 to 30 years ago and then faded out of popularity for a time. When I prepare them for dinner parties or for catered events, sometimes just to experiment, they go over fabulously. Try bringing them back at your next party with Spinach Congealed Mold or Asparagus Mold on the following page.

Measure out gelatin to equal 4 teaspoons and pour into room temperature broth. Heat broth in microwave or on stove until bubbly and remove from heat. Add mayonnaise, cream cheese, well drained spinach, onions, water chestnuts, egg and bacon and mix well by hand or in a mixer fitted with a metal blade. Place into a 2-quart greased mold, cover and refrigerate for at least 8 hours. Makes 12 to 16 servings.

ASPARAGUS MOLD

1 (3-ounce) package lemon gelatin
1 cup cold water
3 cups water
1/2 pound fresh asparagus
1 teaspoon salt
1 cup celery, 2 stalks, chopped
1/2 cup white vinegar
1 (2-ounce) jar pimento, drained
3 green onions, peeled and chopped
1 (5-ounce) can water chestnuts, drained and chopped
1/4 cup almonds, slivered
1/4 cup mayonnaise
1/2 teaspoon salt

Dissolve gelatin in 1 cup cold water then heat on stove or in microwave until bubbly and set aside. In a medium pot over high heat, place water and let boil. Chop asparagus spears into 1/2-inch pieces. Add salt and asparagus to water. Cook for 3 minutes and drain well. Combine gelatin, asparagus, celery, vinegar, pimento, onions, water chestnuts, almonds, mayonnaise and salt. Pour into a 2- or 3-quart greased mold and refrigerate covered for at least 8 hours. Can be made 1 to 2 days in advance. Men even enjoy this one. Makes 12 to 16 servings.

BLOODY MARY ASPIC

2 packages unflavored gelatin
4 tablespoons cold water
2 pints tomato juice
1 tablespoon lemon juice
1 teaspoon Worcestershire sauce
1 teaspoon celery salt
Hot sauce

DRESSING:
1 (8-ounce) package cream cheese, softened
1 (14 1/2-ounce) can artichoke hearts, drained
1 tablespoon lemon juice
2 tablespoons mayonnaise
1 tablespoon parsley, fresh chopped or 1/2 teaspoon dried

Dissolve gelatin in cold water and heat on stove or in microwave until bubbly. Combine gelatin mixture, tomato juice, lemon juice, Worcestershire, celery salt and hot sauce and mix well by hand or in food processor fitted with metal blade or in a mixer. Pour into a greased 1 1/2- to 2-quart mold and refrigerate for at least 8 hours. Can be prepared 1 to 2 days in advance. **To make dressing:** In a mixer or by hand, combine cream cheese, artichoke hearts, lemon juice, mayonnaise and parsley and mix well. Can be made 1 day in advance. When serving, place mold on green leaf lettuce and place dressing in the middle or side. Makes 12 to 16 servings.

TOMATO BASIL ASPIC

1 (11-ounce) can tomato soup
1 envelope unflavored gelatin
1/4 teaspoon salt
1 cup cottage cheese
1/4 cup mayonnaise
3 fresh basil leaves, chopped
1 cup celery, chopped
2 green onions, peeled and chopped
1 teaspoon lemon juice

Combine cold tomato soup, gelatin and salt and heat on stove or in microwave until bubbly. Place cottage cheese, mayonnaise and basil in a food processor fitted with a metal blade, or blend in blender or hand blender. Add to tomato mixture and set off heat. Add celery, green onions and lemon juice. Pour into a 3-cup greased mold and refrigerate for at least 8 hours. Can be prepared 1 to 2 days in advance. To serve, unmold and serve with a side of mayonnaise. Makes 8 to 12 servings.

Serving Tip:

Individual congealed salad molds are quite beautiful for a fixed plate luncheon. Investing in some tiny molds is ideal for kitchen inventory. Vegetable cooking spray is the secret to easy removal of any congealed mold from its dish.

Using frozen artichokes instead of canned artichokes can be more economical, however frozen artichokes can be rather tough. Using canned artichokes will give the best outcome in most dishes.

Tip of the Trade:

In Italy, a pot of basil in a young lady's window is said to be an invitation to her lover to visit her. There are more than 100 varieties of the basil family and it is related to the herb mint.

♦

MOLDED POTATO SALAD

1 1/2 pounds potatoes, peeled and diced 1/4-inch cubes
3 cups water
1/2 teaspoon salt
1/2 cup celery, trimmed and chopped
3 green onions, peeled and chopped
2 tablespoons vinegar
1 cup chicken broth
1/2 cup white wine
2 envelopes unflavored gelatin, 4 teaspoons
1/2 cup mayonnaise
2 teaspoons prepared stone ground or Dijon mustard
1/2 teaspoon salt

Chop potatoes and cover with water and salt in a medium pot. Bring to a boil and cook for 10 to 15 minutes over medium high heat. Potatoes should still be a little firm. Drain and cool. Mix potatoes, celery and onion. Add vinegar and broth. Dissolve gelatin in cold wine and heat in microwave or stove until bubbly. Add gelatin, mayonnaise, mustard and salt to potatoes. Pour into a greased 4-cup mold and refrigerate for 8 hours. Can be prepared 1 to 2 days in advance. To serve, unmold onto green leaf and garnish with dill and parsley. Surrounding with deviled eggs will make a beautiful Southern picnic dish. Makes 12 to 16 servings.

WINE CHERRY MOLD

1 (16-ounce) can cherries, reserve juice
3/4 cup reserved juice from cherries and water to measure
1 (3-ounce) package cherry gelatin
1/2 cup zinfandel wine or champagne
1 (4-ounce) package cream cheese, softened
1/2 cup walnuts, chopped
1/2 cup sour cream

♦

Dissolve gelatin in cold cherry juice, adding enough water to make 3/4 cup. Heat gelatin mixture in microwave or on the stove. Combine gelatin, cherries, wine and cream cheese in a food processor fitted with a metal blade or a blender, and process for 2 to 3 seconds. Stir in walnuts and sour cream and pour into a greased 4-cup mold. Cover and refrigerate for at least 8 hours. Can be made 1 to 2 days in advance. To serve, unmold onto green leafy lettuce and serve with a side of mayonnaise with fresh cherry garnishes. Makes 6 to 10 servings.

Serving Tip:

Serve fruited molds at the end of a buffet before the bread and relishes.

CRANBERRY CONGEALED SALAD

A recipe from the collection of my client, Mrs. Dianne Matthews, Marietta. Traditionally served at her family Thanksgiving meal.

1 pound whole fresh cranberries
2 whole oranges, seeds removed
2 cups sugar
3 (3-ounce) packages raspberry gelatin
1 (8-ounce) can crushed pineapple
1 cup pecans or walnuts, chopped
1 cup celery, chopped
3 cups water

Grind cranberries and oranges in a food processor fitted with a metal blade. Add sugar. Set aside. Mix gelatin with 3 cups hot water and juice from pineapple. Chill slightly. Add pineapple, nuts and celery to cranberry mix. Mix with gelatin and congeal covered in refrigerator for at least 8 hours. Makes 12 to 16 servings.

Tip of the Trade:
Gelatin Stages

Gelatin has different jellying stages. Steps taken during preparation of making gelatin should be done when it is at the proper consistency.

Chill to partially set:

The gelatin is the consistency of unbeaten egg whites. This allows any fruit or nuts added to stay consistently throughout the mold rather than all sink or float.

Chill until almost firm:

The gelatin would flow to one side or the other if tipped, but looks as if it is congealed. This stage is used for layering salads.

Chill until firm:

The gelatin can hold a distinctive cut and will not slide or move when tilted. It is ready to unmold.

◆

Spiced Pickled Peaches

*1 20-ounce can canned
peaches with syrup
1/2 cup white or cider
vinegar
3/4 cup brown sugar
12 whole cloves
6 whole allspice*

*Bring all ingredients to a
simmering boil for 15 minutes.
Easily canned and preserved
for use as a relish, side dish
or in Pickled Peach Mold.
If using in a mold, the
whole allspice and cloves
can be simmered with
peaches in a tied piece
of cheesecloth or a tea holder
for easier removal.*

*Pickled Peaches can be bought in
the canned or bottled form in the
canned fruit section of markets
and grocers.
Making homemade pickled peaches
takes little time and effort. The
recipe works well with either
homemade or store-bought pickled
peaches. Wonderful for the
holiday season.*

CRANBERRY EGGNOG SALAD

**1 (3-ounce) package vanilla pudding
1 (3-ounce) package lemon gelatin
2 cups cold water, divided
1 3-ounce package cranberry gelatin
1 tablespoon lemon juice
1 cup whipping cream
1 cup commercial egg nog beverage
1/2 teaspoon nutmeg
1 teaspoon brandy**

Dissolve vanilla pudding and lemon gelatin in 1 cup cold water and heat on stove or in microwave until bubbly and set aside. Dissolve cranberry gelatin in 1 cup cold water and lemon juice and heat on stove or in microwave until bubbly. Refrigerate cranberry gelatin to cool down to room temperature. Whip the whipping cream with a hand blender or in a mixer fitted with a metal whip and fold into pudding mixture along with egg nog, nutmeg and brandy. Place 1/2 pudding mixture in a 2 1/2-cup mold and freeze for 15 to 20 minutes or chill for 30 minutes until almost firm. Remove from freezer and add cold cranberry mixture. Place in freezer to set for 10 minutes or chill until almost firm. Top with remaining pudding mixture, cover and refrigerate for at least 8 hours. Makes 10 to 14 servings.

HOLIDAY PICKLED PEACH MOLD

**1 cup pickled or spiced peaches, reserve juice
1 (3-ounce) package lemon or orange gelatin
1 cup pickled peach juice and water to measure
1 cup lemon-lime soda
1/2 cup chopped pecans**

Chop pickled peaches and reserve juice. Strain the juice. Reuse the pickled peach juice and add enough water to obtain 1 cup and disslove gelatin in it. Heat gelatin mixture on stove or in microwave until bubbly. Remove from heat and add soda and pecans. Place in a greased 2 1/2-cup mold and refrigerate covered for at least 8 hours. Can be made 2 to 3 days in advance. A perfect winter holiday side dish. Makes 6 to 10 servings.

PINEAPPLE CONGEALED SALAD

1 (3-ounce) package lemon gelatin
1 package unflavored gelatin, 2 teaspoons
2 cups pineapple juice
2 tablespoons lemon juice
2 cups fresh pineapple or
  1 (22-ounce) can pineapple, drained
2 carrots, peeled and grated
1/2 cup almonds, slivered
1/4 cup celery
1 cup mini marshmallows
1 cup whipping cream
1 (8-ounce) package cream cheese, room temperature

Soften lemon gelatin and gelatin in cold pineapple juice and heat on stove or in microwave until bubbly. Remove from heat and transfer to a mixer. Combine gelatin with lemon juice, pineapple, carrots, nuts, celery, marshmallows, whipping cream and cream cheese. Mix all ingredients well and pour into a greased 4-cup mold. Refrigerate covered for at least 8 hours. Can be made 1 to 2 days in advance. Unmold before serving. Makes 12 to 16 servings.

◆

CREAMY APRICOT MOLD

2 envelopes unflavored gelatin
1/2 cup sugar
1/4 teaspoon salt
2 1/4 cups apricot nectar
1/4 cup water
1 1/4 cup white wine
1 cup sour cream

Measure out gelatin to equal 4 teaspoons and place with sugar, salt, apricot nectar and water. Place on stove and heat until bubbly. Remove from heat and add white wine and sour cream. Mix well and place in a greased mold, cover and store in refrigerator. Can be made 2 to 3 days in advance. Unmold and serve with tiny sliced fresh fruit. Makes 8 servings.

STRAWBERRY SALAD

A recipe from the collection of Mrs. Marie Barnes Rambo

1 (3-ounce) package strawberry gelatin
1 cup boiling water
1 (8-ounce) can crushed pineapple, reserve juice
1 (10-ounce) package frozen strawberries,
  thawed, reserve juice
1 cup juice, reserved juices with other fruit juice to measure
1 (8-ounce) package cream cheese, room temperature
1/2 cup nuts, chopped

Mix gelatin with boiling water to dissolve. Strain juice from pineapple and strawberries to make 1 cup. (Other juice can be added if needed to equal 1 cup.) Add fruit juice to gelatin. Stir in fruit. Pour gelatin into desired greased 2-quart mold or greased 9 x 9 baking dish and place in refrigerator to start congealing process. Break cream cheese into bite-size pieces and roll into balls. Roll each individually in chopped nuts. When gelatin begins to thicken, place each ball decoratively into gelatin. Cover and continue refrigerating for 8 hours and up to 48 hours. Makes 6 to 8 servings.

Tip of the Trade:

We have taken for granted the little prepared gelatin mixes that are available to us at the grocers. In looking through cookbooks of the '20s and '30s, great details were given on how to prepare the plain gelatin with the fruit just to make a clear salad. Next time you combine a package with hot water and then cold water, think of how instant our lives have become and how deligently a cook had to work in the kitchen just a few years ago.

Using wine or Champagne in any fruited gelatin dish will give a wonderful subtle flavor and bite to the recipe. Add it in the same amounts as water.

◆

Celebrating *The Morning Harvest*
Eggs, Cheese, Grains and Tarts

Anne Mullins Rigdon

SWISS SAUSAGE AND EGGS

A recipe inspired from the collection of Mrs. Joan Greene, shared from the recipes of Marsha Collier

8 slices bread with crust, diced
1/4 cup butter or margarine, melted
1 pound mild ground pork sausage
1 cup Swiss or gruyere cheese, grated
1 cup sharp Cheddar cheese, grated
6 eggs
3 cups whole milk
1 teaspoon prepared mustard
1/2 teaspoon salt
1/4 teaspoon pepper

Place chopped bread in a greased 9 x 13 baking dish. Pour melted butter over bread and toss gently. Cook pork sausage in a medium skillet over medium heat until brown. Drain sausage well and place over cubed bread. Sprinkle grated cheeses evenly over sausage. In a mixer fitted with a metal whip or a food processor fitted with a metal blade, combine eggs, milk, mustard, salt and pepper. Mix eggs well and pour over sausage. Cover tightly and refrigerate for at least 4 hours and up to 24 hours. Bake at 325 degrees for 30 minutes covered and then another 20 to 30 minutes uncovered. Makes 8 to 10 servings.

Deviled Eggs:

When boiling eggs, never use fresh eggs, they will not peel. Start the egg in cold water and bring to a soft boil for 12 to 15 minutes. Drain water and peel immediately under running cold water. This prevents gray discoloration of the yolks. Slice the egg in half lengthwise and remove yolk. Combine yolk with 1/4 teaspoon salt and 1/4 cup mayonnaise to every 12 egg yolks. Fill mixture back into whites and cover and refrigerate until ready to use. Sprinkle top with paprika or place an olive or almond slice on top.

Tip of the Trade:

Monterey Jack cheese is an excellent cheese for egg dishes. Cheddar cheese is not a satisfactory cheese for egg dishes because it tends to separate at hot temperatures.

CHICKEN SCALLOPED EGGS

4 tablespoons butter or margarine
1 pound fresh button mushrooms, trimmed and washed
3 green onions, peeled and chopped
4 tablespoons sherry
2 (10 1/2-ounce) cans cream of chicken soup
1 (8-ounce) carton sour cream
2 tablespoons plain all-purpose flour
9 to 10 hard-boiled eggs
1 (6 to 8-ounce) can sliced water chestnuts, drained
3 cups chicken, cooked and diced into cubes
1 1/2 cups bread crumbs
3 tablespoons butter or margarine, melted

In a medium skillet or in a microwave safe dish, melt butter and cook mushrooms and onions for 3 to 5 minutes until tender. Drain vegetables from their juices. Combine mushroom mixture, sherry, soup, sour cream, and flour and mix well. Boil eggs for 15 minutes over a soft boil and peel immediately after cooking to prevent browning of yolks. Slice into five rings. In a greased 9 x 13 pan, place sliced hard-boiled eggs. Layer water chestnuts and chicken over eggs. Spread soup mixture over chicken. Mix together bread crumbs and 3 tablespoons melted butter. Sprinkle over top of casserole. Ingredients can be prepared in advance, but assemble 1 to 2 hours before serving. Bake at 350 degrees for 35 to 45 minutes, uncovered. Serve warm. Makes 10 to 12 servings.

Menu Suggesiton:
Breakfast Before A Garden Tour

Fruited Mixed Greens with Madeira Dressing,

Tomato Grits,

Croissants and Fruited Muffins,

Spiral Honey Ham,

Fresh Juices and Coffee

Menu Suggestion:

A Brunch for Twelve

Creamed Chicken Sauce,

Fresh Fruit,

Buttermilk Biscuits,
Butter and Preserves,

Bakery Purchased
Danish and Pastries,

Mimosas with a dash of
Peach Schnapps,

Orange Juice and Coffee

Tip of the Trade:

Ham, Shrimp and Artichoke
Soufflé is not suggested for
large crowds due to the egg whites
needing to be folded
within an hour of cooking,
and because of its needing
to be served immediately
after being brought from
the oven. It is a perfect recipe for
parties of 12 or less.
When making this sauce for the
soufflé, it can be made in the
microwave rather than the stove, if
desired. The sauce is rather thick
before folding in the egg yolks and
egg whites. You will be very
pleased with yourself when this
beautiful dish comes out
of the oven.

PIE DISH SOUFFLÉ

1 commercial pie crust sheet or prepared shell
1/4 cup butter
1/4 cup plain all-purpose flour
1/2 cup half and half
1/2 cup milk
6 ounces Monterey Jack cheese, grated
4 eggs, divided
1/3 pound ham, diced fine
1/4 pound shrimp, cooked, peeled and diced
1 (14 1/2-ounce) can quartered artichokes, drained
2 green onions, peeled andchopped
1/2 teaspoon cream of tartar

Place commercial crust in a greased 9-inch deep dish pie plate and scallop edges with fingers. In a medium saucepan, melt butter and add flour to make a roux or paste. Pour in half and half and milk and stir with a whisk constantly over medium high heat until thickened. Add cheese and stir until melted. Cool slightly and gently whisk egg yolks and fold into sauce. Place diced ham, diced shrimp, artichokes and onions evenly in pie crust. In a mixer fitted with a metal whip, whip egg whites with cream of tartar until stiff. Fold egg whites into cream mixture and pour into pie plate. Bake at 375 degrees for 40 to 45 minutes. Serve with Creamed Chicken Sauce. Makes 4 to 6 servings.

CREAMED CHICKEN SAUCE

3/4 cup butter or margarine
3/4 cup self-rising flour
2 3/4 cups milk
1/2 teaspoon salt
1/4 teaspoon white or black pepper
1 cup chicken, cooked and diced
1 (2-ounce) jar dried beef, chopped
2 cups button mushrooms, sliced
2 tablespoons butter or margarine

In a medium saucepan over medium heat, or in a microwave safe dish, melt butter and add flour to make a roux or paste. Add milk and heat, whisking until thickened, making sure to scrape the bottom of pan to keep from burning. If using microwave, heat in 3-minute intervals while whisking between cooking time until thickened. Add spices, chicken and chopped dried beef. Dried beef can be chopped easily with kitchen scissors or shears. In a skillet over medium heat, melt butter and add mushrooms. Cook for 3 minutes until tender and drain. Chicken sauce can be made 1 day in advance and stored without the mushrooms. Mushrooms should be added right before serving and additional milk might need to be added for desired consistency. Serve warm with Pie Dish Soufflé or as a gravy with Buttermilk Biscuits. Makes 6 to 8 servings.

Tip of the Trade:

Without the chicken, dried beef, and mushrooms, this is just simple, white gravy. Serve white gravy with buttermilk biscuits, scrambled eggs, cheese grits, sausage and bacon to your family on a special weekend morning.

SAUSAGE GRITS

3 cups water
1 teaspoon salt
1 cup grits
4 ounces processed cheese spread
1 (12-ounce) can evaporated milk
3 eggs, slightly beaten
1 pound cooked and drained sausage, any type
1/2 teaspoon parsley flakes

Bring water to a boil with salt and add grits while stirring. Lower temperature, cover and cook for 8 to 12 minutes. Remove from heat and add cheese. When cheese has melted, add evaporated milk. Add eggs and stir well. If using link sausage, chop fine or pulse two to three times in a food processor fitted with a metal blade. If cooked, ground sausage is used, drain well before adding. Pour into a 9 x 9 greased baking dish or 2-quart casserole and store covered in refrigerator for up to 1 day. Bake covered for 25 to 35 minutes at 375 degrees and an additional 10 to 15 minutes uncovered. Makes 6 to 8 servings.

Tip of the Trade:

When I make this dish, I like to use a fully cooked mild Cajun link sausage. I slice and chop before adding to the dish. Follow the cooking directions given with any sausage chosen before preparing this dish.

◆

Menu Suggestion:

A Christening Brunch

Artichoke Bites,

Fresh Fruit Salad,

Spinach and Orange Salad,

*Buttermilk Biscuits
with
Creamed Chicken Sauce,*

Sour Cream Coffee Cakes,

*Coconut Cake with Coconut
Pecan Frosting*

Tip of the Trade:

*Lowcountry regions which include
the coastal and low lying
regions of Georgia and more
importantly South Carolina, give
the host the freedom to
use grits as a side dish
any time of the day. It
is common of their heritage
and traditions to serve
grits with shrimp and other
shellfish as well as poultry
and meats.*

CHARLESTON SHRIMP AND GRITS

3 3/4 cups water
1 cup real grits
1 teaspoon salt
8 ounces Swiss cheese, grated
8 ounces Monterey Jack cheese, grated
1 garlic clove, peeled and crushed
1 cup whipping cream
8 eggs
1/4 teaspoon red pepper
4 green onions, peeled and chopped
10 ounces ham, chopped
1 pound shrimp, cooked, peeled and deveined

In a medium saucepan, bring water to a boil. While stirring, pour grits in with salt. Let cook according to package directions. Remove grits from heat and add cheese and garlic. Stir until cheeses have melted. In a mixer fitted with a metal whip or in a bowl with a whisk, beat whipping cream and eggs until smooth. Add to slightly cooled grits and stir well. Add red pepper, green onions, ham and shrimp and pour into a greased 9 x 13 dish. Can be made 1 day in advance and stored covered in the refrigerator. Bake at 375 degrees for 50 to 60 minutes. If premature browning of top of dish occurs, cover with aluminum foil during half the cooking time. This dish can be frozen before or after cooking, thawed and cooked or reheated. Makes 10 to 12 servings.

Serving Tip:

*Serve 9 x 13 Pyrex dishes out of holder for the best look
when presenting on entertaining tables.*

◆

Serving Tip:

Capture a private moment with your loved one with a breakfast for two after the children have left for school or on a relaxing weekend morning. If feeling festive, start out with a mimosa or Bloody Mary.
Don't forget breakfast in bed for a special occasion or a loving gesture. Add fresh flowers and linens or the morning paper to the tray.

Menu Suggestion:
Late Breakfast for Two

Fresh Fruit,

Toasted English Muffins,

Butter and Strawberry Jam,

Coffee

CHEESE MIGAS FOR TWO

2 tablespoons butter or margarine, divided
2 (6-inch) corn tortillas chopped
1 tablespoon butter or margarine
1/2 onion, peeled and chopped, (1/4 cup)
1/2 tomato, seeded and chopped
1/4 cup bell pepper, chopped
2 eggs
2 tablespoons milk
1/2 teaspoon salt
1 tablespoons butter
1/2 cup Monterey Jack cheese, grated
2 tablespoons sour cream

Tip of the Trade:
Chili Peppers

Adding finely chopped chili peppers to Cheese Migas will give any morning a big boost.

Anaheim peppers are red or green, cone shaped and mild to medium hot.
Poblano or Pasilla peppers are dark green, long and triangular and are mild to hot. These dry well.
Jalapenos are green, smooth and shiny, mild when raw but when left to redden and then dried, they become very hot.
Serrano are bright green or red, hot to very hot and are sometimes pickled. Will work in vinegars or oils to give dishes a kick.

In a medium skillet, place 1 tablespoon butter and fry corn tortilla pieces very quickly. Remove from pan leaving grease. Melt 1 tablespoon butter with leftover grease and add onion, tomato and pepper. Cook for 3 to 5 minutes on medium low heat. Remove vegetables and set aside. In a bowl or in a mixer, beat eggs, milk and salt together until smooth. In the same skillet, melt remaining 1 tablespoon butter and add eggs, letting cook slightly to form a bottom. Sprinkle 1/2 of cheese over eggs. Add tortillas and vegetables and keep folding eggs over, forming a distorted omelet. When eggs are fully cooked, serve immediately. Sprinkle with remaining cheese and a dollop of sour cream. Makes 2 servings.

◆

Menu Suggestion:
A Reunion Brunch

Broccoli Salad,

Tomato Basil Aspic,

*Fresh Cut Melons
and Strawberries,*

Cheese Biscuits,

Sausages and Ham,

Frozen Pecan Coffee Cakes

Menu Suggestion:
Late Brunch with Friends

Fruited Pasta Salad,

Marinated Poached Asparagus,

Angel Biscuits,

*Pound Cake Cookies,
Strawberries and Sorbet*

HOT CHEESE SOUFFLÉ

7 slices white bread, cubed with crust
1/2 cup butter or margarine, melted
8 ounces hot pepper Monterey Jack cheese, grated
3 eggs, beaten
2 cups milk or 1 cup half and half and 1 cup milk
1/2 teaspoon Worcestershire sauce
1/2 teaspoon dry mustard
1/4 teaspoon salt

Cube white bread leaving on crusts. Pour melted butter on bread and stir gently. In a greased 9 x 9 pan or greased 2-quart soufflé dish, evenly place 1/2 of bread cubes topped with 1/2 cheese. Repeat this process using all the cheese and all the bread. In a mixer fitted with the metal whip or a bowl whisking by hand, combine eggs, milk, Worcestershire, mustard and salt. Pour into casserole, cover and refrigerate for at least 4 hours and up to 24 hours. Bake at 350 degrees for 35 to 50 minutes. Check dish during half the cooking time. If top browning is too dark, cover with greased aluminum foil for remaining cooking time. This is a wonderful accompaniment to meats for dinner or lunch. Grated American or Cheddar cheese can be substituted for Monterey cheese for an old fashioned soufflé taste. Makes 4 to 6 servings.

RICH QUICHES

1 pie crust
3 ounces Monterey Jack cheese or Swiss cheese, grated
1/2 cup vegetable of choice (see directions)
3 eggs
1/4 cup whipping cream
3/4 cup half and half
1/2 teaspoon salt

◆

Prepare pie crust in a greased dish of choice. A glass pie dish is the most attractive for serving. To make individual quiches for passing, grease muffin tins and with a cookie cutter, cut crust sheets into 1 1/2-inch circles for mini muffin tins or 3-inch circles for large muffin tins. Press into desired pan. Scallop edges for larger pies. Place cheese in bottom of uncooked crust. Drained cooked spinach, artichokes, chopped seeded tomatoes, shredded summer squash or zucchini, cooked mushrooms and cooked onions all work well for a vegetable choice. Combinations of your choice not exceeding 3/4 cups work well. Divide vegetables evenly between quiches on top of cheese.

In a mixer fitted with a metal whip or with a blender or food processor fitted with a metal blade, combine eggs, whipping cream, half and half, and salt. Pour batter over cheese but only filling crust 3/4 full. Bake in a 350-degree oven for 35 to 45 minutes for larger pies and down to 15 to 25 minutes for smaller muffins. Cooked crab, shrimp, ham or sausage all work well with this dish with or without vegetables. The egg custard is a wonderful base for any ingredient of choice. Makes 24 miniature quiches or six brunch servings.

DINNER GRITS

2 cups water
3/4 teaspoon salt
1 cup chicken broth
1 cup milk
1 cup grits

In a medium pot, bring water, salt, broth and milk to a soft boil. Add grits while stirring and cover to cook for 8 to 12 minutes. Remove from stove, leaving covered, and let sit for 5 to 10 minutes before serving. Serve with Shrimp Scampi or other favorite fish or chicken dish. Can make ahead and reheat in microwave if desired. Add milk for desired consistency. Best made right before serving. Makes 4 servings.

Tip of the Trade:
Quiche and Omelet Combinations

Spinach, Wild Mushroom and Baby Swiss with Bacon

Grated Yellow and Zucchini Squash with Cheddar and Tomatos

Hot Pepper Jack with Bell Peppers, Onions and Sausage

Canandian Bacon and Mushroom with Havarti Cheese and Sunflower Sprouts

Shrimp and Crab with Bacon and Cheese

Asparagus with Gruyere and Fresh Herbs

Goat Cheese and Tomato with Fresh Basil

Tip of the Trade:

Grits can be bought in several ways. Real grits cook almost as fast as quick grits. Do not be afraid to try coarser, stone ground grits in place of real or regular grits in any recipe.

◆

Tip of the Trade:

The recipe for Tomato Grits was inspired by a beautiful inn in Asheville, North Carolina. The chef of the time had been trained in Charleston and served grits similar to this with many of his casual dinner dishes.

If egg dishes are retaining water while baking in oven, uncover and raise the temperature to 375 to 400 degrees to evaporate the excess water.

TOMATO GRITS

3 cups water
3/4 cup real grits
1 teaspoon salt
1 cup tomatoes, chopped
2 ounces cream cheese
3/4 cup Colby, Swiss or Monterey Jack cheese, grated
1 egg

Boil water in a medium saucepan. Add grits while stirring with salt. Simmer for 15 to 20 minutes, covered. Place tomatoes, cream cheese, cheese and egg in a food processor fitted with a metal blade and pulse for 3 to 5 seconds. Add mixture to cooked grits and stir well. Pour into a greased 9 x 9 pan and bake at 375 to 400 degrees for 35 to 50 minutes uncovered. Cool for 5 minutes before serving. Makes 4 to 6 servings.

Tip of the Trade:
Easy Saturday Brunch

*Spiral Sliced Ham,
Biscuits or Croissants,*

Fresh Fruit,

Wine Cherry Mold,

Waffles with Syrups and Butter,

Bakery Sticky Buns

BAKED CHEESE GRITS

3 1/2 cups water
3/4 teaspoon salt
1 cup grits
1/4 cup butter or margarine
3 ounces nippy cheese or garlic cheese spread
3/4 cup grated sharp Cheddar cheese
3 tablespoons Parmesan cheese
1 teaspoon Worcestershire
1/4 teaspoon garlic powder
1/2 cup whipping cream or 1/4 cup milk
1/4 cup milk
2 eggs, slightly beaten

◆

◆

In a medium saucepan, bring water to a boil with salt. While stirring, add grits. Cover and cook for 3 to 5 minutes or according to package directions. Remove from heat and add butter, nippy cheese spread, Cheddar cheese, Parmesan cheese, Worcestershire and garlic powder. Stir until cheese is melted. Add cream, milk and eggs and mix through. Pour grits into a greased 9 x 9 pan or a 1 1/2- to 2-quart greased casserole. Dish can be refrigerated covered for up to 1 day at this point. Bake at 375 degrees for 45 to 60 minutes. A wonderful side dish at any time of day. Makes 6 to 8 servings.

FLUFFY WILD RICE

1 (8-ounce) package pure wild rice
3 1/2 cups water
1 teaspoon salt
2 cups long grain white rice
3 1/2 cups water
1 teaspoon salt
4 tablespoons butter or margarine
1 clove garlic, peeled and crushed
1/2 sweet yellow onion, peeled and chopped
1/2 to 3/4 cup slivered almonds, toasted

In a medium pot, place wild rice with 3 1/2 cups water and 1 teaspoon salt and bring to a boil. Cook according to package directions, around 35 minutes. Drain rice in colander and rinse with cold water. Meanwhile, bring remaining 3 1/2 cups water to a boil with 1 teaspoon salt in a medium pot over medium heat. Add white rice and simmer covered on low for 15 to 20 minutes, or according to package directions. Rinse in a colander with cold water and drain well. Combine all rice in a microwave-safe dish or heavy storage bag. In a small saucepan, melt butter and cook garlic and onion for 3 to 5 minutes over low heat until transparent. Pour over rice and toss with toasted almonds. Add salt and pepper to taste. Rice can be refrigerated covered at this point until ready to serve, up to 2 days. Reheat in microwave and serve warm. Makes 12 servings.

Tip of the Trade:

Cheese Grits is one of my most popular recipes. I have even seen Northerners sneak to get a second helping. Adding cooked shrimp to this dish is fantastic.

When cooking any egg dish, make sure the middle has cooked and set before removing from oven.

Tip of the Trade:

Wild rice is not actually a rice, but a seed of a water grass that grows in the Northern part of our country and around the Great Lakes of neighboring Canada. It is commonly cooked with other grains rather than by itself.

For Storing:

Storing rice in resealable bags not only is practical for storing in refrigerator, but it helps keep dishwashing down to a minimum during party. It simply can be reheated right in the bag in microwave or even tightly sealed in bag placed in boiling water.

♦

FRUITED RICE

3 tablespoons butter or margarine
1/4 cup green onion, peeled and chopped
1/2 cup celery, chopped
1 cup white uncooked long grain rice
1 (14 1/2-ounce) can chicken broth
3/4 cup milk
1/2 teaspoon salt
1/8 teaspoon pepper
1/2 cup chopped almonds (or other favorite nut)
1/8 cup dried cranberries
1/4 cup dried apricots, diced
1/2 cup purple grapes, halved
1/4 teaspoon cinnamon

Melt butter in a medium skillet and cook onion and celery for 2 to 3 minutes. Add rice and cook for 2 minutes while stirring constantly. Add broth, milk, salt and pepper. Cook covered for 10 to 15 minutes. Remove from heat, and when rice is just tender, remove 1/2 the rice and drain under cold water. This will give the rice a fluffy texture. Add dried fruits to hot rice and stir well. Combine all rice together and store in a bowl or storage bag until ready to serve, up to 2 days. Reheat rice in microwave, toss with grapes and cinnamon and serve in a crystal or china serving bowl with a bunch of purple grape garnishes. Makes 4 to 6 servings.

RICE WITH WINE AND PARMESAN

1/4 cup butter or margarine
1 onion, chopped
1 garlic clove, crushed
1 cup rice, uncooked
1/8 cup white wine

INGREDIENTS CONTINUED NEXT PAGE

♦

1 (14 1/2-ounce) can chicken broth
1/4 cup water
1/2 teaspoon salt
1/2 cup Parmesan cheese, grated

In a medium skillet that can be covered, melt butter and add onion and garlic. Cook for 2 to 3 minutes. Add rice, stirring for an additional 2 minutes. Add wine, chicken broth, water and salt. Cover and cook for 25 minutes. Stir in grated Parmesan cheese and serve warm. If making in advance, reheat rice in microwave without Parmesan cheese. Parmesan should be added right before serving. Makes 4 to 6 servings.

ZESTY ORANGE RICE

2 tablespoons butter or margarine
3 green onions, peeled and chopped
1 cup long grain rice, uncooked
1 1/3 cups chicken broth
1 1/3 cups orange juice
1 to 1 1/2 tablespoons orange peel, grated from 1 orange
1 orange, zest from
1/2 teaspoon salt
Dash white or black pepper
1 tablespoon parsley, fresh snipped
1/4 cup fresh chopped watercress, optional

In a large skillet that can be covered, melt butter and add onions. Cook for 3 to 5 minutes. Add rice and stir over medium low heat for 1 to 2 minutes. Add broth, orange juice, orange peel, orange zest and spices. Cover and cook 20 to 35 minutes. Serve warm. If refrigerating and reheating, add more butter and spices, if desired. Can be reheated in microwave before serving. Toss fresh chopped watercress after cooking or reheating, if desired. Makes 4 to 6 servings.

Tip of the Trade:

White rice has a neutral flavor. It can be bought in several ways which are described below. Keep in mind while cooking the various cooking times of the different rice and make necessary changes to the recipes as needed.

Parboiled or Converted Rice *has been steamed in the hull which takes the vitamin to the center of the grain. It is less sticky but takes longer to cook.*

Instant Rice *has been processed, cooked and dehydrated, making the cooking time very short.*

Long Grain Rice, *because of their length, tend to stay fluffy and separate from each other while cooking.*

Tip of the Trade:

Substitute the Italian grain, risotto, in Zesty Orange Rice, if desired. When adding the liquid in the recipe directions, add 1/2 the liquid, heated, to risotto and boil, and then add remaining liquid, heated. Finish cooking as recipe suggests.

Tip of the Trade:

The harvest day, Thanksgiving, nationally known was consecrated in 1621 by the Pilgrims at Plymouth, Massachusetts. It is a holiday that belongs to our entire country. It is a holiday we do not have to split due to regions, religion or background. It brings families together in fellowship and thanksgiving.
An entire menu of the first celebration was never found in any writings, but the food is known to be plentiful with turkey being one of the main entrees served.

Stuffing of the turkey in some families and regions is usually done inside of the turkey's cavity. In my family, it traditionally is done as a separate dish. The Cornbread Dressing is a combination of our family recipes.

CORNBREAD DRESSING

2 1/2 cups cornmeal
1 1/4 teaspoon salt
1 teaspoon sugar
3 eggs
1 1/4 cups buttermilk
2 teaspoons baking powder
1/8 cup oil
2 cups chicken broth
3/4 cup crumbled or cubed bread
1/2 cup butter or margarine
1 onion, chopped
3/4 cup celery, chopped
4 eggs
1/3 cup buttermilk
1/2 teaspoon salt
1/2 teaspoon pepper
1/4 teaspoon dried marjoram, optional
1/4 teaspoon dried thyme, optional
1/4 teaspoon dried sage, optional

Make cornbread by mixing cornmeal, salt, sugar, eggs, buttermilk and baking powder in a bowl or in a mixer. In an iron skillet or in a 9-inch glass or metal baking pan, place oil and set in a 400-degree oven for 2 to 5 minutes. Remove from oven and add cornbread batter. Cook for 25 to 35 minutes, uncovered. Remove cornbread and crumble to make 3 cups. Place in a large bowl or mixer. Add chicken broth and bread crumbs to cornbread and set aside. In a small skillet, melt butter and add onions and celery. Cook for 2 minutes. Add onions and celery to cornbread and mix with eggs, buttermilk and spices. Pour into a greased 9 x 13 pan or greased 3- to 4-quart casserole. Can be made 2 days in advance and stored covered in refrigerator. Bake for 30 to 45 minutes at 375 degrees, uncovered. Makes 12 to 16 servings.

Menu Suggestion:
*Business Luncheon
Vegetarian*

Rice Crispy Wafers,

*Uncle Ryland's
Cream of Crab Soup,*

Spinach and Orange Salad,

Marinated Asparagus,

Tomato Basil Aspic,

Grandmother's Apple Cake,

Orange Spiced Tea

Serving Tip:

Tarts work beautifully on a dinner or lunch buffet or on a fixed plate. On a buffet, have two trays, one for serving and one for replenishing. Large muffin-size tarts were used in 90 percent of my catered tart recipes. They were very popular with my clientele and their guests.

ARTICHOKE TARTS

1 pie shell sheet, uncooked
1 tablespoon butter or margarine
1/4 cup onion, chopped
1/4 cup celery, chopped
1 garlic clove, crushed
1 (14 1/2-ounce) can artichokes, drained well
3/4 cup Monterey Jack cheese, grated
1/4 cup sour cream
1/4 cup ricotta cheese
1/4 cup cornmeal
1/4 cup whipping cream
1/4 teaspoon salt
1 egg

L ay pie sheet onto surface and cut into 3-inch circle with cookie cutter. Place individual pastries in 12 greased individual muffin tins or tart pans. As an alternative, the whole sheet can be placed in one greased 9-inch-deep dish pie pan or tart pan. In a medium skillet, melt butter and cook onion, celery and garlic for 2 to 3 minutes. Add artichokes and cook an additional 2 minutes. In a mixer or bowl, cream together cheese, sour cream, ricotta cheese, cornmeal, whipping cream, salt and egg. Add vegetables and stir well. Scoop mixture into pie shells 3/4 full. Avoid overfilling past the pastry. Bake at 350 degrees for 20 to 40 minutes depending on size. Makes 8 to 12 servings.

Tip of the Trade:

Artichokes originated from an Arabian word meaning thistle, which became what we know through a long line of name changes.

It is a member of the sunflower family, and is truly a thistle. If left to flower in the garden, it blooms a beautiful blueish, violet flower. California produces artichokes and its Monterey County is known as the **Artichoke Capital** *of the World.*

♦

Menu Suggestion:

*Club Meeting and
Dinner Buffet*

Marinated Beef Tenderloin,

Chicken Rice and Vermicelli Salad,

Fruit Salad,

Wine Cherry Mold,

*Moist Carrot Cake and
Chocolate Chip Rum Cake*

Basic Pastry:

*1 1/3 cups plain
all-purpose flour
1/2 cup cold margarine
or butter
1 teaspoon salt
2 to 4 teaspoons ice water*

*Place flour in a food processor
fitted with a metal blade. Do not
turn on and add butter, which has
been cut into six pieces, and salt.
Turn machine on and add
ice water 1 tablespoon at
a time. Stop processing
as soon as the dough forms
into a ball. Dough may be rolled
to use immediately or stored
sealed in refrigerator.
Makes one crust.*

SPINACH AND ARTICHOKE TART

1 pie crust sheet
1/3 cup sunflower seeds, ground (or other favorite nut)
1/2 cup Cheddar cheese, grated
1/8 teaspoon red pepper
2 eggs
1 cup chopped fresh spinach
1 (3-ounce) can artichokes, drained
1 cup ricotta cheese
1/2 cup Feta cheese, crumbled
3 tablespoons Parmesan cheese
1/2 teaspoon salt

Place pie shell in a 9- to 10-inch greased tart or pie pan or cut sheet with a 3-inch cutter and place in 12 greased individual tart or muffin pans. Sprinkle sunflower seeds on crust and press in gently. Sprinkle Cheddar cheese over seeds. In a food processor fitted with a metal blade, combine eggs, spinach, artichokes, ricotta, Feta, Parmesan and salt. Process until mixed. Pour into pie shell and place in a 375-degree oven for 30 minutes for small tarts and 40 to 50 minutes for large tarts. Makes 8 to 12 servings.

Serving Tip:

Tarts can be used in place or in addition to a starch or bread. They easily can be prepared in advance and even frozen and reheated on baking sheets, making party preparation easier on a hostess.

♦

GOAT CHEESE TARTS WITH RED PEPPER SAUCE

1 (9 to 10-inch) pie crust sheet
8 ounces goat cheese
1 (8-ounce) package cream cheese, room temperature
2 eggs
1/3 cup whipping cream

1 red pepper, seeded and chopped
1/2 cup onion
3 tablespoons oil
1 (4-ounce) package cream cheese
1/8 cup whipping cream
1/2 teaspoon salt

Place pie shell into a greased 9-inch tart pan or a greased 9-inch pie plate. Individual tarts can be substituted by cutting pastry into 3-inch circles with cookie cutter and placing in 12 large greased muffin tins or 12 large greased tart pans. Mix together in a food processor fitted with a metal blade, or in a mixer fitted with the metal whip, goat cheese, cream cheese, eggs and whipping cream. Pour batter into desired pastry shell 3/4 full and bake at 350 degrees for 20 to 35 minutes. Cooking time will vary, depending on size of tart. Top of tarts should be set but not browned.

To make sauce: In a medium skillet, cook red pepper and onion in oil for 6 to 8 minutes. Place vegetables in a food processor fitted with a metal blade. Add cream cheese, whipping cream and salt to vegetables and purée pulsing six to eight times. Serve Goat Cheese Tarts warm or at room temperature with Red Pepper Sauce. Red Pepper Sauce can be thinned with additional cream or milk to desired consistency. Makes 10 to 12 servings.

◆

TEXAS TART

Tip of the Trade:

This Texas Tart has a hint of the South by adding a grit crust to a spicy quiche-like filling.

Substitute a can of tomatoes and green chilis for green chilis in recipe, if desired.

1 1/2 cups milk
1/2 teaspoon salt
1/2 cup grits
1/2 cup Monterey Jack cheese, grated
1 tablespoon butter or margarine
1 egg

1 1/2 cup Monterey Jack cheese, grated
3 eggs
1/2 cup cottage cheese
1/2 cup sour cream
1 (4-ounce) can green chilis, drained
1/4 teaspoon salt
1/4 teaspoon ground cumin
1 tomato, chopped
2 green onions, peeled and chopped
3 whole chives, optional

Menu Suggestion:
Fall Football Brunch

Lemony Bloody Marys,

Butternut Squash Soup,

Sunflower Salad,

Fresh Fruit Salad,

Wine Cherry Mold,

*Zucchini Blueberry Muffins,
Pecan Cheese Scones*

In a small saucepan, boil milk with salt. Add grits while stirring. Cook for 5 to 8 minutes until grits are thickened. Remove from heat. Add 1/2 cup grated cheese and butter and stir until melted through. Add egg and stir well. Cool slightly and scoop into a greased 8-inch springform pan. Form grits along bottom and slightly up sides to mold a crust. **For filling:** Combine 1 1/2 cups Monterey Jack cheese, eggs, cottage cheese, sour cream, green chilis, salt and cumin. Stir well and pour into grit crust. Filling might come over crust and this is fine. Sprinkle top of tart with tomatoes and green onions. Lay long chive sprigs into a star on top as garnish. Can refrigerate covered for up to 1 day at this point. Bake at 350 degrees for 45 to 55 minutes. If middle is not set and a little watery, bake last 10 to 15 minutes at 375 degrees. Remove from oven and let sit 5 to 10 minutes before removing from springform pan and slicing to serve. Can be stored in refrigerator after cooking and reheated at 350 degrees in pan, if desired. Wonderful buffet or fixed plate dish. Makes 6 to 8 servings.

◆

A Garden of Celebrations
Vegetables and Fruits

Anne Mullins Rigdon

◆

This Marinated Beans recipe is an easy way to serve beans because it can be made in advance with no need for heating. It cannot spoil on the buffet table, making it perfect to set out for long lengths of time. Try sprinkling crumbled bacon on top for a real treat.

Snap Beans are less pricey than asparagus most of the year, making it an economical dish. Asparagus and Snap Beans work quite well served together, and asparagus can be substituted in this recipe easily by cutting down the cooking time.

MARINATED BEANS

2 pounds fresh snap green beans
6 cups water
1 teaspoon salt
1 red or Vidalia onion, peeled and sliced in thin rings
1/3 cup walnut oil or vegetable oil
1/2 cup cider vinegar
2 tablespoons honey
1/4 cup fresh chopped parsley
1/8 cup fresh chopped dill
1/2 cup cashews, walnuts or almonds, toasted

Snap stem end off beans and leave whole. Cook beans in boiling water with salt for 8 to 10 minutes. Remove from heat and drain well in colander. In a large bowl combine beans, onion, oil, cider vinegar, honey, parsley, dill and nuts. Toss well, cover and refrigerate for at least 24 hours and up to 2 days. Beans can be served warm or cold. Drain beans from some of marinade before serving on a green leafy lettuce lined platter or a vegetable serving bowl for a beautiful presentation. Makes 8 to 12 servings.

SOUTHERN BEANS

Half White Runners are the favorite Southern bean by those who garden or farm. Whenever in season, substitute for pole beans.

2 pounds pole beans or other favorite green bean
1 garlic clove, peeled and crushed
1 cup bell pepper, seeded and chopped
1 small onion, peeled and chopped
1 tablespoon butter or margarine
1 teaspoon salt
1/4 teaspoon dried basil
1 teaspoon sugar
2 cups chicken broth

◆

String pole beans and break into 1-inch pieces. Soak beans in cold water for as long as possible, up to 24 hours. In a pot large enough to hold beans, cook garlic, bell pepper and onion in butter for 3 minutes. Add salt, basil, sugar and broth. Drain beans, add to pot and cook for 25 to 35 minutes. Serve warm. Can be stored in refrigerator covered or in sealed bags and reheated on stove or microwave. Drain beans of juice and serve out of a vegetable bowl. Makes 4 to 6 servings.

SNAP BEANS WITH ALMOND BUTTER

8 tablespoons butter or margarine
1 cup almonds, slivered or sliced
2 small leeks or green onions, peeled and chopped
3/4 teaspoon salt
1/2 teaspoon pepper
1 1/2 teaspoon plain all-purpose flour
1 1/2 cups chicken broth
1 tablespoon white wine vinegar
3 tablespoons wine, port, Madeira or sherry
3 pounds snap green beans, stem end removed, leave whole
Water to cover
1/2 teaspoon salt

In a small pan or skillet, melt butter and add almonds and onions. Cook for 3 minutes, adding salt and pepper. Add flour to pan and stir until mixed through and paste-like. Add broth, vinegar, and wine and stir or whisk until sauce is thickened over medium heat. Remove from heat. Snap beans should be left whole and have stem side removed. Place beans in large pot and cover with water, adding 1 teaspoon salt. Boil beans in water for 8 to 10 minutes. Remove beans from water and place in serving dish. Top with sauce. Can be stored covered in refrigerator for up to 2 days and reheated in microwave for 5 to 8 minutes on high. These work well stored in sealed bags reheated in microwave before placing in desired serving dish. Pecans can be substituted in the sauce and served over broccoli, cauliflower, Brussel sprouts, asparagus or potatoes. Makes 8 to 12 servings.

Serving Tip:

A china vegetable bowl or, for larger crowds, a green leafy lettuce lined platter for placing Snap Beans in these recipes will work beautifully. When placing in desired container, take the time to place beans all in the same direction for a prettier presentation. Serve these unsnapped recipes with tongs rather than a spoon.

Tip of the Trade:

If beans are out of season or slightly old, boil with a little sugar to enhance their natural flavors.

*Beans are a very ancient vegetable. They have been found even as far back as the Bronze Age and are mentioned more than once in the Bible. In their history, they have been offered to gods, have been thought of as mystical, thought of as unclean, to cloud vision, to keep ghosts away and even to call spirits.
They have been used as ballots, as proverbs and in expressions.
Beans have been fed to the high and mighty noblemen as well as fed to livestock.
A very versatile vegetable.*

♦

Tip of the Trade:

*When choosing a vegetable
accompaniment for a meal, let the
season be your guide. Remember,
freshness will aid in any vegetable
before or after cooking. Taking the
time to shop at a farmer's market
or picking from your own garden
will enhance any menu.*

FANCY GREEN PEAS

1 cup water
4 cups early frozen English peas or fresh English peas
2 leeks, chopped
1/4 cup butter or margarine
1 teaspoon sugar
1/2 teaspoon salt
1/2 cup iceberg lettuce, grated
1 celery stalk, grated
1 carrot, grated
2 tablespoons cream

Bring water and peas to a low boil and cook on medium low heat with leeks, butter, sugar and salt for 20 to 25 minutes. Water should be cooked out almost completely, so watch for easy burning near last 5 minutes of cooking. Remove from heat. Before serving, add grated vegetables and cream. Serve warm. Can be stored in refrigerator for up to 2 days and reheated. Makes 6 to 8 servings.

VEGETABLE CREAM SAUCE

2 tablespoons butter or margarine
1 teaspoon grated onion
2 tablespoons plain all-purpose flour
1 1/2 cups light cream or 1 1/4 cups milk
3/4 cup Cheddar cheese, grated
1/2 teaspoon paprika

Tip of the Trade:

*Vegetable Cream Sauce and
Mock Cheese Sauce are
very rich, but can really get
the cook out of a bind if
more guests show up
than planned. A
vegetable covered with a
sauce will go a little
further than one without.*

Melt butter or margarine in a medium saucepan and add onion. Stir for 1 to 2 minutes and add flour. Stir flour well to make a paste or roux. Add cream and stir over medium to medium low heat with a whisk until mixture is thickened. Add cheese and paprika. Stir until cheese is melted. Additional cream or milk can be added by tablespoonfuls for desired consistency. Serve with steamed broccoli, cauliflower and carrots or other favorite vegetables as a side sauce. Makes approximately 2 cups.

♦

MOCK CHEESE SAUCE

1/2 cup mayonnaise
1/4 cup sour cream
1/2 cup medium Cheddar, grated, or other favorite cheese
2 tablespoons Parmesan, romano or asiago cheese, grated
1 tablespoon milk, lemon juice, or sherry

Stir ingredients together in a small saucepan or a microwave-safe bowl. Heat just until melted on stove or for 1 minute or less in microwave. Stir vigorously and serve with vegetables. Makes 4 to 6 servings.

GINGER VEGETABLES

3 tablespoons vegetable or sesame oil
4 carrots, chopped
1/2 pound sugar or snap pea pods, trimmed
1/2 head broccoli flowerets
2 cups red cabbage, shredded
3 green onions, peeled and chopped
1/2 to 3/4 cup chicken stock or broth
2 tablespoons lemon juice
1/2 to 1 teaspoon ground ginger
1/2 teaspoon salt
2 tablespoons sesame seeds, toasted

Place oil in a wok or large skillet and heat over medium heat for 1 minute. Add all vegetables and stir well for 1 to 2 minutes. Add 1/2 cup chicken stock mixed with lemon juice and cook for 3 to 5 minutes. Add remaining chicken stock as needed for cooking to desired tenderness. Add spices. Toss with toasted sesame seeds and serve warm or room temperature. Keeping this warm will ruin its crispness. Best made right before serving. Makes 8 to 12 servings.

Tip of the Trade:

Mock Cheese Sauce is a great secret. Ingredients are easily kept on hand and can hide any vegetable's flaws. Great to use over vegetables that have been cooked longer than planned.

Tip of the Trade:

To sauté is to cook food rapidly. Sauter in French suggests food should actually jump in the pan. Using a large pan with a long handle will allow you to shake, toss and remove to and from heat while cooking. Using just a little oil or vegetable cooking spray allows vegetables to be quickly cooked which will help retain their nutrients. Broth, wine or water can be added by 2 tablespoonfuls to add a little steam. Spices should be added at the end. Hollandaise Sauce, Mock Cheese Sauce or Vegetable Cream Sauce can be served on the side, if so desired.

♦

Tip of the Trade:

Marinated vegetables will 'cook' or soften in the vinegar dressings during storage.

Lemon juice is famous for discoloring vegetables. It causes green vegetables to brown. Make sure the lemon juice is mixed in the dressing to avoid this happening.

The marinade in Marinated Asparagus can be used on any cold vegetable as a dressing or marinade. Great on mushrooms that have been cooked in broth and then chilled or a mixed steamed vegetable salad.

Serving Tip:

Fresh or steamed asparagus facing in the same direction into a circular fan style, flower side out in a footed crystal or glass compote is truly beautiful. Garnish one side with herbs and white flowers and serve with a side of Hollandaise, Vegetable Cream Sauce or Curry Cream Mayonnaise.

POACHED MARINATED ASPARAGUS

2 pounds asparagus spears
1/2 cup lemon juice
1/2 cup apple cider vinegar
1/2 cup sugar
2 tablespoons oil
1 teaspoon salt
1/2 teaspoon seasoned pepper
Medley of fresh herbs
1/2 onion, sliced into thin rings

Trim asparagus and wash. Place flowerets on one side and bunch together with a rubber band or large twist tie. Place asparagus standing flower side up in a small, tall saucepan. Fill water to 1-inch from top of asparagus. Bring to a slow boil for 3 to 5 minutes and drain well. Place asparagus in a dish. In a small saucepan, mix together lemon juice, vinegar, sugar and oil. Bring to a simmer until sugar is dissolved and pour onto asparagus. Sprinkle with salt and pepper. Lay desired herb leafs on top of asparagus with large onion rings. These will be removed when serving or used as garnishes. Cover and refrigerate for at least 4 hours and up to 48 hours. Serve chilled on green leafy lettuce leaves. Makes 8 to 10 servings.

MARINATED CANNED ASPARAGUS

A recipe from the collection of Jenny Nucholls, Marietta

1 pound and 3 ounces of canned asparagus
Juice of 1/2 lemon
1/2 cup cider vinegar
3/4 cup sugar
1 tablespoon seasoned pepper blend

Drain asparagus reserving juice and place flat in a dish. Mix together lemon juice, vinegar, sugar, salt and pepper and pour over asparagus. Use reserved juice only to cover all asparagus in marinade. Cover and refrigerate for at least 8 hours. Drain well before serving chilled on green leafy lettuce. Makes 8 to 12 servings.

STEAMED ASPARAGUS WITH HOLLANDAISE

1 1/2 pound fresh asparagus spears
1/2 cup butter or margarine
2 egg yolks
1/2 teaspoon salt
1 1/2 tablespoons lemon juice
1/2 cup sour cream

Trim the ends off asparagus. Bunch asparagus with flower side up with rubber bands or twist tie. Place in steamer flower side up and steam covered for 3 to 5 minutes. Remove and place on towels to drain. Asparagus also can be poached or blanched in water. Bundle asparagus standing flower side up is a small, tall saucepan. Fill water 1-inch from top of asparagus. Boil for 3 to 5 minutes and drain on towels. Keeping flowers from getting wet will make for a prettier presentation.

For Hollandaise Sauce: In a small saucepan or double boiler, melt butter on very low heat. Remove from heat and whisk in egg yolks, salt and lemon juice. Return to low heat and stir until thickened. Do not leave the stove. When thickened, remove from heat and immediately add sour cream. Serve warm over asparagus. Trying to keep vegetables warm will ruin the crispness of the vegetables. Refrigeration for 1 day and quick reheating in microwave works well. Sauce can be made 1 day in advance and reheated. Use the sauce on other favorite dishes. Makes 4 to 6 servings.

Tip of the Trade:

Asparagus, a sprout-like vegetable, is the cousin of the orchid and is of the lily family. It has 120 species, but the garden asparagus is the only edible form. Asparagus has a medicinal property called rutin, which is a factor in preventing small blood vessels from rupturing. In addition, it is the fanciest vegetable a cook can serve at his or her table. Small round spears are ideal if available.

Tip of the Trade:

One pound fresh asparagus, 16 to 20 spears, equals 2 cups chopped pieces.

Ice water will freshen limp asparagus, however, do not soak the tips, only the stems.

The sour cream in the Hollandaise Sauce gives this recipe a creamy, mild flavor. If a strong lemon taste is desired, reduce the amounts of sour cream.

Tip of the Trade:

To gut out vegetables to fill, simply slice the vegetable in half or cut out stem. Remove the seeds or part of the pulp. Bell peppers and tomatoes do not require any prior cooking before filling, but potatoes, zucchini and yellow squash do need cooking. Brush with oil and bake at 350 degrees for 10 to 15 minutes. Fill the vegetable and store covered in refrigerator for up to one day until ready to cook and serve. A cheese or cracker crumb topping works well. Also, seasoning the vegetable before filling will bring out the flavors.

Tip of the Trade:

Spinach leaves can be curled or flat. New Zealand spinach is a nice flat variety. Avoid leaves that are limp or damaged, or that have a bad odor.

GOAT CHEESE SPINACH AND RICE

3 cups fresh chopped spinach
1 cup rice, cooked
3 ounces goat cheese
4 ounces sharp Cheddar cheese, grated
1 egg
1/3 cup milk
1 tablespoon onion, grated
1/2 teaspoon white Worcestershire sauce or white wine
1/2 teaspoon salt
1/4 teaspoon pepper
1 cup butter cracker crumbs
Vegetable oil cooking spray

Chop spinach in a food processor fitted with a metal blade. In a bowl, combine spinach, rice, goat cheese, sharp cheese, egg, milk, onion, Worcestershire and spices. Mix well and spread in a greased 6 x 6 baking dish. Sprinkle with butter cracker crumbs and generously spray crumbs with vegetable oil cooking spray. Can be refrigerated for up to 2 days covered at this point. Bake uncovered for 20 to 30 minutes at 350 degrees. This is a wonderful filling for gutted out squashes or tomatoes. Makes 6 to 8 servings.

Serving Tip:

Pewter serving pieces work wonderful when entertaining. They can be placed in the oven with the vegetable already placed in bowl. Simply remove from oven and serve.

Tip of the Trade:

One 10-ounce package of frozen spinach will make about 1 1/2 cups after draining. Fifteen cups or 1 1/2 pound fresh spinach will make 1 1/2 cups cooked.

Tip of the Trade:

When cooking vegetables, a general rule can help. If it grows covered in the earth, root vegetables, start cooking in cold water and cover. If it grows on top of the earth, uncovered by soil, start in boiling water and cook uncovered.

SPINACH ARTICHOKE STUFFED TOMATOES

4 to 5 Roma tomatoes or small tomatoes
1 (10-ounce) package frozen chopped spinach, thawed
1 (14 1/2-ounce) can artichokes, drained well
1 (4-ounce) package cream cheese
1/3 cup mayonnaise
1/4 cup Parmesan cheese, grated
1/2 teaspoon salt
Hot sauce

Slice Roma tomatoes in half lengthwise and gut out the middle. Place on paper towels to drain. In a mixer fitted with a metal whip or food processor fitted with the plastic blade, combine spinach, artichokes, cream cheese, mayonnaise, Parmesan, salt and hot sauce to taste and mix or process well. Add 1 drop of hot sauce at a time to taste. Fill Roma tomatoes with spinach mixture and place on a baking sheet. Tomatoes can be covered and refrigerated at this point for up to 2 days. Bake at 350 degrees for 15 to 20 minutes. Filling should just be heated through. Overcooking will make a tomato mess. Serve warm or at room temperature. Substituting another can of artichokes for the spinach also makes a wonderful stuffing. Makes 6 to 8 servings.

Tip of the Trade:

When selecting tomatoes for stuffing, choose ones that are not fully ripe, but still red. They should have a firm feel to them when touched, and have no soft spots or bruises. Roma tomatoes have been chosen for this recipe because they are small and naturally a firm tomato. Any variety can be used, according to availability or choice. I love using small tomatoes from my garden in the summer months.

◆

SOUTH GEORGIA OKRA GUMBO

A family recipe from the collection of Hall Rigdon

1 pound butter beans, fresh shelled or frozen
1/2 teaspoon salt
2 strips bacon, uncooked or 1 strip fat back
Water to cover
8 to 10 whole tomatoes, peeled or
**   3 (14 1/2-ounce) cans whole tomatoes, with juice**
4 to 6 ears fresh corn, cut from the cob
3 cups fresh okra, trimmed and chopped

In a large saucepan, place butter beans with salt, bacon or fat back and water to cover. Fresh beans cook 45 to 60 minutes on a low simmer or cook frozen beans according to package directions. When fully cooked, drain beans of excess water and place back on stove on medium low heat. Immediately add tomatoes to beans and simmer for 15 to 30 minutes. Add corn and okra to the pot. Cook for 10 to 15 minutes just until okra is tender. Gumbo should not be soupy. Serve over 6 to 8 cups of white rice or with 1 recipe Cornbread, page 52. To present, place white rice on plate, bowl or large platter, mold the rice into a shallow bowl and spoon vegetable gumbo into center of rice. Cornbread should be sliced into wedges and served to the side or on the bottom of the gumbo in large bowls. Adding 1 1/2 to 3 cups cooked and diced chicken, cooked and shelled shrimp or crawfish or ham is a wonderful addition to make this side dish into an authentic Southern meal. Adding other vegetables, like onions, celery and bell peppers, is optional. They should be cooked in a little oil before adding. Potatoes are a traditional vegetable and can be added. They should be cooked and added at the beginning with the beans. Gumbo in the South was made to make use of summer vegetable crops. Traditionally, tomatoes and okra are always used, with other vegetables being flexible. Makes 6 to 8 servings.

Although the South Georgia Gumbo is a family recipe, Hall remembers it being made by his family maid and cook, Gertie, at his South Georgia home.

Tip of the Trade:

To peel a fresh tomato, skewer the whole tomato and hold over a gas flame, turning until the skin splits. Cool and peel.

Another method is to cut a shallow x-shape slash at the bottom of the tomato and drop in boiling water for 5 to 10 seconds. Remove, cool and peel.

Tip of the Trade:

Tomatoes are of South American origin. They come in many varieties and were derived from the Aztec word Tomatl.

◆

Summer squash is absolutely, entirely and traditionally a Southern vegetable. It's easy to grow in the South and wonderfully versatile. It can be eaten raw, sautéd, boiled, broiled, made into pudding and casseroles and even breads.

If you were to plant one single seed in a garden or even a pot, one plant will produce many squash in just a very short time.

Tip of the Trade:

Yellow or soft skin squash, which includes the variety of zucchini, should be kept in the refrigerator for storing. They should be bought or picked small and fresh. The entire squash of this variety can be eaten, skin and all, unlike the winter squashes.

OLD SOUTHERN SQUASH CASSEROLE

3 pounds yellow summer squash
1/2 onion, chopped, 1/4 cup
Water to cover
1 teaspoon salt
1 tablespoon sugar
1/4 cup butter or margarine, melted
2 eggs
1/2 teaspoon salt
1/4 teaspoon pepper
1 to 2 cups bread crumbs or butter cracker crumbs
1/8 to 1/4 cup butter or margarine, melted

Trim squash and cut into 1/2-inch pieces. Place in a medium pot with onions and just cover with water. Add 1/2 teaspoon salt and boil over medium heat for 10 minutes and drain well. Pressing in colander will drain out most water. Combine warm squash with sugar, 1/4 cup butter, eggs, salt, pepper and 1/2 cup bread crumbs. Pour into a greased 9 x 13 baking dish or a greased 2-quart casserole. Mix together remaining bread crumbs with melted 1/4 cup butter and sprinkle on top of squash. The amount of bread crumbs depends on the dish size. Can be refrigerated for up to 2 days at this point. Bake at 350 degrees uncovered for 20 to 30 minutes. Makes 8 to 10 servings.

Tip of the Trade:
Recipe Alternative

Adding 1 cup grated American cheese, processed cheese or mild Cheddar cheese to the Old Southern Squash Casserole works well. Almonds crushed with the cracker crumbs on the topping taste good. Also, half yellow squash and half zucchini bring color to the dish.

♦

My catering clientele shared with me their unique styles of Southern entertaining, and their love of good food. My regular clients are wonderful cooks but have found they could better enjoy their parties if I could come in and help. It was always a joy trading cooking secrets, techniques, ideas and menus with them and, in turn, I can now share them with you with treats such as Southern Squash Crêpes.

Tip of the Trade:

Four medium squash or 1 1/4 pounds will equal approximately 3 cups chopped squash.

The smaller the summer squash, the more tender it will be. Avoid soft marks or brown spots when choosing.

SOUTHERN STYLE SQUASH CRÊPES

A recipe from the collection of my client and friend, Mrs. Patsy Dupree

SQUASH MIXTURE:
3 cups yellow squash, trimmed and sliced
2 medium onions, peeled and chopped
1 tablespoon bacon grease, optional
1/4 teaspoon salt
1 egg, beaten
1 (8-ounce) carton sour cream

CRÊPES:
3 eggs
2 tablespoons plain all-purpose flour
1 tablespoon water
1 tablespoon milk
1 pinch salt
1 1/2 teaspoons butter
1 cup extra sharp Cheddar cheese, grated

Add bacon grease to a small amount of water and simmer squash and onions covered over medium to medium low heat for 6 to 8 minutes. Drain well. Stir in salt. Blend in egg and sour cream and mash well. Set aside. **To make crêpes**, mix eggs, flour, water, milk and salt together to make a thin batter. Keep batter covered and refrigerated from 3 hours to overnight. In a small skillet over medium heat, melt 1/4 teaspoon of butter in pan. When butter bubbles, pour in enough batter to cover bottom of pan with a thin coating. Keep the pan moving. After 1 minute of cooking, turn the crêpes . Cook until browned. Stack crêpes between foil or waxed paper.
To fill, place 2 tablespoons of the squash mixture into each crêpes and fold twice into a triangular shape. Place filled crêpe on lightly greased baking sheet. Sprinkle each crêpe with cheese. Bake in a 350-degree oven until cheese melts, approximately 15 minutes. Crêpes freeze beautifully. Makes 6 servings.

♦

WHIPPED BUTTERNUT SQUASH

4 pound butternut squash
1/2 cup butter or margarine
3/4 cup instant potato flakes
1 1/2 cups brown sugar, divided
1/2 cup plain all-purpose flour
1 cup walnuts, chopped well
1/3 cup butter or margarine, room temperature

Winter squash has very strong skin and does not require refrigeration for storage. It has a much longer pantry life than regular squash. When selecting these squash from the markets, the skin should never be soft and they should be heavy for their size.

Cut butternut squash in half, using a very strong knife or small-tool saw. If the squash is too hard for you, pierce and place in microwave whole in a sealed plastic bag for 10 to 20 minutes to make for easier carving. Remove seeds and place squash side down in a microwave-safe dish or baking dish. Cover with 3 cups water and cover microwave dish with plastic wrap or oven dish with aluminum or a top. Place in microwave on high for 10 to 20 minutes or in oven at 350 degrees for 40 to 50 minutes, until squash is soft. (Cooking time might vary if placed in microwave for easier carving). Remove and scoop squash from skin. Mix together in a mixer or hand mixer squash, butter, potato flakes and 1/2 cup brown sugar. Place in a greased 9 x 9 baking pan or greased 2-quart casserole. In a separate bowl, combine 1 cup brown sugar, flour, walnuts and 1/3 cup butter. Sprinkle this on top of casserole. Squash can be refrigerated at this point for up to 2 days. Bake in a 350-degree oven for 25 to 35 minutes. Serve warm. Can also be made with acorn squash or sweet potatoes. Makes 8 to 10 servings.

The word squash was shortened from an Algonquin Indian work called isquonterquasher in 1634. This word means "something you eat raw." The Pilgrims preferred the taste of the vegetable cooked rather than raw and began including it in their diets. Today's kitchen offers wonderful recipes for winter squash.

Serving Tip:

Potato and Squash Casseroles keep well covered in a warm oven and reheat wonderfully. This makes serving time very flexible, making last-minute preparation a step easier.

♦

Tip of the Trade:

The Whipped Butternut Squash and Creamy Winter Squash and Potato Medley are very similar to our sweet potato casseroles. Serve them in place of the traditional dish to add flair and originality to your entertaining tables, especially during the winter holidays.

Ground cinnamon or nutmeg can be added (about 1/2 teaspoon) to Creamy Winter Squash, if desired.

In French cooking, the milk is always brought to a steam when adding to squash, pumpkin and, especially, potatoes.

Tip of the Trade:

Vegetable casseroles can be kept warm in a low oven until ready to serve. To help with oven space, remove the top rack and stack 9 x 13 casseroles T-shaped or crisscrossed on top of each other. This works especially well if several casseroles of the same dish are needed, or during holidays, when large amounts of food are being prepared.

CREAMY WINTER SQUASH AND POTATO MEDLEY

1 acorn squash
1 butternut squash
1 sweet potato
1/2 cup butter or margarine
1 cup evaporated milk
1 cup brown sugar
2 eggs
1 teaspoon vanilla
1/2 teaspoon salt
2 to 3 cups mini marshmallows

Pierce all vegetables once with a fork. Place each in individual sealed plastic bags. Place in microwave and cook on high or medium high for 15 minutes. Check potato for softness and turn. Continue baking at 10-minute intervals and check softness of vegetables between each interval. The butternut squash, being the largest, might take the longest. Cut butternut squash in half after 30 minutes of cooking. If it has not cooked, return to bag and continue cooking for 5-minute intervals until soft. Cut all vegetables in half. Scoop out sweet potato, remove seeds from acorn and butternut squash and scoop vegetable from rind. Place in a mixer or bowl where a hand blender or mixer can be used. Combine vegetables with butter, milk, sugar, eggs, vanilla and salt. Mix or blend well. Place in a greased 9 x 9 baking dish or greased 2-quart casserole. Can be refrigerated at this point for up to 2 days. Bake at 350 degrees for 35 to 45 minutes. During the last 10 minutes of cooking, sprinkle marshmallows on top and finish cooking uncovered. Makes 6 to 10 servings.

Vegetable dishes work best on a buffet or serving family style. They are not recommended for fixed plate meals.

♦

CORN CHIPAIGUACU

A recipe from the collection of Betsy Rambo

1 large onion, peeled and chopped
1 cup vegetable oil
6 ounces cream cheese, room temperature
2 cups milk
8 slices firm white bread, cubed or crumbled
2 teaspoons salt
1/2 teaspoon pepper
6 eggs, lightly beaten
2 (16-ounce) cans whole kernel corn, drained
2 (16-ounce) cans cream corn

In a large pot, sauté or cook the onions in the oil until soft. Remove from heat. Add the cream cheese and milk, and stir until the cream cheese is soft and melted (will still have some lumps of cheese). Add the remaining ingredients, mixing well. Pour into a 9 x 13 casserole dish. Bake at 375 degrees for approximately 1 hour or until a knife inserted into the middle comes out clean. This recipe can be halved and freezes well. Makes 10 to 15 servings.

EASY CORN PUDDING

A recipe from the collection of my friend, Eleanor Knox, Marietta

2 cups corn, frozen, canned or fresh
1 tablespoon plain all-purpose flour
3 tablespoons sugar
2 eggs
3/4 teaspoon salt
3/4 cup milk
1/4 cup butter or margarine

In a blender, place corn, flour, sugar, eggs, salt and milk. Mix 10 seconds on high speed. Pour into a greased baking dish and dot top with butter. Bake at 375 degrees for 45 minutes uncovered. Makes 4 to 6 servings.

Tip of the Trade:

*Chipaiguacu is pronounced chip-a-wa-soo.
This recipe was served at the former restaurant Birdies, owned in part by a wonderful cook, Betsy Rambo. It was located off the pier on St. Simons Island, Georgia.*

Fresh Corn Cookery:

If fresh corn on the cob is planned with a menu, it should be boiled in a pot in salted water or 1/2 salted water and 1/2 milk, sweetened with 1 tablespoon sugar. Soft boil for 10 minutes. Cooking any longer will make the corn taste starchy.

Tip of the Trade:

Placing corn in the blender or blending with a hand blender gives canned or frozen corn an immediate fresh taste.

◆

Sweet potatoes are more nutritious than the yam which is easily mistaken for this beautiful orange potato. They do not store as well or as long as the white potato and should be bought and cooked fresh so they do not lose their flavor.

The Apricot Sweet Potatoes recipe has an unique flavor and would work well any time of year. Perfect for late Summer or Autumn months.

APRICOT SWEET POTATOES

3 pounds sweet potatoes, peeled and diced
1 teaspoon salt
1/2 cup dried apricots, chopped
1 (15-ounce) can Mandarin oranges, drained well
1/3 cup brown sugar
2 tablespoons apricot brandy
2 tablespoons preserves, apricot or orange
3 tablespoons butter or margarine, melted
1/2 cup almonds, pecans or walnuts, chopped

Peel and dice sweet potatoes. Cook in boiling, salted water for 8 minutes. Drain well and place 1/2 of the potatoes in a greased 2-guart casserole. Sprinkle apricots on top. Drain oranges well and lay over apricots. Top with remaining potatoes. In a bowl combine remaining ingredients. Place on top of casserole. Can be stored covered for up to 2 days, if desired. Sprinkle 2 extra tablespoons brown sugar on top. Bake at 350 degrees for 35 to 45 minutes until bubbly on edges. Makes 8 to 10 servings.

HOLIDAY SWEET POTATOES

A recipe from the collection of my husband's mother, Mrs. Sue Alred Rambo

Holiday Sweet Potatoes are very sweet and rich. They can easily be made with canned sweet potatoes, however using fresh potatoes will give more flavor and a thicker consistency.

3 cups sweet potatoes
1 cup sugar
1/2 teaspoon salt
2 eggs
2 3/4 tablespoons butter or margarine
1/2 cup milk
1 teaspoon vanilla
TOPPING:
1 cup light brown sugar
1/3 cup plain all-purpose flour
1 cup nuts, chopped
2 3/4 tablespoons butter or margarine, room temperature

◆

If using fresh sweet potatoes, bake until done, peel and mash. Canned sweet potatoes need to be drained and mashed to equal 3 cups. Combine potatoes with sugar, salt, eggs, butter, milk and vanilla. Mash with potato masher until smooth or mix in a mixer fitted with a metal whip until smooth. Pour into a greased 9 x 13 baking dish. In a separate bowl, combine brown sugar, flour, nuts and butter and mix to a crumble by hand or in a mixer fitted with a metal whip. Sprinkle on top of casserole. Cover and refrigerate for up to 1 day at this point, if desired. Bake in a 350-degree oven uncovered for 35 to 40 minutes. Makes 6 to 8 servings.

ROSEMARY POTATOES

A recipe from the collection of my friend, Patricia Collins Simpson

1 1/2 pounds new potatoes
4 garlic cloves, unpeeled
4 tablespoons olive oil
1/2 teaspoon salt
4 sprigs fresh rosemary, not chopped
3 tablespoon white wine vinegar
2 1/2 tablespoons prepared Dijon mustard
1/4 teaspoon pepper
3 tablespoons oil
2 green onions, peeled and thinly sliced

Cut potatoes in 1 1/2-inch chunks. Mix potatoes with garlic, oil, and 1/4 teaspoon salt until they are well coated. Lay rosemary sprigs on top. Prepare grill, placing rack 5 inches from coals or set on medium heat. Make a pan with heavy duty foil by folding up edges. Grease handmade pan and lay on grill. Cover and grill 25 to 30 minutes. Can be placed in a 350-degree oven on greased, foil lined baking sheet for 25 to 35 minutes if grilling is not convenient. Meanwhile, whisk together vinegar, mustard, remaining salt and pepper. Gradually add oil while whisking and set aside. After potatoes have cooked, discard rosemary from tray. Squeeze grilled cloves from skin, crush between plastic wrap and add to dressing. Toss dressing with potatoes and green onions. Can be reheated in oven. Spray top of potatoes with vegetable cooking spray before reheating. Serve warm to room temperature. Makes 4 servings.

Tip of the Trade:
Mashing Potatoes

Russet potatoes mash well. Peel and dice potatoes. Cook in salted boiling water until tender. Drain well and immediately place back in pot or in a mixer. Mash or whip with butter, hot milk and sour cream. Add cooked or roasted garlic and Parmesan, if desired. Potatoes can be stored after mashing in refrigerator and reheated in microwave, if desired.

Tip of the Trade:

The rosemary plant is an herb and perennial. Some varieties can reach up to 6 to 7 feet long. It is hardy and can be grown in pots or gardens. The very aromatic smell adds to most meats as a garnish and is a perfect herb for potatoes, chicken and lamb.

Rosemary Potatoes are as good baked as grilled. A delicious Southern vegetable accompaniment to any menu.

Russet and long white potatoes are also suitable varieties for roasting or baking with this recipe.

♦

When baking a regular or sweet potato, wash skin thoroughly and oil with vegetable cooking spray, shortening or oil. Sprinkle white potatoes with salt and wrap either variety in foil. Bake in a 400-degree oven for 50 to 90 minutes. Sweet potatoes cook faster than regular baking potatoes. Potatoes are best opened and mixed with butter as soon as possible after baking. If left to sit too long, they become hard and rubbery. A potato can be kept hot in an oven or in a cooler for up to 1 hour after cooking. If keeping in a cooler, place a regular brick or an oven brick in the oven while baking and then place it in the cooler with the potatoes.

A sweet potato can be served with butter, brown sugar and cinnamon or nutmeg. They are delicious with Salmon, Gingered Pork or Teriaki Chicken.

A regular potato can be served with butter, sour cream, cottage cheese, grated cheese, chives, steamed broccoli, cheese sauce, hollandaise, or chili. A baked potato bar works well for a business luncheon with a salad or combination salad bar.

MADEIRA NEW POTATOES

2 pounds new potatoes
1/4 cup butter or margarine
1/4 cup oil
1/4 cup Madeira wine or port wine
1 teaspoon wine vinegar
1 tablespoon orange peel, grated
4 teaspoons corn starch
1 cup strong orange juice
1 tablespoon lemon juice
1 teaspoon chopped fresh rosemary
1/2 teaspoon dried chopped parsley

New potatoes can be peeled in the center for presentation purposes or cut in half. Place potatoes in boiling water for 6 to 10 minutes. Carefully drain potatoes and toss with butter in a greased baking dish. In a medium saucepan or in microwave, combine oil, Madeira, vinegar, and orange peel. Dissolve cornstarch in orange juice and add to saucepan or microwave with lemon juice and simmer, while whisking, for 3 minutes. Pour the hot sauce over potatoes and sprinkle with herbs. Can be stored covered in refrigerator at this point. Bake in a 350-degree oven for 25 to 35 minutes. Serve warm with fresh rosemary garnishes. Makes 10 to 12 servings.

APRICOT GLAZED CARROTS

2 pounds carrots
3 tablespoons butter or margarine
1/4 cup apricot preserves
2 teaspoons lemon juice
1 teaspoon orange peel, grated
1/4 teaspoon ground nutmeg
1/4 teaspoon salt
1 tablespoon brandy

♦

Peel and cut carrots into tiny julienne strips using a large serrated or jagged cutting tool. Bring 3 cups salted water to a boil and cook carrots for 3 minutes. Drain carrots well. In a large skillet, melt butter and add preserves, lemon juice, orange peel, nutmeg, salt and brandy. Add carrots and serve warm. Can be stored for up to 2 days in refrigerator covered. Storing in a storage bag and reheating in microwave works well. Makes 8 to 10 servings.

Serving Tip:

Carrots are beautiful served out of a light and delicate vegetable server, crystal or cut glass bowl. It can be garnished with slices of oranges or lemons.

CRANBERRY APPLES

A recipe from the collection of my great aunt, Margaret Carpenter

6 Granny Smith apples
1 (12 to 16-ounce) package fresh cranberries
2 tablespoons corn starch
1 1/2 cups brown sugar
2 tablespoons butter or margarine, melted
1 (8-ounce) jar apricot preserves
1 1/2 teaspoon vanilla
1 cup walnuts, chopped

Peel and core apples and slice into 16 pieces each or dice. In a greased 9 x 13 baking dish, place one half sliced apples. Wash and drain cranberries and lay one half on top of apples. Repeat this procedure. Dissolve cornstarch in 4 tablespoons cold water. Mix together corn starch solution, brown sugar, melted butter, apricot preserves and vanilla. Pour over cranberries and apples. Sprinkle with chopped walnuts. Can be refrigerated covered for up to 2 days at this point. Bake at 350 degrees for 55 to 65 minutes. Makes 12 to 14 servings.

Tip of the Trade:

For a special twist, add dried cranberries (about 1/4 cup) to the Apricot Glazed Carrots while cooking.

Carrots contain a great deal of natural sugar and are available all year round, which makes them economical. The best carrots are young and slender. If they still have their greens, remove them. They rob the vegetable of nutrients. Unless the outer portion of the carrot is brown and old, there is no need to peel it. Just scrub well before preparing.

Carrots add color to a buffet or plate. Not everyone takes a serving of carrots, so be careful on amounts.

Tip of the Trade:

Invest in a 9 x 13 holder of some type to fit your lifstyle and entertaining formality. Pottery, pewter, silver or basket weave can be found at craft shows, department stores and specialty stores. If the holder has a glass insert, purchase extra ones to use for replenishing or in case of breakage.

WARM BRANDIED FRUIT

1/2 cup butter or margarine
1/2 cup sugar
2 tablespoons cornstarch
1 cup brandy
6 cups fruit, canned and fresh mixture

In a medium saucepan, melt butter and add sugar. Dissolve cornstarch in room-temperature brandy, stirring well and add to saucepan. Heat for 5 to 8 minutes until thickened, stirring over medium heat. Set aside. Prepare fruit. Using canned pineapple, pears, and peaches works well. Adding fresh pineapple, fresh apples, fresh pears is outstanding. Using fresh cherries or berries is wonderful, however, add these just before serving so not to discolor fruit. Using a combination of canned and fresh fruit makes a beautiful combination and presentation. Place all fruit with the exception of fresh berries or cherries in a greased 2-quart serving dish. Pour sauce over fruit. Can be refrigerated for up to 2 days at this point. Bake in a 350-degree oven for 20 to 30 minutes. Stir in fresh berries and cherries. Serve warm. Makes 10 to 12 servings.

Tip of the Trade:

Warm Brandied Fruit can be served with simple chicken or pork dishes. Using a fruited liqueur brandy will give a sweeter taste than regular brandy. Best if served with a slotted spoon in a footed holder or chafing dish.

SCALLOPED PINEAPPLE

3 cups bread crumbs
1/2 cup butter or margarine, melted
1/2 to 1 1/2 cups sugar
1/2 teaspoon salt
2 tablespoons plain all-purpose flour
3/4 cup cream
1 (14-ounce) can crushed pineapple with juice
1 tablespoon brandy

Mix together crumbs and butter. Add sugar, salt, flour, cream, pineapple and brandy and mix well. Pour into a greased 9 x 9 baking dish or greased 1 1/2- to 2-quart casserole. Dish can be refrigerated for up to 1 day at this point. Bake at 350 degrees for 25 to 35 minutes. Makes 4 to 6 servings.

Tip of the Trade:

Scalloped Pineapple makes an unique covered dish. It also works well on a holiday table. Good with ham, chicken and pork.

The amount of sugar varies with the recipe, so the cook can judge the best sweetness needed to accompany the menu appropriately.

Hearty Celebrations
Poultry, Meats, Seafood and Vegetarian

Anne Mullins Rigdon

♦

Menu Suggestion:
A Summer Menu

Crab Mornay with Crackers,

*Rosemary Potatoes
with Garlic,*

*Green Salad with Creamy
Port Dressing,*

Strawberry Congealed Salad,

*Pound Cake Cookies,
Ice Cream or Sorbet with
Raspberry Purée*

Wine Suggestion:

California Reisling

Menu Suggestion:
An Autumn Dinner

Fruited Rice,

Tomato and Basil Aspic,

*Green Salad with
Honey Mustard Dressing,*

Fruit Cobbler with Ice Cream

CHARCOAL MARINATED CHICKEN BREAST

A recipe from the collection of Patricia Collins Simpson

2 1/4 to 3 boneless, skinless chicken breast halves
3 cloves garlic, peeled and crushed
1 1/2 teaspoons salt
1/3 cup brown sugar
3 tablespoons stone ground or course mustard
1/4 cup cider vinegar
Juice of 1 lime or 1 teaspoon bottled juice
Juice of 1/2 lemon or 1/2 teaspoon bottled juice
6 tablespoons olive oil
Black pepper

Place chicken in a large, heavy sealed bag with all other ingredients. Refrigerate 8 hours or overnight. Turn over bag in refrigerator and marinate for at least 1 hour to 8 hours more. Chicken needs to be drained from marinade for about an hour before cooking. Prepare grill to medium setting or medium coals and grill approximately 4 minutes on each side or until middle of chicken is no longer pink. Slice into strips and serve. Wonderful in rice salads, served Fahita style or as a main dish. Makes 6 to 8 servings.

TERIYAKI CHICKEN

2 1/4 pounds boneless, skinless chicken breast halves
1 cup soy sauce
3 tablespoons corn starch
1 cup wine
3/4 cup sugar
1/8 cup Worcestershire sauce
3 tablespoons vinegar
1/4 cup orange juice
3 tablespoons oil
1 garlic clove, peeled and crushed, optional

♦

Wine Suggesiton:

*Buttery Chardonnay,
Washington State*

lace chicken breasts in a greased baking pan. In a medium saucepan, place soy sauce. Dissolve cornstarch in wine and add to pan with sugar, Worcestershire, vinegar, juice, oil and garlic. Heat until sugar is dissolved and sauce is thick. Cool sauce and pour over chicken. Marinate for at least 4 hours and up to 24 hours in refrigerator. Grill over medium coals for 10 to 15 minutes one side and 8 to 10 minutes second side. Keep a spray bottle at hand because the sugar and oil in sauce could cause flames. For good grill marks, do not move chicken after placing on racks. Baste with sauce occasionally. If serving sauce with meat, heat again to a boil before serving to kill bacteria. Makes 6 servings.

Tip of the Trade:

Grill meats up to 1 day in advance and reheat covered in oven. If drying out is a concern, add 1/4 cup water, wine or boiled marinade to chicken while reheating.

OATMEAL CRUSTED CHICKEN

A recipe from the collection of my husband's mother, Mrs. Sue Alred Rambo

1/2 cup butter or margarine
1/4 teaspoon garlic powder
3/4 cup 3-minute oats, uncooked
1/4 cup Parmesan cheese, grated
1/4 cup almonds, slivered
2 tablespoons dried minced parsley
1 teaspoon salt
1/4 teaspoon dried thyme
1/8 teaspoon pepper
6 boneless, skinless chicken breast halves

Menu Suggestion:
A Southern Meal

Ricotta Cheese Ball and Crackers,

Apricot Brandied Sweet Potatoes,

Francy Green Peas,

Cheese Sour Cream Muffin Bread,

Chocolate Caramel Squares

Wine Suggestion:

Oregon Pinot Gris

elt butter with garlic powder on stove or in microwave. In a separate shallow bowl, combine oats, Parmesan, almonds, parsley, salt, thyme and pepper. Chicken breasts should be without skin and preferably filets. Dip chicken breasts first in butter mixture and then in oat mixture. Place in a 9 x 13 greased baking dish and bake uncovered for 55 to 65 minutes at 375 degrees. Temperature reading from middle of chicken breasts should read 185 degrees. Do not turn chicken while cooking. Makes 4 to 6 servings.

◆

Menu Suggestion:
A Fall Celebration

Fluffy Wild Rice,

Fresh Beans or Peas,

Mixed Greens and Cherry Tomatoes with Creamy Russian Dressing,

Pecan Cheese Scones,

Cranberry Cheesecake

Wine Suggestion:

Piesporter Spatlese

HONEY BUTTER CHICKEN

A recipe from the collection from my husband's mother, Mrs. Sue Alred Rambo

3 pounds boneless, skinless chicken breast halves
1/2 cup butter or margarine, melted
1 cup all-purpose flour
1 teaspoon paprika
1/2 teaspoon salt
1/4 teaspoon pepper
SAUCE:
1/4 cup butter or margarine, melted
1/2 cup honey
1/4 cup lemon juice

Prepare chicken. Small breast halves work well. Place butter in a 9 x 13 baking pan. Mix flour, paprika, salt and pepper together in a shallow bowl. Roll chicken in mixture and place with butter in pan. Cover and bake at 400 degrees for 30 minutes. Meanwhile mix butter, honey and lemon juice together. After chicken has baked for 30 minutes, remove from oven. Turn chicken over, pour sauce on chicken and return to oven uncovered for 25 to 35 more minutes or until meat thermometer has reached 185 degrees. Makes 4 to 6 servings.

JERK CHICKEN IN RUM

Menu Suggestion:
A Caribbean Buffet

Green Salad with Lime Vinaigrette,

Grilled Vegetables,

Ginger Fruit,

Orange Balls,

Ice Cream with Almond Caramel Sauce

3 1/2 pounds chicken
2 tablespoons fresh rosemary sprigs, snipped
3 tablespoons fresh parsley, snipped
1 tablespoon fresh basil leaves, snipped
1/4 cup prepared mustard
1/2 cup strong orange juice
1/4 cup rum
1 tablespoon apple cider vinegar
1 onion, sliced
1 lemon, sliced
Commercial jerk seasoning

◆

Place chicken breasts in a greased baking dish. Mix together rosemary, parsley, basil, mustard, orange juice, rum and vinegar. Pour over chicken. Place onion slices and lemon slices over chicken. Cover and chill to marinate for at least 4 hours or overnight. Bake in a 350-degree oven, covered, for 40 to 50 minutes. Temperature reading with meat thermometer should be 185 degrees. Remove from oven and remove chicken from sauce, placing on serving platter or green leafy lettuce. Sprinkle chicken with desired amount of jerk seasoning. Serve with the lemons and onions as garnish. Can be presented warm or room temperature. Makes 6 to 8 servings.

Tip of the Trade:

A spicier jerk seasoning can be served on the side. For entertaining, mild seasonings are the safest. Steamed shrimp or other shellfish would go nicely with the Caribbean Dinner.

APRICOT CHICKEN

10 to 12 boneless, skinless chicken breast halves
1 (8-ounce) jar commercial Russian dressing
2 (4-ounce) jars apricot baby food
1 tablespoon minced onions
1 teaspoon orange peel, grated
1 teaspoon lemon peel, grated
2 tablespoons honey or brown sugar
1/2 teaspoon salt
1/8 teaspoon pepper
1/2 teaspoon parsley flakes, or 1 teaspoon fresh snipped
2 tablespoons fruited liqueur, optional
1 tablespoon fresh chopped thyme sprigs, optional

Place chicken breasts in a greased 9 x 13 baking dish. Mix together all other ingredients and pour over chicken. Bake covered for 40 minutes at 350 degrees. Remove from sauce to serve over green leaf lettuce or on a china platter with fresh herbs. Serve warm or room temperature. A wonderful oven bag dish. Use fresh chives in the place of minced onions in the spring and summer months. Makes 8 to 10 servings.

Menu Suggestion:
Grandparents for Dinner

Rice Crispy Wafers,

Rice,

Broccoli, Cauliflower and Carrots with Vegetable Cream Sauce,

Scalloped Pineapple,

Spinach and Artichoke Tarts,

Apple Cake

Wine Suggestion:

Napa Valley Chenin Blanc

♦

Menu Suggestion:

A Dinner Buffet

Squash Rounds,

*Tossed Salad with
Peppercorn Dressing,*

Zesty Orange Rice,

Baked Tomatoes,

*Creamy Apricot Mold with
Fresh Fruit,*

*Amaretto Cheesecake,
Whipped Cream,
Pecan Flavored Coffee,
Amaretto Liqueur,*

Wine Suggestion:

White Macon Village

Tip of the Trade:

*Pounding of chicken breasts
sometimes scares cooks away from
a recipe. If the right chicken mallet
is used, it is very easy. Lay several
breasts on a large piece of plastic
wrap or waxed paper and cover
with another piece. Pound with a
flat heavy mallet at the same time.
A mallet has a handle and a heavy
3-inch circle piece with a flat
bottom.
It can be used to crush nuts,
crumbs and husbands.*

ELEGANT CHICKEN FLORENTINE

6 boneless, skinless chicken breast halves
1 (10-ounce) package frozen chopped spinach, thawed
1/4 cup onion, chopped
4 tablespoons butter or margarine
4 tablespoons plain all-purpose flour
1 cup whole milk
1/2 cup chicken broth
1/2 teaspoon salt
2 tablespoons mayonnaise
1/2 cup sour cream
3 tablespoons white wine
2 cups bread crumbs
2 tablespoons butter or margarine, melted

Pound chicken breast by placing filet between plastic wrap and pounding with a mallet or large hammer. Pounding is not necessary but would only add to the elegance of the dish. Drain spinach by pressing in colander or ringing in clean hands. Divide spinach into six portions. Place breasts on a working surface with top side down. Place spinach in middle of breasts. Wrap breasts around spinach. Enclosing breasts completely is not necessary. Place hole side down in a greased 9 x 13 baking dish. In a medium saucepan, cook onion in 4 tablespoons butter for 2 to 3 minutes. Add flour and make a roux or paste, mixing well. Add milk and broth and stir with a whisk for 5 to 8 minutes over medium heat until sauce is thick. Remove from heat and add mayonnaise, sour cream and wine. Pour over chicken. Mix bread crumbs with 2 tablespoons melted butter and sprinkle over dish. Can be stored covered in refrigerator at this point, if desired. Bake for 30 minutes covered at 350 degrees and uncover to cook an additional 10 to 20 minutes. A meat thermometer can be used to check temperature of 185 degrees. Serve warm. Makes 4 to 6 servings.

♦

PESTO CHICKEN WITH CHAMPAGNE SAUCE

8 boneless, skinless chicken breast halves
2 ounces cream cheese, room temperature
2 1/2 cups chopped fresh spinach leaves
1/2 cup chopped fresh basil leaves
1/4 cup fresh parsley
1 tablespoon olive oil
2 tablespoons almonds
2 tablespoons Parmesan
3 tablespoons butter or margarine
3 tablespoons self-rising flour
3/4 cup chicken broth
1 cup champagne or white wine
Salt and pepper
Parmesan
Almonds

Pounding of chicken breasts between plastic wrap is not necessary, but not discouraged. Place breasts on a working surface with top side down. In a food processor fitted with a metal blade, combine cream cheese, spinach, basil, parsley, olive oil, almonds and Parmesan. Process three to four times. Place 2 to 3 tablespoons mixture in the middle of each breasts, using all the mixture. Fold breasts around filling. Place breasts into a greased 9 x 13 baking dish, seam side down. In a saucepan or in a microwave-safe dish, melt butter. Add self-rising flour to melted butter and stir to make a roux or paste. Add broth and champagne and cook on medium heat or on high in microwave until bubbly, stirring with a whisk to smooth. Season with salt and pepper to taste and pour sauce over chicken leaving the top 1/3 portion of breast uncovered. Sprinkle each breast with Parmesan and sliced almonds. Can be stored at this point. Bake at 350 degrees, uncovered, for 40 to 50 minutes. Use a meat thermometer to ensure 185 degrees. The pesto will blend with the sauce, making a delightful sauce to accompany mashed potatoes or pasta. One-half cup commercial pesto mixed with 2 tablespoons almonds, added to cream cheese, can be used as the filling instead of making homemade pesto. Makes 6 servings.

Menu Suggestion:
A Hint of Italy Dinner

Ricotta Cheese Ball with Wafers,

Hazlenut and Goat Cheese Salad with Mixed Greens,

Pasta or Mashed Potatos,

Artichoke Tarts,

Fresh Fruit,

Liqueured Chocolate Mousse

Wine Suggestion:

Burgundian Chablis

Serving Tip:

Using authentic serving dishes, plates, glasses and decorations for regional recipes will help to add flair to a table.
Accompany regional foods with simple dishes to complement their authenticity.

Menu Suggestion:

Bon Voyage Dinner

Crab Artichoke Dip with Wafers and Corn Chips,

Winter Green Salad with Peppercorn Dressing,

Fresh Fruit,

Cheese Stuffed Rolls,

Chess Pie with Raspberry Purée

Wine Suggesiton:

Spanish Red Rioja

Tip of the Trade:

If too much browning occurs on top of casserole, cover with aluminum foil while cooking.

If burning occurs on the bottom, quickly grease a separate casserole. Place 1 to 2 cups of casserole sauce on bottom and scrape the top off burnt casserole. Add additional topping if necessary to hide flaws and keep your fingers crossed.

MEXICAN CHICKEN LASAGNA

A recipe from the collection of Mrs. Betsy Rambo

4 to 6 chicken breast halves, to equal 4 cups, cooked
2 cups sour cream
1 cup diced green chilis or 1/2 cup canned, drained
1 (3 1/2-ounce) can sliced black olives
1/2 to 1 tablespoon jalapeno pepper, chopped, optional
1 pound Cheddar cheese, grated
1 pound Monterey Jack cheese, grated
1 (17-ounce) package flour tortillas, 8-inch

ENCHILADA SAUCE:
2 tablespoons oil
1/2 cup onion, chopped
4 cloves garlic, peeled and crushed
2 cups tomatoes, chopped
1 (15-ounce) can tomato sauce
1 cup chicken broth
1/2 teaspoon salt
1 teaspoon cumin powder
1 1/2 teaspoons chili powder

When preparing chicken, reserve 1 cup broth for enchilada sauce. Mix together diced chicken, sour cream, green chilis, black olives, jalapeno pepper and all but 4-ounces each of cheeses. Reserved cheese will be used to top the casserole. Set aside. **To make enchilada sauce:** Place oil in a medium saucepan and cook onion and garlic for 2 to 3 minutes on medium heat. Add tomatoes, tomato sauce, chicken broth and spices and simmer for 5 to 10 minutes. To assemble dish, grease a 9 x 13 baking dish. Place 1 cup of enchilada sauce in dish. Coat each side of eight tortillas with just enough enchilada sauce to moisten them. Lay two and one-half tortillas on sauce in dish. Layer one third of chicken mixture over tortillas and repeat each step, softening each tortilla in sauce before layering, until the filling is gone. Place a last layer of tortillas on top. Pour remaining enchilada sauce on top and store sealed in refrigerator for up to 1 day, if desired. Bake at 375 degrees for 35 to 40 minutes. Add remaining cheese on top the last 5 minutes of cooking. Serve with shredded lettuce, chopped tomatoes and sour cream, if desired. Makes 10 to 12 servings.

> *Make White Chili a lower-fat dish by thickening with potato flakes or pearls rather than the cheese.*

WHITE CHILI

A recipe from the collection of my friend, Mrs. Angela DuPre

4 to 6 chicken breast halves, to equal 4 cups, cooked
6 cups water
2 teaspoons salt
1 tablespoon olive oil
2 medium onions, peeled and chopped
4 garlic cloves, peeled and chopped or crushed
2 (4-ounce) cans chopped mild green chilis
2 teaspoons ground cumin
1 1/2 teaspoons dried oregano, crumbled
1/4 teaspoon cayenne or red pepper
3 (16-ounce) cans great northern white beans, undrained
4 cups chicken stock or canned broth
3 cups Monterey Jack cheese, grated, about 12 ounces
Sour cream

Place chicken in a heavy, large saucepan or pot. Add water and salt and bring to a low simmer for 35 to 45 mintues. Remove chicken and save broth to use in recipe. In a large pot, place oil with onions and garlic and cook until tender, about 5 minutes. Stir in chilis, cumin, oregano, cayenne and undrained beans. Measure out 4 cups chicken stock and add to pot. Simmer for 10 to 15 minutes. Meanwhile, remove chicken from bones and skin and dice. Measure chicken out to equal 4 cups. Add chicken to pot with cheese. Stir while simmering just until cheese melts. Ladle into bowls and top with a dollop of sour cream. Makes 12 servings.

Tip of the Trade:

With heavier soups, stews and chili, an appropriate bowl needs to be used or they lose their hearty, rustic and casual touch. Pottery bowls, heavy soup cups or deep china soup servers are ideal. Large crusty loaf breads complement them as a side bread. Fall and Winter are the months to serve these dishes.

This or regular chili is wonderful to serve for a casual supper to watch a game or movie. Serve it topped in your own style with oyster crackers, cheese, sour cream, onions, chives, tomatoes and tortilla chips.

Menu Suggestion:
Sunday Supper

Fresh Green Salad with Honey Mustard Dressing,

Sourdough Bread,

Chinese Chews with Butter Pecan Ice Cream

Wine Suggestion:

California Fumé Blanc

♦

Menu Suggestion:

A Christmas Night Dinner

Hot Beef and Walnut Dip with Fresh Vegetables,

Mixed Greens with Sunflower Sprouts and Buttermilk Dressing,

Poached Marinated Asparagus,

Apricot Sweet Potatoes,

Stuffed Celery,

Cranberry Egg Nog Mold,

Coconut Cream Cheese Cake with Coconut Pecan Frosting,

Pecan Pie

Wine Suggestion:

Pinot Blanc

Tip of the Trade:

Commercial pie crust sheets are one of the best pantry items to keep around. They have saved a party more than once for myself and my clients. Keep at least one in the freezer for emergencies or a rainy day.

FAMOUS POT PIE

2 (1-pound) package pie crust sheets
4 pounds chicken breast halves, with skin and bones
9 cups water
1 teaspoon salt
3/4 cup butter or margarine, melted
3/4 cup self-rising flour
1/2 teaspoon pepper

Grease a 9 x 13 baking dish. Using 1-package pie crusts, place sheets of crust side by side, cutting and pressing to make desired rectangle shape. Place pastry in the bottom of the greased dish, bringing sides of pastry up the sides and slightly over rims. Trim off any excess. Place chicken breasts in a large pot with water and salt and cook chicken for 30 to 40 minutes until tender. Remove chicken reserving broth and, when chicken has cooled, tear from bone and chop into bite-size pieces. Place chicken in pie crust. Measure out broth to equal 8 cups adding water, if needed. Place broth in same pot and on a low boil or simmer. Mix together melted butter and flour to make a roux or paste. Add to broth with pepper and whisk until thickened. Cool slightly and Pour broth over chicken. Take two remaining pie crusts and lay side by side. Roll out into a neat rectangle, trimming sides as needed and replacing where needed. Excess crust can be rolled out and used to decorate the top of the dish. Place rectangle on top of chicken and broth and pinch edges together with bottom crust using thumb to imprint. Decorate top with excess crusts, if desired. Simply roll out the extra dough and cut into shapes for the occasion. Baby booties, Christmas wreaths, wedding bells are just a few ideas. This dish can be refrigerated covered with plastic wrap at this point for up to 2 days and cooked when ready. Freezing before or after cooking is fine. Bake at 350 degrees for 35 to 45 minutes uncovered until crust is golden. Serve warm. A delicious Southern meal and a wonderful dish for sick friends. Travels well. Makes 9 to 12 servings

♦

CHICKEN TORTILLA TORTE

6 medium flour tortillas
3 tablespoons butter
1 1/2 cups Monterey Jack cheese, grated
1 cup Cheddar cheese, grated
1/2 cup mayonnaise
1 cup cooked chicken breast halves, diced
1 tomato, seeded and sliced thin
1 (8-ounce) can water chestnuts, drained well and chopped
1/2 red bell pepper, chopped
1/4 cup almonds or pine nuts
1/2 cup Parmesan cheese

Place 1/2 tablespoon butter in a skillet large enough to lay tortilla flat. Heat skillet and butter over medium heat. When butter is bubbly, place one tortilla and fry about 1 minute, until just browned on one or both sides, as desired. Repeat with other five tortillas. Mix cheeses together. Tear off two 2-foot pieces of aluminum foil and lay T-shaped on a baking sheet. Spray entire piece with cooking spray. Lay one tortilla in middle of foil. Spread with 1 1/2 tablespoons mayonnaise and sprinkle with 1 1/2 tablespoons Parmesan. Sprinkle with 1/2 cup chicken, 1/2 can water chestnuts and 1/2 cup cheese. Top with another tortilla. Spread with 1 1/2 tablespoons mayonnaise and 1 1/2 tablespoons Parmesan. Lay tomato slices over and sprinkle with 1/2 cup cheese. Top with another tortilla. Spread with 1 1/2 tablespoons mayonnaise and sprinkle with 1 1/2 tablespoons Parmesan cheese. Top with another 1/2 cup chicken and 1/2 can water chestnuts. Sprinkle with 1/2 cup cheese and top with another tortilla. Spread 1 1/2 tablespoons mayonnaise and sprinkle with 1 1/2 tablespoons Parmesan cheese. Place red pepper and top with 1/2 cup cheese. Top with another tortilla. Finish off with 1 1/2 tablespoons mayonnaise and 1 1/2 tablespoons Parmesan. Add nuts and remaining cheese and top with last tortilla. Sprinkle with Parmesan cheese. Fold foil over and seal. Place in refrigerator until ready to bake up to one day. Bake in a 350-degree oven for 20 to 30 minutes. Remove from foil and place on a platter or cutting board. Slice pizza style with a serrated knife and serve with a side of sour cream or guacamole. Makes 6 to 12 servings.

Menu Suggestion:
Couple Bridal Party

Mexican Crab Dip with Dip Style Corn Chips,

Marinated Eye of Round with Onions and Mushrooms, Potato Rolls with Mayonnaise and Mustard,

Fruited Cabbage Slaw,

Steamed Asparagus with Hollandaise,

Moist Carrot Cake

Wine Suggestion:

Bandol Rosé

Tip of the Trade:

This layered torte gives the feel of a Mexican quesadilla, but is much fancier. Substitute fresh spinach leaves for bell pepper or for water chestnuts for variety.

Serving more than one meat or main dish is an old Southern tradition and is very practical with large crowds. It might be a little more costly, but really takes care of any taste variety you might have among guests. Count on each person having some of both.

Menu Suggestion:

Impressive Supper Club Buffet

Cheese Wafers with Pepper Jelly,

Marinated Beef Tenderloin,

Fluffy Wild Rice,

*Fruited Green Salad with
Madeira Dressing,*

*Dinner Rolls,
Whipped Butter,*

Banana Pudding

Wine Suggestion:

Marsanne from the Rhone Valley

Tip of the Trade:

*A supper club can be started easily
with a few phone calls. A group of
six to 12 couples can gather
together once or every other month
for dinner. The hostess is
responsible for the main course,
beverages and the bar. The
remaining club members bring the
appetizers, side accompaniments
and dessert. Each dinner rotates
at a different club member's home.
A wonderful way to organize to see
friends at least once in a while
without being too much of a
workload on one hostess.*

POPULAR CHICKEN SHRIMP AND ARTICHOKE

3 pounds chicken breast halves, with skin and bones
1 pound shrimp, cooked and peeled
1 (14 1/2-ounce) can quartered artichokes, drained well
1/2 cup butter or margarine
1/3 cup self-rising flour
1 cup chicken broth, canned or reserved stock from chicken
1/3 cup milk
1/2 cup half and half or milk
1/4 cup sour cream
1 1/2 tablespoons sherry wine
2 cups Cheddar cheese, grated or
   2 cups bread crumbs
3 tablespoons butter or margarine, melted

Place chicken in a large pot covered with water with 1 teaspoon salt. Cook covered over low heat for 35 to 45 minutes. Remove chicken, reserving 1 cup broth. Remove chicken from bones and chop. Layer chicken, artichokes and shrimp in a greased 9 x 13 baking dish. In a medium saucepan or microwave-safe dish, melt butter and add flour to make a roux or paste. Add milk, half and half or broth and microwave in 3-minute intervals on high, whisking between each, or keep on medium heat and scrape bottom of pan often to keep from burning. Remove from heat when thickened and stir in sour cream and sherry to taste. Pour sauce over chicken and shrimp. Can be refrigerated uncovered until chilled and then covered and stored for up to 1 day at this point. Bake at 350 degrees covered for 35 to 50 minutes. Edges should be very bubbly and middle warm. Remove from oven and sprinkle top with cheese. Return to oven just until cheese melts. If bread crumbs are desired in the place of cheese, mix together crumbs with melted butter and sprinkle on casserole before baking in same degree oven. Serve warm. Makes 6 to 8 servings.

BAKED CHICKEN SALAD

2 tablespoons self-rising flour
2 tablespoons butter or margarine
1 cup milk
5 to 7 chicken breast halves, to equal 5 cups, cooked
1 1/2 cups celery, chopped
1/2 cup almonds, slivered
1/2 cup mayonnaise
1/2 cup sour cream
1/8 cup green onions or sweet onion, chopped
Juice of 1 lemon
2 teaspoons fresh tarragon, optional
Salt and pepper, to taste
1 1/2 cups Monterey Jack or Cheddar cheese, grated

In a medium saucepan or a microwave-safe dish, melt butter and add flour to make a roux or paste. Pour in milk and heat on stove top or microwave, stirring occasionally until thickened. Keep stove top on medium heat and scrape bottoms often to keep from burning. In a large bowl, mix together sauce, diced chicken, celery, almonds, mayonnaise, sour cream, onion, lemon and spices. Pour into a greased 9 x 13 baking dish and cover. Dish may be refrigerated for up to 1 day at this point. Bake in a 350-degree oven, covered, for 30 to 40 minutes. Remove from heat and sprinkle cheese on top. Return to oven for 5 to 10 more minutes, uncovered. Serve warm. Makes 8 to 10 servings.

Serving Tip:

Serving outdoors is a beautiful way to entertain. Use remnants of beautiful fabrics cut and sewn into squares on round tables with a neutral cloth to the ground. Use casual china and colored glassware with outdoor lanterns and garden flower arrangements. Tiny votive holders with citronella candles can be lit to repel insects.

Menu Suggestion:

A Business Luncheon

Tomato and Roasted Red Pepper Soup,

Poached Marinated Asparagus,

Cheese Biscuits (filled with honey ham),

Creamy Lemon Custard with Sour Cream Pound Cake, Fresh Berries

Beverage Suggestion:

Orange Spiced Tea

Wine Suggestion:

New Zealand Sauvignon Blanc

Tip of the Trade:

Two whole chicken breasts uncooked, 10 ounces each, will make about 2 cups cooked, chopped chicken. A 2 1/2- to 3-pound fryer will make 2 1/2 cups. The fryer, however, will have white and dark meat. Using only white chicken will be the best quality and prettiest presentation of any chicken dish.

Menu Suggestion:
Bridal Luncheon

*Luncheon Sangria
served as guests arrive,*

Squash Rounds,

*Traditional Frozen Fruit Salad,
Fruit Garnish,*

Spinach and Artichoke Tarts,

Rice Crispy Biscuits,

Strawberry Napoleons

Wine Suggestion:

White Graves

Menu Suggestion:
Special Ladies Luncheon

*Shrimp and Artichoke Cream Soup
with Feta,*

*Spring Greens for Salad
Garnishing,*

*Goat Cheese Tarts with
Red Pepper Sauce,*

Marinated Poached Asparagus,

TANGY CHICKEN SALAD

6 to 8 chicken breasts halves, to equal 4 1/2 cups
5 cups water
1 1/2 cup commercial Italian dressing
1 teaspoon salt
1 3/4 cup celery, chopped, 4 stalks
2 tablespoons sweet salad cubes
3 green onions, peeled and chopped
1 teaspoon parsley
3/4 cup mayonnaise
3/4 cup sour cream
2 tablespoons cider vinegar
1 teaspoon lemon juice
1/4 teaspoon salt
1/2 teaspoon pepper

Place chicken breasts in a large pot with water, Italian dressing and 1 teaspoon salt. Bring to a low simmer, covered, and cook for 30 to 40 minutes. Remove chicken, cool and chop. Broth will not be needed in this recipe. Mix chicken, celery, salad cubes, green onion, parsley, mayonnaise, sour cream, vinegar, lemon juice and spices. Cover and refrigerate for up to one day. The perfect recipe for sandwiches. Plan on one to two breasts halves per person. Makes 4 to 6 servings.

FRUITED CHICKEN SALAD

6 to 8 chicken breast halves, to equal 4 1/2 cups
5 cups water
1 teaspoon salt
Reserved juice from pineapple tidbits
1/4 cup orange juice concentrate
1 (16-ounce) can pineapple tidbits, reserve juice
3/4 cup celery, chopped
1 cup purple grapes, halved, or halved and pitted cherries

INGREDIENTS CONTINUED NEXT PAGE

3/4 cup mayonnaise
3/4 cup sour cream
1/4 teaspoon salt
1/2 teaspoon pepper
3/4 cup chopped macadamias or other favorite nut

Place chicken breasts in a large pot with water, salt, reserved pineapple juice and orange juice. Cook covered for 30 to 40 minutes. Remove breasts from broth. Broth will not be needed in this recipe. Cut chicken breasts to equal 4 to 5 cups. Combine with pineapple tidbits, celery, mayonnaise, sour cream and Macadamias. Refrigerate covered until ready to use, up to 1 day. Best served with fresh fruit garnishes on green leafy lettuce. (If using cherries, add right before serving.) Makes 4 to 6 servings.

LAYERED CHICKEN CORNBREAD SALAD

3/4 cup mayonnaise
3/4 cup sour cream
3 tablespoons milk
2 tablespoons oil
2 tablespoons vinegar
SALAD:
1 recipe Cornbread, (one 8-inch pan)
2 chicken breast halves, to equal 1 3/4 to 2 cups,
    cooked and diced
10 ounces dried 16 bean soup mix, cooked and drained, or
    2 (15-ounce) cans desired beans, drained
2 celery stalks, trimmed and chopped (1/2 cup)
1/4 cup onion, finely chopped
3 to 4 tomatoes, chopped, 1 1/2 to 2 cups
4 ounces Cheddar cheese, grated

Combine dressing ingredients, set aside. In a trifle dish or glass bowl, layer 1/3 of all ingredients in the order given. Place 1/3 of dressing before the cheese layer. Layer until ingredients are all used. Chill for up to 1 day until ready to serve. Makes 8 to 12 servings.

Dessert Suggestion:

*Fresh Fruit with
Low-Fat Lemon Pie*

Wine Suggestion:

White Bordeaux

Menu Suggestion:
Dinner with Old Friends

Soup and Salad,

Marinated Canned Asparagus,

Fresh Fruit,

*Chocolate Ganache with
Pound Cake and Strawberries*

Wine Suggesiton:

Vouvray from Loire

Tip of the Trade:

*In Layered Salad, 3/4 cup fresh
cooked corn or 1/2 cup sliced black
olives can be added if desired.
Omit the chicken for
a vegetarian or side dish.
When layering dressing, keep
1/2-inch from sides of serving bowl
for a cleaner presentation.
Substitute 1 pound frozen beans
for dried or canned, as needed.*

Menu Suggestion:

A Fireplace Dinner

Spinach Puff Pastries,

Caesar Salad,

Ginger Tenderloins,

Apricot Glazed Carrots,

Crunchy Fresh Asparagus Mold,

Southern Loaf Bread,

Buttermilk Pie

Wine Suggestion:

South Australian Sémillon

Menu Suggestion:

A Kitchen Family Dinner

Cheese and Crackers,

Green Salad with Honey Mustard Dressing,

Madeira New Potatoes,

Zucchini Blueberry Muffins,

Caramel Toffee Brownies and Ice Cream

CHICKEN RICE AND VERMICELLI SALAD

1 (6.9-ounce) package chicken rice and vermicelli mix
2 to 4 chicken breast halves, to equal 2 cups, cooked
1 (6-ounce) can water chestnuts, chopped
1/4 cup slivered almonds, toasted
1/4 cup mayonnaise
2 tablespoons vegetable oil
1 tablespoon olive oil or other oil
2 tablespoons apple cider vinegar
2 celery stalks, chopped

Cook rice according to package directions, using 1/4 cup less water than suggested. Cool and combine rice with diced chicken, water chestnuts, almonds, mayonnaise, oils, vinegar and celery. Mix well and chill covered until ready to serve. Makes 6 to 8 servings.

STUFFED TURKEY FILETS

1 1/2 pounds large bonelss, skinless turkey breast half
  or 4 boneless, skinless chicken breast halves
1/4 pound goat cheese
1/4 pound honey maple ham, sliced thin
1/4 cup dry white wine
1/4 teaspoon salt
1/4 teaspoon pepper
1/2 teaspoon parsley
1/4 teaspoon paprika

Place breast on a clean working surface. On the larger end of the breast, cut a pocket with opening at fattest end, or cut in half leaving attached on 2 sides. Stuff pocket with goat cheese and then with ham. Place stuffed turkey pocket side up onto a greased baking dish and pour wine over breasts. Sprinkle salt, pepper, parsley and paprika over breasts. Cover and bake in a 350-degree oven for 45 to 60 minutes. A meat thermometer inserted into the center should read 185 degrees. Remove from oven and cool for 5 to 10 minutes. Can be refrigerated for up to 1 day before cooking. If chicken breasts are substituted, cooking time will be 35 to 45 minutes. Slice and serve. Makes 4 to 6 servings.

Oven Roasting Times:

A turkey breast will need to cook 25 minutes per pound, unstuffed. A whole turkey will need 30 to 35 minutes per pound, unstuffed and a whole hen will need 20 minutes per pound unstuffed

---

SMOKED TURKEY BREASTS

4 pound boneless turkey breast
Cinnamon sticks, apple, pear, orange, lemon
1 (14 1/2-ounce) can chicken broth, brought to a boil

Prepare smoker with coals. Ignite coals according to package directions. In water bin of smoker, place one or more of the fruit selections, floating in water. Slicing them will give flavor. When coals have died down, place water on smoker. Place thawed turkey breasts onto rack of smoker. Some turkeys come with roping tied around. Leave roping on but adjusting roping 1/4-inch from its original position will make easier removal. Cover smoker and cook for 5 hours. Additional coal might be added once during cooking. Remove from smoker, place in deep baking pan and pour hot chicken broth over turkey. Cover turkey with foil until cooling is complete. This will make turkey moist and make for less breakage during slicing. Turkey will be very pink from smoking. Wonderful for sandwiches and for tailgates. Makes 4 to 6 servings.

Wine Suggesiton:

Californian White Meritage

Tip of the Trade:

Chicken and meat or pork roasts can be smoked as well. You can also use a marinade before smoking.
Adding a flavorful wood chip to coals can add an unique taste. Fruit pieces add a delicate flavor and need to be added to water during smoking. Do not be afraid to experiment with your smoker.

Menu Suggestion:
A Tailgate Picnic

Sandwich Breads, Mayonnaise and Mustards,

Molded Potato Salad,

Broccolli Ramen Salad,

Sliced Fresh Melons,

Chocolate Caramel Bars

Wine Suggestion:

Alsation Pinot Gris

♦

Menu Suggestion:

*An Outdoor Birthday
Dinner Buffet*

Artichoke Bites,

Hot Fruit Relish,

Tortellini Pasta Salad,

*Steamed Asparagus and Carrots
with Curry Cream Mayonnaise,*

Fresh Corn Salad,

Bloody Mary Aspic with Dressing,

*Pound Cake with Fresh Berries and
Creamy Lemon Custard*

Wine Suggestion:

Sonoma Red Zinfandel

Tip of the Trade:

*The above menu works well in case
of rain for an outdoor party. The
food can be transformed easily to
eating in your lap during a storm
if needed because there is minimal
cutting needed and it can be eaten
with just a fork. All of the recipes
can be served room temperature,
which makes an easy party.*

MARINATED TURKEY

4 to 6 pound boneless turkey breast
1 cup apple juice
1/2 cup orange juice concentrate
1/4 cup lime juice
2 tablespoons lemon juice
1/4 cup vegetable oil
3 tablespoons vinegar, any variety
1/2 cup white wine

Boneless turkey breasts usually come frozen. Thaw in refrigerator 1 to 2 days. Never thaw at room temperature. Unwrap turkey. Some brands come wrapped in a roping. Leave the roping on, but adjust it from the original position by 1/4-inch. Just slide it over a little to make an easier removal after cooking. Place turkey in a heavy bag or roasting pan to marinate. Pour apple juice, orange juice, lime and lemon juice, oil, vinegar and wine on turkey. Marinate for 12 to 24 hours. (If thawing in refrigerator, this is a wonderful time to place turkey in marinade.) Cook turkey covered or in roasting bag in marinade for 1 hour and 15 minutes at 325 degrees. Temperature reading of turkey middle should read 185 degrees on a meat thermometer. Remove from pan and remove roping. Refrigeration will help in better slicing, but slicing immediately is fine. Serve with Hot Fruit Relish. Makes 6 to 8 servings.

HOT FRUIT RELISH

1 papaya, peeled and chopped
2 peaches, peeled and chopped
2 tablespoons lemon juice
4 kiwi, peeled and chopped
1/2 sweet onion or 3 green onions, chopped
1 orange or red bell pepper, seeded and chopped
1 medium banana pepper, seeded and chopped fine
1/4 cup fresh chopped Cilantro

♦

Make relish as close to serving time as possible for better texture and color. Chop papaya and peaches and toss in lemon juice. Add other ingredients and serve with Marinated Turkey as a relish. If making in advance, draining might be necessary before serving. Makes 6 to 8 servings.

FAMILY TURKEY

1 large oven bag
2 tablespoons flour
1 (10-pound) turkey
1 onion, peeled and sliced
2 cups white wine or Madeira wine
1/4 cup oil
1 teaspoon lemon pepper or pepper blend
1/4 cup apple cider vinegar or white wine vinegar
1/2 teaspoon salt

Remove giblets from turkey cavity and rinse turkey in cold water. Slice onion, sprinkle onion with salt and pepper and place in turkey cavity. Fresh herbs or turkey livers also can be stuffed in cavity for additional flavors. Place flour in oven bag, hold tightly and shake to coat inside. Place bag inside roasting pan and place turkey in middle, inside of bag. In a medium saucepan or in microwave, boil wine, oil, lemon pepper, vinegar and salt. Pour boiling wine over turkey. Skin should shrink to seal. Seal bag with provided tie. Place turkey into a 400-degree oven and bake for 2 hours 45 minutes sealed. Remove from oven and place a meat thermometer into thickest part of breast right through bag. Thermometer temperature should reach 185 degrees. Return to oven with thermometer in place until done. Cool for 10 minutes and up to 40 minutes before slicing. Turkey Gravy recipe follows on page 156. Makes 6 to 8 servings.

Tip of the Trade:
Entertaining Outdoors

Setting the seating tables and a bar outside with the buffet set up on the regular dining table works remarkably well. Hot bread and dessert can be served outside to guests at their seats. Champagne can be served with dessert for toasts or birthday wishes.

Menu Suggestion:
Thanksgiving Dinner

Cornbread Dressing,

Turkey Gravy,

New Southern Pole Beans,

Holiday Sweet Potato Casserole,

Cranberry Apples,

Angel Biscuits,

Cheesecake Rogét

Beverage Suggestion:

Winter Tea

Wine Suggestion:

Burgundian Mercurey

Tip of the Trade:

The giblets can be cooked with the turkey. After cooking, the gizzard and liver can be chopped well and added to the Turkey Gravy along with the boiled egg. This makes the traditional Giblet Gravy that is part of many Thanksgiving meals.

TURKEY GRAVY

6 tablespoons butter or margarine
4 tablespoons self-rising flour
3 cups broth or drippings
Salt
Pepper
2 hard-boiled eggs, chopped

In a medium skillet, melt butter and add flour to make a roux or paste. Stir in broth, which can be canned or made from the drippings taken from the pan of the cooked turkey. Cook until thickened and smooth. A hand-held blender can help with the smoothness. Add salt and pepper to taste. Fold in hard-boiled eggs and serve with Turkey and Cornbread Dressing.

Menu Suggestion:
Before the Mountain Hike

Cheese Straws,

Butternut Squash Soup,

Broccolli Salad,

Tortellini Pasta Salad,

Waldorf Salad,

Amaretto Cheesecake

Wine Suggestion:

Fendant or Johannisberg du Valais

TURKEY CRÊPE TORTE

1 recipe basic crêpes
1/4 cup mayonnaise
4 ounces cream cheese, room temperature
5 ounces fresh spinach leaves
1/2 cup Parmesan cheese
1/2 pound turkey, shaved
10 ounces Monterey Jack cheese, sliced thin

Twelve crêpes will be needed for this recipe. Mix together mayonnaise and cream cheese. Remove stems from spinach. Lay two crêpes on working surface, side by side to make two tortes. Place 1 tablespoon mayonnaise mixture on each crêpe. Place layer of spinach leaves on top of mayonnaise and sprinkle with Parmesan cheese. Top each with another crêpe. Spread this crêpe with 1 tablespoon mayonnaise and a layer of turkey. Sprinkle with Parmesan. Top with another crêpe and top with cheese. Top with another crêpe and spread with 1 tablespoon mayonnaise and then spinach. Sprinkle with Parmesan and top with another crêpe. Spread with mayonnaise and top with whatever is left. Sprinkle with Parmesan and cheese. Top with a crêpe and sprinkle tops with Parmesan. Can store covered in refrigerator at this point for up to 1 day. Bake at 350 degrees uncovered on a greased baking sheet. Cool or refrigerate before slicing. Serve chilled or room temperature, slicing pizza style. Makes 6 to 8 servings.

TENDERLOIN MADEIRA

1 (3-pound) beef tenderloin
1/4 cup soy sauce
1/4 cup olive oil
1/4 cup Madeira wine or port

SAUCE:
2 tablespoons butter or margarine
3 tablespoons self-rising flour
1 (14 1/2-ounce) can beef broth
1/2 cup Madeira wine
1 teaspoon lemon juice
2 tablespoons tomato paste

Place roast in a heavy plastic bag or dish and pour soy sauce, olive oil and 1/4 cup wine over roast. Marinate roast 4 to 12 hours, covered, in refrigerator. Bake for 25 to 30 minutes at 425 degrees, covered, in a greased foil lined baking pan. Keep a meat thermometer in the roast. Poke the thermometer through the foil or roasting bag into middle of roast. Tenderloins will overcook very fast. When it has reached the temperature you desire, usually medium rare, 150 degrees, remove from oven and unwrap from foil. Do not slice tenderloin until it has cooled for at least 20 minutes and up to 1 hour. **To make sauce**: Melt butter in a medium saucepan over medium high heat. Add flour to make roux or paste, stirring well. Pour in broth, Madeira, lemon juice and tomato paste. Stir until bubbly and thickened. Serve warm over roast or as a side sauce on a buffet. Roast can be served room temperature using green leaf lettuce or herbs as a platter liner. Makes 4 to 6 servings.

Meat Temperatures:

140 degrees F - Rare
160 degrees F - Medium
170 degrees F - Well Done
Pork - 185 to 190 degrees

Menu Suggestion:
A Valentine's Dinner

Champagne,

Shrimp Pâté Mold,

Mixed Greens with Artichoke Feta Dressing,

Hot Cheese Soufflé,

Cranberry Congealed Salad,

Mint Chocolate Decadence,

Brandy

Wine Suggestion:

Carneros Pinot Noir

Tip of the Trade:

Vacuum packed roasts are available in most supermarkets. Have the butcher trim the fat before weighing for 3 pounds.

◆

Menu Suggestion:

Fund-raiser Lunch Buffet

Shrimp Crab and Artichoke Salad,

Fresh French Beans,

Tiny Rich Vegetable Quiches,

Rolls,
Mayonnaise and Mustards,

Apple Pie with Spiked
Whipped Cream

Wine Suggestion:

Italian Barbera

Tip of the Trade:

It is unrealistic to try to keep food hot on a buffet. Start out with the dishes hot and replenish when needed with hot food. It's the best anyone can do.

TENDERLOIN ROQUEFORT

1 (3 to 4-pound) beef tenderloin
2 tablespoons olive oil
1/2 teaspoon salt
1/2 teaspoon pepper
SAUCE:
1/2 cup butter or margarine
1 celery stalk, chopped fine
1/4 cup onion, chopped fine
2 cloves garlic, crushed or minced
1/4 cup plain all-purpose flour
1 cup whole milk or half and half
2 ounces Roquefort cheese or bleu cheese, crumbled
1/4 cup sour cream

Have the tenderloin trimmed at the market of all fat to measure 3 to 4 pounds. There should be no visible white marks on the roast. Place roast in a roasting pan or in a foil-lined baking dish. Spray pan or foil with cooking spray. Oil the roast with olive oil and sprinkle with salt and pepper. Cook covered in a 375-degree oven for 30 to 45 minutes until temperature reaches 150 degrees with a meat thermometer. Middle of tenderloin should never reach above 160 degrees. Guest who prefer medium well can eat off ends of roast that will be less pink. Remove roast from oven and immediately uncover to stop cooking. Wait at least 20 minutes and up to 1 hour before slicing.

To make sauce: In a medium saucepan, melt butter over medium heat. Cook celery, onion and garlic in butter for 2 minutes. Add flour and stir until smoothed of flour lumps to make a roux or paste. Add milk and stir until thickened. Add bleu cheese and heat through. Add sour cream. Serve warm with roast. Roast can be room temperature and served on a bed of leafy lettuce or herbs. Serve warm sauce on the side. Makes 6 to 8 servings.

◆

◆

Serving Tip:

Holiday trimming-the-tree parties are wonderful to gather friends. Have guests bring gifts or donations for a local children's charity to start the true meaning of Christmas spirit for close friends, a club or organization. Children can string popcorn and cranberries or exchange small gifts among themselves. Caroling afterwards will bring smiles to neighbors and friends.

MARINATED BEEF TENDERLOIN

1 (3-pound) beef tenderloin roast
1/3 cup soy sauce
1/3 cup white wine
3 tablespoons oil
2 tablespoons brown sugar
1 tablespoon vinegar

Have all fat trimmed from roast at market or by butcher to equal 3 to 4 pounds. Lay roast in a heavy sealed bag or roaster and pour all ingredients over roast. Marinate roast covered or sealed in refrigerator for at least 4 hours and up to 24 hours. Place roast in roasting pan with marinade. Cover with aluminum foil and place meat thermometer in middle of roast poked through the aluminum foil. Bake at 375 degrees for 30 to 40 minutes or until middle of roast reaches 150 degrees. Let cool for 20 minutes and up to 1 hour before slicing with an electric knife or sharpened meat knife. Serve in roast form on green leafy lettuce. Great marinade for other roasts too. Makes 6 to 8 dinner servings and 12 to 15 cocktail buffet servings.

◆

Menu Suggestion:

Perfect Dinner Buffet

Crab Mornay Baked in Individual Shells or Texas Tart

Marinated Poached Asparagus,

Spinach Congealed Mold,

Fresh Fruit,

Rolls,
Mayonnaise and
Horseradish Sauce
or
Angel Biscuits,

Chocolate Chip Rum Cake,

Wine Suggestion:

Dolcetta d'Alba

Tip of the Trade:

Select meats from a market or butcher will be far better than those from chain grocers. If market meats are available, take advantage of their quality. It will spoil you and your guests and be quite worth the extra costs.

MARINATED EYE OF ROUND WITH MUSHROOMS AND ONIONS

1 (4-pound) eye of round roast
1 1/2 tablespoons cracked black pepper
3/4 teaspoon meat tenderizer
1 pound button mushrooms
1 (14 1/2-ounce) can chicken broth
1 sweet onion, sliced into thin rings
1/4 cup olive oil
1/8 cup red wine vinegar
2 tablespoons white Worcestershire sauce
3 tablespoons wine
1 teaspoon soy sauce
1 teaspoon parsley

Save the wrapper from roast so grocery or market deli will slice on commercial slicers. Commercial slicing is not necessary, but will make a more elegant presentation of this dish. Roll roast in cracked pepper and tenderizer and place on a roasting pan and cover. Cook for 1 hour 15 minutes in a 375-degree oven or until it reaches 160 degrees on a meat thermometer. Remove from heat and cool to room temperature. Refrigerate covered for up to 1 day. After meat is chilled, have it sliced very thin, but not shaved. This might take some time and patience with a electric or hand knife. Most market delis will do this if receipt or proof of purchase is shown. Try to keep meat in roast form even after slicing for prettier presentation. (Onions slice well on a commercial slicer too.) Place mushrooms in a saucepan with broth and boil for 5 to 8 minutes. Drain well. Place roast in a dish and place mushrooms and onions on and around meat. Mix oil, vinegar, Worcestershire, wine, soy sauce and parsley and pour on roast and let marinate for 4 to 24 hours. To serve, drain slightly and place on leafy lettuce with fresh rosemary sprigs. Wonderful dinner buffet or cocktail buffet dish. Makes 8 to 10 servings.

◆

STEAKS WITH PORT WILD MUSHROOM SAUCE

4 rib eye, New York strip or filet mignon steaks
1/4 cup butter or margarine
1 teaspoon fresh rosemary or thyme sprigs, chopped
1 small onion, chopped
8 ounces wild mushroom assortment or
    button mushrooms, cleaned and trimmed
2 tablespoons self-rising flour
1/4 cup port wine
1/4 cup beef broth
1/8 cup milk or cream
1/2 teaspoon salt

Marinate steaks with equal amounts of white wine Worcestershire, soy sauce and port or other favorite marinade. Marinating is optional and can be done 2 to 24 hours in advance. Cook steaks by broiling or grilling 5 to 7 minutes on each side. **To make sauce**: In a large saucepan or skillet, melt butter and cook herbs, onion, and mushrooms for 3 minutes. Add flour and stir until flour lumps are smooth. Add wine and broth and stir until thickened over medium heat. Add milk and salt and serve warm over steaks. Additional milk can be added by tablespoonfulls for desired consistency. Wild mushrooms that work well are: chanterelle, porcini, morels, fairy ring and portebella. Can be served with any beef or pork roast. Any wine can be used, however, port gives this a sweet flavor that no other wine may give. Makes 4 servings.

> *Grilling is not always the easy way out. It can be a time-consuming, smoky, hot job. Husbands have been known to do it well and some not so well. Keep in mind the help you will need at the grill and don't be afraid to do it before guests arrive.*

Menu Suggestion:
A Casual Summer Gathering for Clients

Toasted Pecan Salad with Chevre Dressing,

Sweet and Easy Corn Pudding,

Broccoli with Mock Cheese Sauce,

French Bread,

Frozen Sorbet with Fresh Fruit,

Liqueurs and Brandy

Wine Suggestion:

Bordeaux Pauillac

Tip of the Trade:
Government Inspected Stamping on Meats

Prime
- the finest quality and priciest.
Choice
- high quality and the best buy.
Commercial
- tougher meats but flavorful for stews and soups.
Utility
- low grade and not recommended for the at-home cook.

Menu Suggestion:
Dinner in the Library

Four Cheese Loaf with Wafers,

Sunflower Salad,

White Rice,

Artichoke Stuffed Bread Loaves,

Low-Fat Lemon Pie

Beverage Suggestion:

*Small Open Bar
Dark Ales*

Wine Suggestion:

Dry Creek Zinfandel

Tip of the Trade:

Serving Latin Pepper Steak in the summer is a nice change and a great way to use up all the garden peppers that seem to accumulate. This dish is for relaxed and casual entertaining.

Place meat in freezer for 30 minutes before cooking so that it can be sliced or cubed easily.

LATIN PEPPER STEAK

2 pounds boneless chuck or round steak
Tenderizer
2 tablespoons oil
1/2 cup beef or chicken broth
1/2 cup beer
1 tablespoon soy sauce
1 tablespoon Worcestershire sauce
1 teaspoon brown sugar
1 sweet onion, chopped
1 clove garlic, peeled and crushed
1 red bell pepper, seeded and sliced
1 yellow bell pepper, seeded and sliced
1 green bell pepper, seeded and sliced
1 teaspoon hot chili pepper, chopped fine or grated
3 tablespoons corn starch
1 (14-ounce) can diced tomatoes
1/2 teaspoon salt
1/4 teaspoon ground cumin
1/4 teaspoon dried oregano

Prepare meat by slicing diagonally into 2-inch-long strips. Tenderize meat and let sit for as long as possible or overnight, covered in refrigerator. In a large pot, cook meat in oil until browned on outside edges. Add broth, beer, soy sauce, Worcestershire, brown sugar, onion and garlic and simmer with meat over medium heat for 20 minutes. Add sliced bell peppers and chili pepper to pot. Dissolve cornstarch in can of tomatoes by just stirring right into can and add to pot with salt, cumin and oregano. Simmer for 5 minutes and serve warm over white rice. One recipe will need 5 to 6 cups cooked white rice. Pork or venison can be substituted for meat. Makes 4 to 6 servings.

Remember to use the resources of your market butcher or meat department. They will prepare, slice, ground or trim meats to your exact specifications.

Serving Tip:

Looking through picture cookbooks of the 60's will give you ideas on how to serve a meat loaf. Leafy lettuce and red tomato wedges on a white platter worked well for the housewives on a budget in their day.

OLD SOUTHERN MEAT LOAF

1/2 pound lean ground beef or ground round
1/2 pound ground lean all-white turkey
1/2 pound ground lean pork
1/2 onion, chopped, 1/4 cup
2 eggs
2/3 cup milk
1 teaspoon Worcestershire sauce
3/4 cup bread crumbs
1 cup sharp Cheddar cheese, grated
1 teaspoon salt
1/2 teaspoon pepper
1/2 cup ketchup
2 tablespoons brown sugar
1 teaspoon Worcestershire
1 teaspoon dry mustard

The types of ground meats used are flexible, however, 1 1/2 pounds in total should be used no matter what types of meat are picked from the market. In a large bowl, combine ground beef, turkey, pork, onion, eggs, milk, Worcestershire, bread crumbs, Cheddar cheese, salt and pepper and mix well. This can be mixed with a mixer fitted with a metal whip or with clean hands. Form mixture into a loaf and place in a greased large loaf pan or greased 2-quart dish. Mix together ketchup, brown sugar, Worcestershire and dry mustard in a separate bowl and place on top of meat loaf. Loaf can be stored covered for up to 1 day at this point. Cook uncovered at 350 degrees for 35 to 40 minutes. Makes 4 to 6 servings.

Menu Suggestion:
Dinner for Mom and Dad

Spinach and Orange Salad,

Mashed Potatos,

Snap Beans with Almond Butter,

Sliced Tomatoes and Spring Onions,

Fudge Sundae Cake

Wine Suggestion:

Dry Creek Cabernet

Tip of the Trade:

Meat Loaf is not something you want to serve with all guests, but it's wonderful as a family dinner. It is old fashioned, economical and easy, so the cook can also sit down and enjoy the family. The leftovers can be used the next day with toasted bread, mayonnaise and fresh tomato slices in a meat loaf sandwich.
For a variety, try Pork Meatballs in meat loaf form, page 41.

◆

Menu Suggestion:

A Southern Italian Dinner

Crab Filled Mushrooms,

*Mixed Greens with Artichoke
Feta Dressing,*

*Italian Bread with Olive Oil and
Cracked Black Pepper*

Wine Suggestion:

Italian Barbaresco

Tip of the Trade:

*The sausage sauce could be a little
watery becuase each brand of
tomatoes is different. If this has
occured, simmer sauce uncovered
rather than covered.*

Menu Suggestion:

A 1950's Dinner in the Diner

*Raw Vegetables with Hot Beef and
Walnut Dip,*

Hot Dogs and Hamburgers,

Cole Slaw and Potato Salad,

Chips,

*Chocolate Malts
Bottled Cokes, Straws and
Salted Peanuts*

ITALIAN SAUSAGE AND ZUCCHINI SPAGHETTI

1 pound Italian sausage or
  1/2 pound Italian sausage and 1/2 pound ground turkey
1 onion, peeled and chopped
1 or 2 garlic cloves, peeled and crushed
2 (14 1/2-ounce) cans diced tomatoes
1 cup firm button mushrooms, sliced
2 thin zucchinis, trimmed and sliced into 1/8-inch circles
8 ounces spaghetti, cooked to package directions

Remove Italian sausage from its casing and combine it with turkey (if substituting), onion and garlic in a large skillet that can be covered. Cook while stirring over medium heat until sausage (and turkey) are completely cooked. If meats are hard to manage, add 1/2 cup water for easier breakage of meat. Drain meat from grease and liquids and return to skillet. Add both cans of tomatoes with juices. Cover and simmer for 20 to 25 minutes. Add sliced mushrooms and cook for 10 to 15 minutes more, uncovered. Dish can be cooled and refrigerated covered at this point if preparing up to 1 day in advance. Bring to a simmer 5 minutes before serving and toss in zucchini rounds. Place cooked drained spaghetti on a platter and top with sausage sauce. Garnish with Italian parsley and serve warm. Makes 4 to 6 servings.

CHILI BAKE

1 tablespoon oil
1/3 cup celery, chopped
1/2 cup onion, chopped
1 clove garlic, peeled and crushed
3 tablespoons plain all-purpose flour

INGREDIENTS CONTINUED NEXT PAGE

◆

3 tablespoons fresh Cilantro, chopped
1/2 teaspoon dried parsley
1 (16-ounce) can chili, with or without beans
1/2 cup bread crumbs
1/3 cup sour cream
1 (14-ounce) can diced tomatoes or 2 tomatoes, chopped
1 1/2 cups Monterey Jack or Cheddar cheese, grated

In a medium skillet, place oil with celery, onion and garlic and cook for 2 to 4 minutes over medium heat. Add flour, Cilantro and parsley. In a greased 9 x 9 baking dish, place chili topped with bread crumbs. Layer onion mixture and then sour cream on top of bread crumbs. Pour well drained tomatoes over sour cream and top with cheese. Can be refrigerated for up to 1 day at this point. Bake in a 350-degree oven uncovered for 20 to 25 minutes Appearance for a party dish may require more fresh tomatoes and fresh Cilantro on top. Makes 8 to 10 servings.

BOURBON PORK

2 (1 1/2-pound) pork tenderloin roasts
1/2 cup soy sauce
1/2 cup bourbon
1/2 cup white wine
1/4 cup brown sugar
1/4 cup vegetable oil
1/8 cup apple cider vinegar
1/2 teaspoon salt
1/2 teaspoon pepper

Place pork tenderloins in a greased baking pan or roasting pan that can be covered with a lid or aluminum. Mix remaining ingredients together and pour over pork. Marinate for 8 to 24 hours in refrigerator. Turn tenderloins over before cooking. Cook roasts in marinade at 350 degrees covered for 30 to 40 minutes. Temperature should read 160 to 170 degrees. Cool to room temperature before slicing. Wonderful for cocktail buffets or dinner buffets. Serve room temperature or chilled over green leaf lettuce. Great steak marinade to use before grilling. Makes 6 to 8 servings.

Serving Tip:

Decorate for a 1950s Diner party with old single records, large yellow potted football mums, black and white checked tablecloths and red and yellow napkins. The hamburgers and hot dogs can be catered in by a local restaurant grill for large parties. Don't forget fried pies, if you can find them. For the Southern Italian meal on the opposite page, red and white checked tablecloths, candles melted in old wine bottles, large linen napkins and oversized white Italian pottery plates will start you on party decorations.

Menu Suggestion:
A Cajun Dinner Buffet

Baked Artichoke Loaf

Jambalaya,

Salad with Lime Vinaigrette,

Fresh Fruit,

Crescent Rolls,

Pecan Pies,

Brulot Flavored Coffee

Wine Suggestion:

Central Coast Petite Syrah

Menu Suggestion:
*A Wonderful Wedding
Party Dinner*

Cheese Wafers with Pepper Jelly,

*Crab and Artichoke Dip
with Crackers,*

Full Bar,

*Fresh Green Salad with Tomato
Goat Cheese Dressing,*

Fruited Pasta Salad,

Southern Squash Crêpes,

Pineapple Congealed Salad,

Angel Biscuits,

Strawberry Shortcake

Wine Suggestion:

*Côte de Beaune
Champagne with Dessert*

Menu Suggestion:
An Autumn Dinner

*Cilantro Corn Dip with White
Corn Chips and Raw Vegetables*

CONTINUED NEXT PAGE

GINGER TENDERLOINS

2 (1 1/2 pound) pork tenderloins
2 tablespoons cornstarch
2/3 cup soy sauce
2/3 cup brown sugar
3 cloves garlic, peeled and crushed
2 tablespoons vinegar
1 tablespoon powdered ginger

Place tenderloins in a greased baking dish. Dissolve cornstarch in soy sauce and then place over medium heat in saucepan. Add brown sugar, garlic and vinegar to pan and simmer until thickened and bubbly. Add ginger and pour over pork. Marinate for 6 to 24 hours covered in refrigerator. Cook roasts, covered, in a 350-degree oven for 30 minutes. Uncover and continue cooking for 30 to 40 minutes or until temperature of middle of pork has reached 165 to 170 degrees. Cool for 10 to 15 minutes before slicing. Serve warm or room temperature. Garnish with rosemary. Great with steamed carrots. Makes 6 to 8 servings.

SPICY GRILLED PORK

A recipe from the collection of Patricia Collins Simpson

1 (12-ounce) pork tenderloin
1/4 cup soy sauce
3 tablespoons brown sugar
1 teaspoon ground cumin
1 teaspoon dry mustard
1/2 teaspoon sweet paprika
5 cloves garlic, sliced
2 tablespoons chopped fresh parsley or 3/4 teaspoon dried

◆

Prepare tenderloin by tucking in small end of tenderloin and tying well in place with kitchen string. Place tenderloin in a heavy sealed bag or small pan for marinating in sauce. Combine soy sauce, sugar, cumin, mustard, paprika, garlic and parsley in bag with tenderloin. Push all air out of bag and seal tightly. Marinate for 1 hour to overnight in refrigerator. Set grill on medium temperature or prepare to medium coals. Oil grill and set 5-inches from coals. Grill for 10 minutes, basting and turning once during this grilling time. Can be baked at 375 degrees for 15 to 20 minutes, or until reaches 165 degrees, as an alternative to grilling. Let sit for 5 minutes before slicing. Makes 2 to 4 servings.

OYSTER STUFFED QUAIL

12 quail, cleaned and rinsed
24 to 36 oysters
1 egg
2 tablespoons milk
1 cup cornmeal
1 cup self-rising flour
12 slices of bacon

Wash quail with cold water and clean well. Keep oysters refrigerated while preparing ingredients. Select farm-raised oysters from a market and use the same day as preparing. Place egg and milk in a shallow dish and mix well. Place cornmeal and flour in a separate shallow dish and mix well. Dip oyster first in egg mixture and then in cornmeal mixture. Place 2 to 3 oysters depending on size, inside each quail cavity. Wrap each quail in one piece of raw bacon. Place quail uncovered in a 350-degree oven for 35 to 45 minutes or until meat thermometer reaches 185 degrees when inserted into the middle of quail. Makes 6 to 12 servings.

Shrimp Pasta Salad,

Spinach and Orange Salad,

Whipped Butternut Squash,

Dinner Rolls,

Almond and Brandy Tart with Fresh Fruit

Wine Suggestion:

South African Shiraz

Menu Suggestion:
An Elegant Formal Dinner

Shrimp Pâté,

Spring Greens with Lime Vinaigrette,

Marinated Beef Tenderloin,

Madeira Potatoes,

Spinach and Artichoke Stuffed Tomatoes,

Liquered Chocolate Mousse with Crème Anglaise

Wine Suggestion:

Chianti Classico

◆

Menu Suggestion:
Summer Luncheon Celebration

Luncheon Sangria as guests arrive,

*Chilled Avocado and
Cucumber Soup,*

Texas Tart,

Fresh Fruit,

Cheese Biscuits,

Low-Fat Lemon Pie

Wine Suggestion:

Burgundian Meursault

Tip of the Trade:

*When purchasing seafood of any
kind, always buy from a reliable,
government approved market or
supplier. It should, in most cases,
be purchased and prepared for
eating or frozen the same day as
buying. Have the clerk provide ice
around your choices for
transporting home for the best
safety. Keep refrigerated or iced
down until ready to cook and do
not leave out in room temperature
for more than 1 hour.*

SHRIMP CRAB AND ARTICHOKE SALAD

1/2 pound crab, white lump
1 pound shrimp
1/2 pound sugar snap peas, snapped, or
   1 (6-ounce) can water chestnuts
1/2 cup celery, sliced
3/4 pound baby asparagus, chopped 2-inch pieces
1 (14-ounce) can quartered artichokes, drained
1 (3-ounce) can sliced black olives, drained
1/8 cup oil
2 tablepoons vinegar
1/4 cup sour cream
1/2 cup mayonnaise
1 tablespoon lemon juice
3/4 cup crumbled Feta cheese

Toss crab to remove excess shells. Cook shrimp by steaming or boiling in salted water or court bouillon. Remove tails and peeling from shrimp. If shrimp is bought cooked and frozen, steam well to remove water retained with freezing. Place snap peas and asparagus in boiling salted water for 1 to 1 1/2 minutes. Remove and drain. Mix together crab, shrimp, peas, celery, asparagus, artichokes and olives.
To make dressing: Mix together oil, vinegar, sour cream, mayonnaise, lemon juice and Feta. Mix with salad and chill for 1 hour. If preparing 1 day in advance, keep seafood separate from the vegetables in storing. Drain any juices from seafood and vegetables before tossing with dressing. Dressing should not be added until 1 to 2 hours before serving. Serve on green leafy lettuce with a side of lemon. Makes 4 to 6 servings.

> *Try peeling shrimp raw instead of cooked. It is much
> easier. Start at the large end and peel the shell away and
> then romove the tail, if needed. Small to medium shrimp
> usually do not have to be deveined.*

◆

Menu Suggestion:
A Wedding Reception

Cheese Straws,

**Smoked Eye of Round with
Rolls, Mayonnaise, Mustard and
Horseradish,*

*Breaded Chicken with
Apricot Sauce,*

*Steamed Asparagus with
Hollandaise,*

Artichoke Tarts,

Fresh Fruit,

Creamy Apricot Mold,

Crescent Cookies,

*Cream Cheese Pound Cake Iced
with Buttercream Icing*

Wine Suggestion:

Barrel Fermented Sauvignon Blanc

Shellfish Cookery:

*Bring court boullion or water to a slow medium boil in a
large pot before adding shellfish.
Maine or Rock Lobster cooks 15 to 20 minutes.
Prawns cook for 5 to 7 minutes, have 8 per person.
Crayfish or crawfish cook for 5 to 8 minutes,
have 15 per person.
Jumbo shrimp cook for 3 to 5 minutes, have 5 to 9 per
person cocktail servings or 1/2 pound for dinner.
Mussels, clams and cockles cook until shell is open,
have 10 per person.*

SHRIMP PASTA SALAD

1 cup shrimp, small
8 ounces sea-shell pasta
2 green onions, peeled and chopped
2 celery stalks, trimmed and chopped
2 tablespoons mayonnaise
2 1/2 tablespoons oil
1 1/2 teaspoons lemon juice
1 teaspoon fresh thyme
1/2 teaspoon dried parsley
1/4 teaspoon salt
1/4 teaspoon pepper or pepper blend

Prepare small shrimp by steaming or boiling in court bouillon or salted water. Remove all shells and tails. If using precooked frozen shrimp, steam for 2 to 3 minutes to remove excess water retained during freezing process. Cook pasta according to package directions, using the lowest cooking time given. Rinse with cold water and drain well. Place shrimp, pasta, onions and celery in a bowl and toss. Add mayonnaise, oil, lemon juice, fresh thyme, parsley, salt and pepper. Chill covered until ready to serve. If storing overnight in refrigerator, 1 tablespoon of mayonnaise might need to be added to obtain creamy texture again.

Tip of the Trade:

**Follow directions for the Smoked
Turkey, page 157, to smoke an eye
of round or other desired roasts.*

Menu Suggestion:
Elegant Cocktail Buffet

*Cold Crab Mousse with
Butter Crackers,*

*Smoked Turkey Breasts and
Marinated Beef Tenderloin
with
Rolls, Hosrseradish Sauce, Stone
Ground Mustard,*

*Oyster Rockefeller or Pork
Meatballs with Peach Sauce,*

*Ricotta Red Pepper Dip
with Snow Peas, Carrots,
Asparagus and Celery Sticks,*

Pesto Cheesecake with Wafers,

*Toffee Dessert Dip with
Fresh Fruit Display
Strawberry Tree*

Wine Suggestion:

Seyval Blanc

Tip of the Trade:

*How many shrimp per pound
depends on size. Average number
per pound are: Jumbo - 11 to 15,
extra large - 16 to 20, large 21 to
30, medium - 31 to 35, small - 36
to 40 and miniature - 60 to 100.*

MARINATED SHRIMP WITH CAPERS AND LEMONS

3 pounds shrimp
2 white or yellow onions, peeled and sliced thin
1/2 cup vegetable oil
1/2 cup olive oil
1 (3-ounce) bottle capers, drained
5 tablespoons white Worcestershire
1/8 teaspoon red pepper or 1/4 teaspoon pepper blend
4 lemons sliced
1/2 cup apple cider vinegar
1/2 cup sugar

Cook shrimp by steaming or by boiling in court bouillon or salted water until pink. If cooked and frozen shrimp are used, steaming for 2 to 3 minutes will remove excess water retained during freezing. Peel shrimp and remove tails, if you wish. For cocktail buffets, leaving tails on can be attractive and an easy eating alternative to forks. Refrigerate shrimp until ready to use. Mix together white onions, oils, capers, Worcestershire, pepper and lemons. In a small pot in a microwave-safe dish, combine vinegar and sugar. Cook on stove or microwave until bubbly and sugar dissolved. Add to vegetables and toss in shrimp. Let marinate for 6 to 24 hours. Use within 24 hours. Drain and serve on leaf lettuce or with picks for a cocktail buffet. Makes 6 to 8 dinner and 12 to 15 cocktail servings.

Create a tiered server for shrimp on a buffet table by using two matching or complementary punch bowls or bowls. Place larger bowl first and fill 1/3 with ice. Place second bowl on ice and fill with shrimp. Additional ice can then be filled around edges. Kosher rock salt will keep ice from melting as fast and green leafy lettuce can be placed under shrimp. Garnish with edible flowers.

BAKED MADEIRA SHRIMP

2 pounds shrimp, uncooked
1/2 cup oil
1/8 cup Madeira wine, sherry or white wine
2 cloves garlic, peeled and crushed
1 teaspoon lemon juice
1 teaspoon orange peel, grated
1 tablespoon juice from orange
1/2 teaspoon lemon pepper
1/2 teaspoon salt

Shrimp can be bought with or without peels. Buying shrimp raw is essential. Grease a 9 x 13 baking dish and lay peeled and cleaned shrimp in dish. Refrigerate shrimp while making the sauce. Mix together oil, Madeira, garlic, lemon juice, orange peel and juice and spices. Pour over shrimp and place in refrigerator to marinate until ready to cook. Place in a 375-degree oven covered for 10 minutes. Remove from oven, stir well but carefully and leave uncovered. Cook an additional 4 to 6 minutes. (Can finish off on grill, if desired.) All shrimp should be pink. Try to avoid overcooking shrimp. It becomes very tough and curled when overdone. Serve warm or at room temperature. A wonderful chicken or salad topper. Scallops can be substituted. Makes 4 to 6 dinner servings and 10 to 12 cocktail portions. Serve with Lime Mayonnaise.

LIME MAYONNAISE

1/2 cup mayonnaise
1/2 cup sour cream
2 tablespoons lime or lemon juice
1 teaspoon lime or lemon peel, grated
2 green onions, chopped fine

Mix all ingredients together and chill until ready to serve. Can be prepared up to 2 days in advance. Wonderful with shrimp or fish. Makes 1 cup.

Menu Suggestion:
Fall Dinner with Neighbors

Butternut Squash Soup,

Tomato Grits,

Sautéd Sweet Onion Rings,

Broccoli Salad,

Strawberry Salad,

Chocolate Chip Rum Cake with Raspberry Purée

Wine Suggestion:

Italian Gavi

Tip of the Trade:

Shrimp should smell of the sea. There should be no visible black spots on their shells. The flesh should be moist and translucent.

Tip of the Trade:

Substitute fresh chopped dill for green onions in Lime Mayonnaise, if desired.

Menu Suggestion:
A Birthday Celebration

Crab Mushrooms,

Dinner Grits,

Field Peas,

Spinach and Orange Salad,

Biscuits,

Moist Carrot Cake with Nutty Cream Cheese Icing

Wine Suggestion::

Stags Leap District Chardonnay

Menu Suggestion:
Outstanding Dinner Buffet

Mixed Greens with Artichoke Feta Dressing,

Spicy Grilled Pork,

Fluffy Long Grain and Wild Rice,

Southern Pole Beans,

Goat Cheese Tarts with Red Pepper Sauce,

Mint Chocolate Decadence Fresh Fruit

SHRIMP SCAMPI

2 pounds shrimp
1/2 cup olive oil
1/2 cup vermouth
2 cloves garlic, peeled and crushed
1 tablespoon dried parsley or 2 tablespoons fresh, chopped
1 teaspoon salt
1/2 teaspoon pepper

Shrimp can be bought with or without skins and tails. Shrimp must be bought uncooked and shells and tails must be removed before cooking. In a large skillet over medium heat, combine shrimp, oil, vermouth and garlic. Cook over medium heat, stirring until shrimp is pink. Add lemon juice and spices. Follow the recipe for Dinner Grits, page 107, to serve with this dish in the place of the traditional white rice. To present, place grits on plate or serving platter making a small dip in the middle. Place shrimp in the middle with juices, and garnish with lemon or fresh herbs. Makes 4 to 6 servings.

APRICOT CURRIED SHRIMP AND SCALLOPS

1 pound shrimp
1 pound sea scallops
1 small onion, peeled and chopped
1/2 cup white wine
1 teaspoon lemon juice
3 tablespoons butter or margarine
3 tablespoons plain all-purpose flour
1/2 to 1 teaspoon curry powder
1 cup cream
1/4 teaspoon salt
4 teaspoons apricot preserves

Wine Suggestion::

Spanish Rioja

Shrimp and scallops should be purchased raw and be free from all shells. In a large skillet placed over medium heat, cook shrimp, scallops and onion in wine and lemon juice. Shrimp should just be pink. In a separate saucepan or in a microwave-safe dish, melt butter. Add flour and curry powder to butter to make a roux or paste. Add cream and heat just until bubbly and thickened, whisking often. Add salt and apricot preserves. Pour sauce over shrimp and scallops and simmer 2 minutes. Serve warm as an entree with rice or on a cocktail buffet with picks or hors d'oeuvres forks. If making as an appetizer, adding 1 to 1 1/2 pounds additional seafood to recipe works well. Makes 4 to 6 dinner servings or 10 to 12 cocktail portions.

SCALLOPS AND SPINACH IN WINE

1 pound sea scallops
1/2 cup white wine
6 tablespoons butter or margarine
3 green onions, peeled and chopped
2 cloves garlic, peeled and crushed
1/2 pound button mushrooms, trimmed and sliced
5 tablespoons self-rising flour
1/2 teaspoon salt
1 1/2 cups half and half or 1 1/4 cup milk
1 cup fresh spinach, finely chopped
1 cup cracker crumbs
2 tablespoons pine nuts or almonds, crushed
Vegetable cooking spray

Tip of the Trade:

Substitute shrimp for scallops in Scallops and Spinach in Wine or use 1/2 scallops and 1/2 shrimp. Chicken can also be substituted, however, add 1/4 cup more half and half to sauce if using chicken. Both chicken and shrimp can be cooked in wine until done, just as recipe suggests.

Menu Suggestion:
Spring Dinner in the Gazebo

Tomato and Roasted Red Pepper Soup,

Fruited Slaw,

Tenderloin Madeira,

Poached Marinated Asparagus,

Spinach and Ricotta French Bread,

Kentucky Pie

Wine Suggestion:

Montrachet from Burgundy

Cook scallops in wine for 3 to 5 minutes. Drain well. In a large skillet, melt butter and cook onions and garlic for 2 minutes. Add mushrooms and cook 2 minutes more. Add flour and salt and mix through. Add half and half and whisk until sauce is thickened. Stir in spinach and scallops. Pour into a greased 9 x 11 baking pan. Sprinkle with a mixture of cracker crumbs and nuts. Spray crumbs generously with cooking spray. Can store covered in refrigerator for up to 8 hours. Bake at 350 degrees for 25 to 35 minutes until bubbly and crumbs slightly browned. Serve with white rice. Makes 4 to 6 servings.

JAMBALAYA

Tip of the Trade:

Jambalaya is from the Louisiana Cajun Country. Like the Spanish Paella, the meat, seafood and vegetable ingredients were used according to the harvest, resources and catch of the freshwater crawfish or ocean catch. There is a difference in Cajun and Creole. Creole began in New Orleans and is more complex than Cajun, which was brought from Southern France. Traditionally, rice is cooked in the Jambalaya pot, but for serving purposes and to keep rice fluffy, heating in microwave before serving works better. Place rice on a large serving platter that has been lined with green leaf lettuce and spoon Jambalaya over. Wonderful served on fixed plates for an entree.

Menu Suggestion:

Uncle Rylands Cream of Crab Soup,

Toasted Pecan Salad and Chevre Dressing,

French Rolls,

Cheesecake Rogét

Wine Suggestion:

Brunello di Montalcino

1/2 stick butter or margarine
2 onions, peeled and chopped
1 1/2 cups celery, chopped
2 green peppers, seeded and chopped
5 cloves garlic, peeled and crushed
6 to 8 ounces smoked cured 81 ham, chopped 1-inch strips
1 pound andouille or kielbasa sausage, cooked
2 (16-ounce) cans diced tomatoes
2 cups chicken broth or fish stock
1 (15-ounce) can tomato sauce
2 tomatoes, seeded and chopped
1 1/2 to 2 pounds chicken, crawfish, or oysters (or mixture)
1 1/2 pounds shrimp, cooked and peeled
2 teaspoons salt
1/2 teaspoon paprika
1 teaspoon thyme
1 to 2 teaspoons black pepper
1/2 to 1 teaspoon red pepper
1 bunch green onions, peeled and chopped
6 to 8 cups cooked white rice

In a large pot sprayed with cooking spray, melt butter and add onions, celery, bell pepper and garlic. Cook for 6 to 9 minutes over medium heat. Add ham and sausage and simmer for 5 to 8 minutes longer. Add 2 (15-ounce) cans tomatoes, chicken broth, and tomato sauce and cook for 15 to 20 minutes over low simmering heat. Add chopped fresh tomatoes. The chicken, crawfish or oyster choice should be free from bones or shells and cooked fully in bite-size pieces. Add to pot with peeled and cooked shrimp. Simmer for 10 minutes while adding all spices. This dish can be refrigerated covered at this point and reheated again on a low to medium low stove. Add green onions 10 minutes before serving. Dish should not cook on the stove more than 15 minutes after meats and seafood have been added to keep from overcooking them. Fresh steamed crawfish, clams or mussels in shells added to dish would make a fabulous presentation. Makes 12 to 16 servings.

Menu Suggestion:
Winning The Lottery Celebration

*Steamed Shrimp with
Cocktail Sauce,*

Raw Oyster Bar,

*Grilled Filet Mignon and
Teriyaki Salmon with
Orange Dill Sauce,*

Rosemary Potatoes,

*Fresh Green Salad with
Peppercorn Dressing,*

*Marinated Green Beans and
Poached Marinated Asparagus,*

South Georgia Okra Gumbo,

Fresh Fruit,

Spinach Congealed Mold,

Dessert Buffet

Wine Suggestion:

Viognier from Condrieu

Tip of the Trade:

*Always use your fingers to pick
through any type crab meat to
remove excess shells.*

Serving Tip:
*Crab Mornay is beautiful cooked in individual shells or
ramekins. There are even edible shells available at specialty
markets and gourmet shops.*

CRAB MORNAY

1/2 cup butter or margarine
1 onion, peeled and chopped
2 celery stalks, trimmed and chopped
1 garlic clove, peeled and crushed
1/2 teaspoon dried parsley
1/4 cup self-rising flour
1 1/2 cups heavy cream
1 1/2 cups chicken broth
1 cup Gruyere cheese, grated or Swiss cheese, grated
1/2 teaspoon lemon rind, grated
1 pound white crab meat, drained and flaked
1 teaspoon lemon juice
2 tablespoons sherry
Milk
Paprika

In a medium to large skillet or pot, melt butter over medium heat and cook onions, celery and garlic for 2 to 3 minutes. Add parsley and flour and stir well to make a roux or paste. Add cream and broth and stir with a whisk. Let heat until starting to thicken. When thick, turn heat to low and add cheese. Whisk until cheese is melted. Sauce can be made at this point up to 2 days in advance. While sauce is hot or reheated and smooth, add lemon rind, crab, lemon juice and sherry. Add milk as needed for desired consistency by teaspoonfuls. This should be served in individual greased shells or a greased 1-quart oven-proof casserole. Sprinkle top with paprika. Dish can be refrigerated covered for up to 24 hours at this point. Bake at 350 degrees for 10 to 25 minutes depending on size of dish. Should be bubbly around edges. Great also on cocktail buffet with wafers. Makes 4 to 6 servings.

Menu Suggestion:

Vacation House Supper

Cranberry Cheese Ball,

Green Salad with Creamy Russian Dressing,

Charleston Shrimp and Grits,

Poached Marinated Asparagus,

Warmed Brandied Fruit,

Gruyere Loaf,

Cake Mix Cake with Lemon Pineapple Filling

Wine Suggestion:

Cru Beaujolais Brouilly

Added Suggestion:

Marinated Tenderloin and Madeira Shrimp would be a magical addition to the above menu.

Tip of the Trade:

Orange Dill Sauce is a very good seafood sauce and highly suggested in place of tartar sauce with any favorite seafood.

TERIYAKE SALMON

2 pounds salmon or tuna filet, 4- to 6-ounce portions
1 cup teriyaki sauce
1/2 cup brown sugar
3 tablespoons chopped candied ginger or
   1 teaspoon ginger powder
1/2 cup orange juice
4 green onions, peeled and chopped
1 tablespoon fresh parsley or 1/2 teaspoon dried
Hot sauce

If skin is still on fish, place fish 3 to 5 inches under a low broil uncovered for 5 to 10 minutes. Remove from oven and skin should peel off easily, or have market skin fish. Place fish in dish brown side down and pour all ingredients over fish. Marinate for up to 24 hours. If you have no time to marinate, cooking fish halfway in marinade will help enhance flavor. (Bake covered in marinade for 5 to 8 minutes at 375 degrees.) Remove fish from marinade and grill, bake or broil. Grilling will take about 8 minutes, turning once if uncooked. Broil 10 minutes on low broil, 5 inches from broiler, uncovered, turning once during cooking. Baking can take 15 to 25 minutes at 375 degrees covered. Thickness of fish will vary cooking times. As a general rule, check fish at one half its cooking time by using a fork and checking for fish flakiness. Serve with Lemon Orange Dill Sauce or Dill Capered Sauce. Makes 4 to 6 servings.

ORANGE DILL SAUCE

1 cup sour cream or plain yogurt
4 tablespoons mayonnaise
2 tablespoons orange juice concentrate
1/4 teaspoon lemon rind
1/4 teaspoon orange rind
1/2 teaspoon fresh dill weed or 1/8 teaspoon dried
1/2 teaspoon lemon juice
1/4 teaspoon salt

Mix all ingredients together and chill covered. Can prepare 2 days in advance. Serve with Teriyaki Salmon, Tuna, Caribbean Grouper or other favorite fish. Makes 1 cup.

FISH WITH PICANTE RELISH

2 pounds grouper, amberjack or roughy filets
1/2 cup white or blush wine
1 lemon
Thyme sprigs
1 tablespoon oil
1 onion, peeled and chopped
1 yellow bell pepper, seeded and chopped
1 jalapeno pepper, seeded and chopped
2 to 3 cloves garlic, seeded and chopped
2 Roma tomatoes, seeded and chopped
2 tablespoons wine
1 (15-ounce) can black-eyed peas, drained well
2 tablespoons fresh parsley or 3/4 teaspoon dried
1/2 cup fesh Cilantro, chopped
1/2 pound fresh spinach leaves

Have market filet and remove skins from fish for you. Choosing a prime cut is worth the extra cost. Foil line or parchment line a baking dish and grease well with cooking spray. Place fish filets in prepared dish and pour wine over filets. Slice lemon and place on fish with thyme sprigs. Cover and place in a 350-degree oven for 25 to 30 minutes. Fish should flake with fork. In a medium saucepan, heat oil over medium heat and cook onion, bell pepper, hot pepper, and garlic for 5 to 8 minutes. Remove from heat and add tomatoes, wine, black-eyed peas, parsley and Cilantro. Place spinach leaves on plate or platter. Spoon fish with some of juices over spinach. Place relish on top of fish.   Relish can be made 2 days in advance. Storing relish really enhances the flavors. Great relish with chicken and pork or can be used as a salad. Makes 4 to 6 servings.

Tip of the Trade:

South Carolina fisherman from Shem Creek gave a tip for grilled fish. They suggested marinating fish in Italian dressing, grill on foil lined grid and before removing from grill, rub top side with apple butter.

Menu Suggestion:
Dinner for Four

Avocado Cucumber Soup,

Fluffy Wild and Long Grain Rice,

Steamed Vegetables with Mock Cheese Sauce,

*Angel Food Cake with Lemon Filling,
Fresh Fruit*

Wine Suggestion:

Côte de Nuits Rouge

The Fish With Picante Relish can be also made by breading and frying the fish in a little oil. Coat the fish with a buttermilk or milk and egg mixture before breading with cracker or bread crumbs.

Menu Suggestion:

Christmas Eve Dinner

Pesto Cheesecake With Wafers,

Hazlenut and Goat Cheese Salad with Mixed Greens,

Dill Capered Sauce,

Tenderloin Roquefort,

Madeira New Potatoes,

Fancy Green Peas,

Whipped Butternut Squash,

Holiday Pickled Peach Mold,

Buttermilk Pie and Chocolate Pound Cake

Wine Suggestion:

Burgundian Chablis

Menu Suggestion:

Welcome Home Dinner

Goat Cheese Spinach and Rice,

Fresh Corn Salad,

Waldorf Salad,

Fruited Muffins

WHOLE SALMON FILET

1 whole 4-pound salmon, market filet
1 onion, sliced in rings
2 lemons, sliced
3 tablespoon capers
2 cups white wine

Have your fish market filet salmon, keeping it whole. There should be two whole filets. If skin is still on fish, line a large cookie sheet with aluminum foil. Fold up edges to hold juices. Spray with cooking spray. Place skin side up on pan and low broil 5 inches from broiler for 5 to 10 minutes. Skin should peel off easily. Line a very large 2-inch-deep pan with foil and then with waxed paper. Spray with cooking spray. Clean hands and forearms well, and using your whole arm length to help protect salmon breakage, flip salmon over to keep gray side down. Place onion rings, lemons, capers and wine over fish and cover. Place in a 350-degree oven for 30 to 40 minutes. Remove fish, cool and refrigerate for up to 24 hours. Using whole arm length again, move salmon carefully to leafy lettuce lined serving platter and garnish with onions, lemons and capers. Refrigeration is necessary to firm fish enough to transfer. This is a wonderfully easy way to prepare any favorite fish or salmon in smaller 4- to 6-ounce portions. Serve with toast points, cucumber slices or large wafers for appetizers. Makes 6 to 8 dinner portions and 25 to 35 cocktail servings.

CARIBBEAN GROUPER

2 pounds grouper filet, 4- to 6-ounce portions
2 tablespoons lemon juice
1 clove garlic, peeled and crushed
2 green onions, peeled and chopped
4 tablespoons rum
2 tablespoons brown sugar
1 teaspoon orange rind, grated
1 teaspoon lime rind, grated
1/4 teaspoon salt
1/4 teaspoon pepper

Grouper is a wonderful white firm fish, however, it is very strong in flavor. Place grouper in a greased baking dish. Fish should be sliced into desired portions before cooking for presentation purposes. Portions larger than 2 inches thick may dry out during cooking, so smaller, thinner portions work best. Mix together lemon juice, garlic, onions, rum, brown sugar, rind and spices. Place one half of sauce over fish and place in a 350-degree oven for 15 minutes. Place oven on low broil and cook an additional 8 to 12 minutes. Fish should be flaky when done. Remove from oven and pour remaining sauce over fish. Serve with lime and orange slices as garnishes and Orange Dill Sauce, page 176. Snapper, halibut, sea bass, red fish, amberjack, pompano or sea scallops can be substituted. Makes 4 to 6 servings.

ORANGE RAINBOW TROUT

2 pounds rainbow trout filet, 1-pound portions
2 tablespoons oil
1/2 teaspoon salt
1/2 teaspoon pepper blend
1/2 red onion
2 tablespoons orange peel, grated
1 orange, sliced

Line a baking dish with aluminum foil or parchment with long pieces so that it can be sealed when baking the fish. Spray with cooking spray and place fish skin side up. Place under a high broil for 2 to 3 minutes. Remove from oven, peel skin off and turn over, placing pink side up, brown side down. Brush with oil and place 1 tablespoon orange peel over fish. Sprinkle with salt and pepper. Slice red onion into rings and place over fish with orange slices. Seal and refrigerate for up to 8 hours until ready to bake. Bake in a 350-degree oven sealed for 20 minutes. Fish should be whiter in color and have a milky juice over when done. In a small saucepan, combine orange juice, remaining orange peel and butter. Heat for 3 to 5 minutes over medium heat. Pour over fish after baking. Remove fish from pan, leaving sliced onions and oranges. Place on a platter with leaf lettuce or fresh herbs. Pewter platters look especially beautiful. Salmon or other variety of trout can be substituted. Makes 4 to 6 servings.

Dessert Suggestion:

Banana Pudding

Wine Suggestion:

Italian Vernancia

Tip of the Trade:

With changing diets, fish has become increasingly popular making market availability to many different varieties. Frozen seafood, as well as overnight mail, have made it possible to eat fresh fish from all around the world.

Menu Suggestion:
Dinner on the Screened Porch

Creamy Winter Squash and Potato Medley,

Crunchy Fresh Asparagus Mold,

Cranberry Apples,

Southern Loaf Bread,

Orange and White Chocolate Custard with Pound Cake

Wine Suggestion:

Grenache Blanc

Menu Suggestion:

A College Reunion

Cheese Soup,

Pasta with Nutty Pesto,

Broccoli Salad,

Cranberry Congealed Salad,

Cheesy Sour Cream Muffins,

Peanut Chocolate Bars

Wine Suggestion:

Puligny-Montrachet

Tip of the Trade:

Fresh fish will have firm flesh, clear eyes, pink gills, shiny scales and little odor. The skin should not feel slippery or sticky.

Cooking a whole fish should not be excluded. Any fish or fish filet can be baked simply in parchment or greased foil with sliced lemons, peppercorns, capers, herbs, onions, carrots, celery and less than a cup of wine, beer, broth, court bouillon or water. Tightly seal and bake in a 350-degree oven. Fish should flake when done.

SOLE WITH VERMOUTH VEGETABLES

2 pounds sole filet,
1 onion, peeled and chopped
1 clove garlic, peeled and crushed
1/2 cup wine
1 cup fish or chicken stock or broth
3/4 teaspoon salt
1/2 teaspoon white pepper
8 tiny new potatoes
2 carrots, julienne
2 zucchini squash, sliced or julienned
1 to 2 yellow summer squash, sliced
2 stalks celery, chopped
1 cup button mushrooms, trimmed and sliced
3 tablespoons chopped fresh parsley
1/3 cup vermouth
2 tablespoons cornstarch

Talapia or orange roughy filet (or other firm white fish) can be used due to market availability. In a greased oven-proof dish, place sole, onion, garlic, wine, stock, salt and pepper. (Line the dish with two large pieces of aluminum foil or parchment paper for good sealing during cooking and easy clean up.) Slice new potatoes the thickness of fish and place around edges of fish. Cover and bake in a 350-degree oven for 15 to 20 minutes. Remove from oven and add carrots, zucchini, squash, celery, mushrooms and parsley. Dissolve cornstarch in vermouth and pour over fish and vegetables. Cook for a remaining 15 to 20 minutes until fish is flaky. Sole is not a readily available fish at the market, but orange roughy, talapia filets, flounder, tarbot and ocean perch work as well. Chicken also works wonderfully in this dish and can be made by adding 15 to 20 minutes to first cooking time. To serve, arrange fish on serving platter with fresh rosemary sprigs or serve right out of decorative baking dish. Makes 4 to 6 servings.

> *Cook fish skin side down even if the skin is removed. This will keep smaller filets from curling when baking and their appearance beautiful. A general rule is to bake 7 to 10 minutes per pound. If grilling or broiling fish, keep portions less than 1-inch thick to keep from charring or drieing out fish. Set oven or grill racks 6 to 8 inches from the coals or heat.*

OYSTERS ROCKEFELLER

A recipe from the collection of my client and friend, Mrs. Carolyn Doxey, Marietta

1 bunch green onions
1 stalk celery, 1 long piece out of bunch
1 bunch parsley
1/2 teaspoon anise seed
2 (10-ounce) packages frozen chopped spinach
1 1/2 pounds melted butter
1/2 cup bread crumbs
4 tablespoons Worcestershire sauce
1 ounce Pernod, or other French wine
Salt
Pepper
Red pepper
4 dozen oysters

In a blender, combine trimmed green onions, celery, parsley, anise seed, spinach that has been defrosted and well drained and butter. Butter should act as the liquid to help grind. Process 3 to 4 seconds but do not purée. Stir in bread crumbs, Worcestershire, Pernod and spices to taste. This mixture can be made 1 day in advance. Oysters should be bought, shucked and served all in the same day. They should be kept on ice even in refrigerator until ready to cook. Place oyster on the half shells in pans lined with rock salt. Place 2 teaspoons sauce on top of each oyster. Bake in a 350-degree oven for 20 minutes. Make 3 oysters per oyster lover for appetizer and 1/2 dozen to 1 dozen for dinner portion. Makes 4 to 6 dinner servings.

Tip of the Trade:

Farm raised oysters are the safest form of oysters to buy, however, a good reputable market will guarantee safest quality. Reject any oyster with an opened or cracked shell. Try freezing oyster in shell for 30 minutes for easier shucking. Use the point of a bottle opener for a shucking tool.

Oysters which are already shucked should be plump and uniform. Their liquid or 'liquor' should be clear.

Menu Suggestion:
Special Date Night Dinner

Mixed Greens with Artichoke Feta Dressing,

Grilled Filet Mignons or Swordfish,

Poached Marinated Asparagus,

Hot Cheese Soufflé,

Angel Biscuits,

Famous Chocolate Pie

Wine Suggestion:

Champagne Brut

◆

Tip of the Trade:

Tartar Sauce can be made by substituting 1 teaspoon grated onion for dill and 2 tablespoons sweet salad relish for capers in Dill Capered Seafood Sauce.

DILL CAPERED SEAFOOD SAUCE

1 to 2 tablespoons fresh dill, chopped
3- to 3 1/2-ounce jar capers, drained very well
1 cup mayonnaise
1 cup sour cream

Chop fresh dill. Drain capers by pressing in colander. Mix together 1 tablespoon dill, capers, mayonnaise and sour cream. If larger capers are used, placing in a food processor fitted with a metal blade and processing one to two times will help texture. Add additional dill as needed. Serve with favorite seafood as a substitution for tartar sauce. Makes 2 cups.

TRADITIONAL COCKTAIL SAUCE

Making homemade cocktail sauce for larger crowds is not only better tasting, but easier on the budget. It stores very well in the refrigerator.

1 (15-ounce) can tomato sauce
1 (5- or 6-ounce) can tomato paste or puree
1 tablespoon horseradish
2 tablespoons Worcestershire
1 1/4 teaspoons lemon juice

Mix all ingredients together and keep for up to 2 weeks sealed tightly in jar in refrigerator. If a thicker sauce is wanted, use tomato paste. A thinner sauce requires tomato puree. Serve with favorite seafood dish. Makes 1 1/2 cups.

◆

VEGETABLE LASAGNA

A recipe from the collection of my mother, Mimi Howard

9 lasagna noodles
1 teaspoon oil
2 cups mushrooms, cleaned and sliced
1 cup carrot, shredded
1 cup onion, peeled and chopped
1 zucchini, halved horizontally and sliced
1 (6-ounce) can tomato paste
2 (8-ounce) cans tomato sauce
1 (2 1/4-ounce) can black olives, sliced
1 1/2 teaspoons dried oregano
1 teaspoon dried basil
1 (10-ounce) package frozen chopped spinach, thawed
2 cups cottage cheese or ricotta cheese
1 (4-ounce) package cream cheese, room temperature
1 tablespoon lemon juice
1 3/4 cups mozzarella cheese, grated
1/4 cup Parmesan cheese

Cook lasagna noodles according to package directions. Lay on towel to dry. In a skillet, place oil over medium heat and add mushrooms, carrots, onions and zucchini. Cook for 3 to 5 minutes. Take vegetables off of heat and add tomato paste, tomato sauce, olives, oregano and basil and set aside. Drain thawed spinach well by pressing in colander or pressing with clean hands. In a bowl, combine spinach, cottage cheese, cream cheese and lemon juice. Spray a 11 x 7 baking dish with cooking spray. Lay 3 noodles on bottom of baking dish. Spread 1/3 of spinach mixture over noodles, spread 1/3 vegetable mixture over, then layer 1/3 mozzarella cheese. Repeat this process two more times and sprinkle top with Parmesan cheese. Can be refrigerated covered for up to 1 day at this point. Bake at 325 degrees covered for 45 to 55 minutes. Spray foil with vegetable cooking spray before covering dish. Makes 6 to 8 servings.

Menu Suggestion:
Dinner For A Crowd

*Vegetables with Ricotta
Red Pepper Dip,*

Sunflower Salad,

Italian Bread,

*Famous Chocolate Pie
and
Low-Fat Lemon Pie*

Wine Suggestion:

Italian Merlot del Piave

Tip of the Trade:

One-dish meals are so practical for busy lives. They give simpler pre-party preparations and require minimal kitchen time before serving. Casseroles always warm well in the oven, leaving no exact serving time.

A pottery baking dish that can be used for your style of entertaining is practical to keep on hand, or a beautiful holder for baking dishes helps jazz up your one-dish meal.

◆

Menu Suggestion:
*Quick and Easy
Italian Dinner*

Green Salad with Italian Dressing,

Garlic Bread,

*Spumoni Ice Cream,
Biscotti*

Wine Suggestion:

Italian Pomino

Tip of the Trade:

*Spumoni ice cream can be ordered
through an ice cream parlor and
sometimes is carried through
markets.
Biscotti can be found in most coffee
shops or specialty bakeries.
Call ahead to order the amounts
you need.*

*Dried pasta made out of durum
wheat, or semolina, is the most
popular way to buy pasta. Dried
pastas will have a very long pantry
life stored in a sealed container in a
dark place. Dried whole wheat
pasta has a pantry life of about
1 month.
Fresh pasta must be wrapped and
refrigerated and should be used
within 5 days or frozen.*

CHEVRE STUFFED PASTA SHELLS

2 tablespoons oil, any type
1 onion, peeled and chopped
1 clove garlic, peeled and minced
1 (28-ounce) can Italian diced tomatoes
2 cups fresh spinach, chopped
1 teaspoon salt
1/2 teaspoon pepper
1 (12-ounce) package jumbo pasta shells
1 cup fresh spinach, chopped
1/4 cup fresh basil
30 ounces ricotta cheese
8 ounces chevre, or other soft goat cheese
8 ounces cream cheese, or goat cheese
1/2 teaspoon salt

In a skillet placed over medium heat, combine oil, onion and garlic and cook for 3 to 5 minutes. Remove from heat. Drain tomatoes and add to vegetables. In a food processor fitted with a metal blade, place 2 cups spinach and pulse several times to chop fine. Add spinach to skillet with salt and pepper. Set mixture aside, this is the topping for the dish. Cook pasta shells in lots of boiling water with salt according to package directions. Breakage can be abundant, so do not be discouraged. In a food processor fitted with a metal blade, combine 1 cup spinach, basil, ricotta, chevre, cream cheese and remaining salt. Pulse several times until mixed. Use this as the filling for shells. Fill shells and place filling side down into two 9 x 13 greased baking dishes. Pour sauce over shells, cover and refrigerate for up to 1 day until ready to bake. Sprinkle Parmesan on top and bake uncovered for 35 to 40 minutes at 350 degrees. Makes 8 to 12 servings.

◆

Tip of the Trade:

Asiago cheese is a little milder and softer than Parmesan cheese, which is a little milder than romano cheese. Any of these cheeses can be substituted easily for the other.

Cooking pasta in advance is practical. After cooking, rinse with cold water, drain and store in refrigerator. When ready to use in a hot dish, rinse with hot water, drain and toss with desired sauce.

PASTA WITH NUTTY PESTO

1/2 cup walnuts
1/4 cup almonds
1/2 cup pine nuts, pecans or almonds
3 tablespoons olive oil
1 cup ricotta cheese or tofu
1 cup packed fresh spinach leaves
3 to 4 fresh basil leaves
1/4 cup milk
1/2 teaspoon salt
1/4 teaspoon pepper
12 ounces pasta
Additional milk, up to 3/4 cup if needed

In a food processor fitted with a metal blade, combine nuts, oil, ricotta, spinach, basil leaves and milk. Process for 3 to 5 seconds until leaves are pesto-like but not puréed. Cook pasta according to package directions. Toss with nutty pesto over low heat until desired consistency. More milk can be added for creamier texture. Add additional milk 1 tablespoon at a time. Can be refrigerated and reheated in microwave when ready to serve. Serve hot. Makes 6 to 8 servings.

Menu Suggestion:
Alfresco Dinner

Ricotta Cheese Ball,

Madeira Shrimp,

Fresh Fruit Salad,

Bloody Mary Aspic with Dressing,

Stuffed Pizza Bread,

Amaretto Cheesecake,
Whipped Cream,

Hazlenut Coffee,
Liqueurs

Wine Suggestion:

Barbera

♦

Menu Suggestion:

Celebrating A Promotion

*Mixed Field Greens with
Peppercorn Dressing,*

Spinach Congealed Mold,

*Fresh Fruit Salad with Nanny's
Fruit Salad Dressing,*

Artichoke Tarts,

Liqueured Chocolate Mousse

Wine Suggestion:

Dolcetto D'Alba

Pasta Shapes:

*Farfalle - Butterflies,
Penne - Tubular shapes, cut
diagonally on ends,
Conchiglie - Shells,
Ditalini - Short Tubes,
Fusilli - Corkscrews,
Orecheitte - small curved disks,
Radiatori - deep ridged accordions,
Rigatoni - large, ridged pasta,
Perciatelli - hollow thick spaghetti,
Pastini - very tiny pasta,
Rotelle - fat spirals or wheels,
Ziti - smooth narrow tubular.*

MEATLESS BOLOGNESE

1 onion, peeled and chopped
1 carrot, peeled and chopped
1 celery stalk, peeled and chopped
1 clove garlic, crushed
1 1/2 teaspoons oil
2 tablespoons Italian parsley, chopped
1 bay leaf
1/2 teaspoon salt
1/2 teaspoon chicken granules or
    1 bouillon or vegetable cube
1/4 cup red wine
1 (14 1/2-ounce) can diced tomatoes
1 (15-ounce) can tomato sauce
2 tomatoes, seeded and chopped
8 ounces pasta, cooked according to package directions

In a large skillet or pot, combine onion, carrot, celery, garlic and oil. Cook for 3 minutes over medium heat. Add parsley, bay leaf, salt, chicken granules, wine, tomatoes and tomato sauce. Simmer for 8 to 10 minutes over medium heat, covered. Stir occasionally. Can be refrigerated covered at this point for up to 2 days and reheated on stove. Before serving, remove bay leaf and add fresh tomatoes. Serve hot over pasta. Makes 4 to 6 servings.

ALMA'S MACARONI AND CHEESE CASSEROLE

A family recipe collection from my client, Dianne Matthews, Marietta

2 cups elbow macaroni
1 stick margarine, 1/2 cup
2 eggs
2 cups milk
12 ounces medium or sharp Cheddar cheese, grated

Cook macaroni according to package instructions, until tender. Drain, transfer to a bowl and salt to taste. Add margarine while noodles are hot and mix. Add beaten eggs to milk and add to macaroni. Stir in grated cheese. Pour into a 2-quart casserole dish. Preheat oven to 350 degrees and cook uncovered for 30 minutes or until it starts bubbling around the edges and is slightly brown. (It will still appear to have too much liquid, but will settle as it cools.) Makes 4 to 6 servings.

VEGETABLE AND CHEESE ENCHILADAS

8 (6-inch) corn tortillas
1 medium zucchini, grated
1 carrot, grated
3/4 cup Monterey Jack cheese, grated
1 cup cooked rice
1/3 cup sour cream
1/4 teaspoon salt
1/2 teaspoon oil, any kind
1/8 cup onion, chopped
1 jalapeno pepper, seeded and chopped
1 (10-ounce) can Cheddar cheese soup or nacho cheese
1/2 soup can of milk
1 cup Monterey Jack cheese, grated
2 tomatoes, seeded and chopped

Prepare corn tortillas by placing 3 tortillas at a time in a sealed bag. Microwave on high for 1 to 1 1/2 minutes. This will keep them from breakage when ready to roll, however, they need to be hot to keep from breaking when rolling. In a bowl, combine zucchini, carrot, 3/4 cup cheese, rice, sour cream and salt. In a medium skillet, combine oil, onion and pepper and cook for 5 minutes. Add to rice mixture. Fill each tortilla with 1/4 to 1/3 cup rice mixture. Roll up and place in a greased 9 x 13 baking dish. In a separate bowl, mix together soup and milk. Pour over tortillas. Sprinkle with cheese and then tomatoes. Bake covered in a 350-degree oven for 35 to 45 minutes. Flour tortilla can be substituted. Serve warm. Makes 4 to 6 servings.

Alma Scott, Dianne Matthews "Mom" since 1967, takes this Macaroni and Cheese Casserole to their family reunion every year. People stand in line to get a serving and there's never a spoonful left. She has shared her recipe with Dianne and it has become one of her family favorites.

Take a break from packaged macaroni and cheese and treat your family to an easy, wholesome dish made from scratch.

Menu Suggestion:
A Fun Business Gathering

Tortilla Chips with Salsa and Cilantro Corn Dip,

(Charcoal Marinated Chicken Breasts,)

Spinach Salad,

Sliced Honeydew, Cantaloupe, Strawberries and Watermelon,

Cheese Stuffed Rolls,

Banana Pudding

Wine Suggestion:

Muscadet

Menu Suggestion:

Sunset Dinner

Shrimp with Orange Dill Sauce,

(Rum Marinated Jerk Chicken),

Sunflower Salad,

Sweet and Easy Corn Pudding,

Tropical Fruit Salad,

Ham and Cheese Puff,

*Creamy Lemon Custard
over Angel Food Cake with
Fresh Strawberries*

Wine Suggestion:

White Macon Village

Tip of the Trade:

*Pasta should be cooked until
al dente, or firm to the bite.
Usually, dried pasta will take
10 to 12 minutes in a boiling pot
of salted water.*

BLACK BEAN PASTA

A recipe from the collection of my friend, Melissa Robertson Worley

8 ounces pasta
2 tablespoons olive oil
2 cloves garlic, peeled and crushed or minced
1/2 cup sweet or yellow onion, chopped
1 small bell pepper, any color, seeded and chopped
1/2 cup button mushrooms, sliced
1 (15-ounce) can black beans, rinsed and drained
1 pound Roma tomatos, chopped
2 teaspoons dried basil or 1 1/2 tablespoons fresh snipped
1/4 teaspoon ground pepper
1/3 cup fresh chopped parsley, or 1 tablespoon dried
1/4 cup fresh Parmesan, grated

Cook pasta according to package directions, drain and rinse with cold water. Drain again and set aside. In a large skillet, place oil with garlic, onion and bell pepper. Cook for 3 to 5 minutes. Add mushrooms, black beans, tomatoes, basil and pepper. Heat for 3 to 5 minutes. Add parsley. Heat pasta in a microwave or with hot tap water in the colander. Place on platter, plate or serving dish. Place vegetables over and sprinkle with Parmesan cheese. (One dinner serving contains 480 calories and 10 grams of fat.) Makes 4 dinner servings and 6 side-dish servings.

Tip of the Trade:

When picking a pasta for a dish, try to match the size and cut of ingredients to the pasta. Use vegetables such as asparagus, carrots, julienned squashes with tubular pastas, with spaghetti, linguini or fettuccine use small chopped or shredded ingredients or sauces to get a taste with every bite and with short tubular pastas, chop the ingredients the same size.

Sweet Celebrations
Cookies, Cakes, Pies and Desserts

Anne Mullins Rigdon

*Overbaking cookies is the most
common problem. Set the timer as
soon as you place the cookies
in the oven. Do not worry if the
cookies look a little
dough-like in the middle.
It will continue cooking after
removing from oven and firm up
with cooling. Have the oven
temperature very well preheated
before baking.*

*Baking sheets should
be flat, strong and
heavy weight. Most importantly,
they should be light in color. Dark
sheets will cause too much
browning on the bottom of the
cookie. Greased aluminum foil,
waxed paper or greased parchment
paper will keep this from
happening if a light colored
pan is not available in your kitchen
inventory. Having two sheets will
allow the cook to prepare one
as the other pan is cooking,
making preparation a little
quicker.*

For Storing:

*Cookies can be frozen for 4 to 6
months. They must be wrapped
and sealed very well and stored in
a sturdy container to prevent
breakage.*

CUT OUT COOKIES

1 cup sugar
1 cup brown sugar or regular sugar
1/2 cup butter or margarine, room temperature
1/2 cup shortening, regular or butter flavored
2 eggs
3 1/2 cups plain all-purpose flour
1/2 teaspoon salt
1/4 teaspoon baking powder
1/4 teaspoon baking soda
1 teaspoon vanilla extract

In a mixer fitted with a metal whip, combine sugar, brown sugar, butter and shortening. Mix well on high until very smooth and lighter in color, about 2 to 3 minutes. Bring speed to low and add eggs one at a time. Measure out flour, salt, powder and soda and add slowly while mixing on low. Bring speed up gradually and add vanilla. Refrigerate for 1 to 24 hours covered. Roll out on a lightly floured surface to 1/4-inch thickness and cut out desired shapes. Sturdy cookie cutters can be used which need to be dipped in flour before each cut. Place cookies on greased baking sheet. Cook 5 to 9 minutes at 350 degrees. Use a spatula to remove from pan when still a little warm. Colored icing can be applied after cooling. Coloring to the cookie dough should be done after adding last ingredient one drop full at a time while mixing. Sprinkles can be added after cutting out and before cooking. Makes 36 small and 24 large cookies.

POUND CAKE COOKIES

A recipe from the collection of Mrs. Jane Smith, Marietta

1 pound butter, no substitutions
2 cups sugar
4 egg yolks, beaten
5 cups plain all-purpose flour
2 teaspoons vanilla extract

In a mixer fitted with a metal whip, cream together butter and sugar until light in color. Add yolks slowly. Lower speed of mixer and add flour. Roll into 1 1/2-inch diameter cylinders on waxed paper. Wrap in plastic wrap and place in refrigerator overnight or for 8 hours. Slice into rounds and place on greased baking sheets. Bake in a 375-degree oven for 10 to 15 minutes. Edges should be slightly browned, however middle will still look slightly dough-like. Store with waxed paper between layers. Makes 36 cookies.

Serving Tip:

To have children decorate cookies: Have cookie dough made or have entire cookie baked for small ones, (3 or under). Colored icings can be placed in foam egg cartons and tiny paint brushes can be used to paint top of cookies. Sprinkles and candies will then stick to top.

CRESCENT COOKIES

3/4 cup margarine, no substitutions
4 tablespoons confectioners powdered sugar
2 cups plain all-purpose flour
2 teaspoons water
1 teaspoon vanilla extract
1 cup pecans or walnuts, finely chopped or crushed
Powdered sugar

Butter does not work as well in this recipe. Cream margarine and sugar together in a mixer fitted with a metal whip. Add flour, water and vanilla and mix well. Add nuts and mix through. With clean hands, pinch off a little of the dough and roll between palms, making ends to a point. Curve into a moon shape and place on a greased baking sheet. Bake for 10 to 12 minutes at 350 degrees. Remove from oven and immediately roll in powdered sugar. A beautiful tea cookie. Also known as wedding cookies, and can be shaped into nuggets if not crescents. Makes 3 to 4 dozen.

Tip of the Trade:

Other extracts can be added to Pound Cake Cookies for unique flavors. Lemon and almond work well. If using lemon extract, a little lemon or orange peel, grated, also can be added, about 1 teaspoon.

Compensate for your oven. They all can't be perfect. If baking is uneven, simply rotate pans while baking. Set the cooking timer for a halfway point to help you remember.

Cookies easily can be taken off the pan with a metal spatula by scraping along the pan. Loosen the cookies from the pan while they are still warm. If they cool and have stuck to the pan, warm back in the oven a little until they can be loosened without breaking.

Crescent Cookies are perfect to serve to children, especially a little girl's tea. The powdered sugar on their little faces and tea dresses go hand in hand. They look beautiful in a silver basket on a wedding table too.

Chinese Chews are not a dainty pick-up dessert. They are more cake or brownie-like and can be eaten with a fork.

CHINESE CHEWS

A recipe from the collection of my husband's grandmother,
Mrs. Marie Barnes Rambo

1/2 cup butter or margarine
2 cups light brown sugar
2 eggs, beaten
1 cup plain all-purpose flour
1 teaspoon baking powder
1 teaspoon vanilla
1 cup nuts, chopped

In a mixer fitted with a metal blade, combine, butter and sugar and whip until light in color. Add eggs and beat well. Add flour, baking powder, and vanilla and mix well. Add nuts and stir through. (Grandmother Rambo would beat completely by hand in her day.) Place in a greased 9 x 9 baking pan and bake in a 350-degree oven for 35 to 45 minutes. The cookies in the middle of the pan will still be a little unfirm. They will rise during cooking and fall during cooling. Let stand until completely cool, cut in squares and serve with a whipped topping or by themselves as a finger dessert. Makes 16 to 24 thick squares.

TINY CHOCOLATE ÉCLAIRS

1 recipe Pâte Choux Puffs, (page 59)
1 recipe Whipped Cream, (page 227)
2 tablespoons instant vanilla pudding
8 ounces semi sweet chocolate bars
1/2 cup pecans, chopped
1/2 cup coconut, grated

Prepare Pâte a Choux Puffs and freeze, if needed. Actual eclairs need to be prepared 24 hours before serving. When ready to fill eclairs, whip cream according to Whipped Cream recipe, adding 2 tablespoons instant vanilla pudding during beating. Place whipped cream in a cookie press fitted with a long, thin pastry tube attachment. Puncture the bottom of the choux puff with this attachment and gently fill whipped cream into each one. Be careful of not applying too much pressure and move cookie press from side to side when filling to assure properly filled pastry. Place on a lined cookie sheet or platter. Melt chocolate in top of double boiler slowly and dip the top of each pâte choux puff into chocolate and then immediately into either pecans or coconut. Refrigerate éclairs, covered, until ready to serve. A delectable treat. Wonderful for teas or coffees. Makes 36 éclairs

This no bake treat is beautiful, easy and freezes wonderfully. A perfect tea finger food. Good served with other treats on a dessert tray.

ORANGE BALLS

12 ounces graham crackers
1 cup walnuts
1 (16-ounce) package confectioners powdered sugar
1 (6-ounce) can frozen orange juice concentrate
1/2 cup butter or margarine, room temperature
1 cup coconut, grated for rolling
1 cup walnut, finely chopped for rolling

Place 10 graham crackers at a time into a food processor fitted with a metal blade and grind. Place in a mixer when complete. Place 1 cup walnuts in a food processor and grind and add to cracker crumbs. Add powdered sugar, orange juice concentrate and butter into mixer and blend all ingredients. Roll into 1/2- to 3/4-inch balls and roll in either coconut or walnuts. Refrigerate until ready to serve. These freeze nicely and serve beautifully. Makes 36 to 48 pieces.

◆

Tip of the Trade:

The botanical name for chocolate is Theobroma cacao, which means, "food for the Gods."

The cocoa tree grows pods containing a pulpy fruit embedded with beans. They are fermented for a week, roasted, hulled and ground. The heart of the bean contains 54 percent cocoa butter. The butter fat is removed with a grinding process invented in the 1800s. Another process brings to us the rich and familiar chocolate color making the powder ready for baking and confection.

For Storing:

Chocolate can be stored, tightly wrapped in a cool, dry place for 6 to 9 months. If the chocolate has been badly stored, it will form grayish sugar crystals on the surface. Chocolate can still be used if this has happened. The texture and flavor will be affected only slightly.

Cocoa powder can be stored in a cool, dark place for up to 2 years. If in a panic, 1 tablespoon melted butter, margarine or oil mixed with 3 tablespoons unsweetened cocoa powder will equal 1 ounce unsweetened chocolate

CARAMEL TOFFEE BROWNIES

1 (16-ounce) box light brown sugar
3/4 cup margarine
3 eggs
1 3/4 cups all-purpose flour
1 teaspoon baking powder
1/2 teaspoon salt
1 teaspoon vanilla
1 1/2 cups milk chocolate toffee bits

In a mixer fitted with a metal whip, cream sugar and margarine. Add eggs one at a time. Add flour, baking powder and salt. Add vanilla and 1/2 of the toffee bits. Pour into a greased 9 x 13 pan and sprinkle remaining toffee bits over mixture. Bake at 325 degrees for 30 to 35 minutes. Cool to room temperature before cutting into squares or cutting out with desired cookie cutter. Chocolate chips can be used in place of toffee bits and nuts can be added, if desired. Makes 4 to 5 dozen.

CHOCOLATE CARAMEL SQUARES

3/4 cup all-purpose flour
3/4 cup quick oats, uncooked
3/4 cup brown sugar
6 tablespoons margarine or butter, room temperature
1/4 teaspoon soda
Dash salt
6 ounces semi sweet chocolate chips
1/2 cup pecans, chopped or macadamias
1/4 cup cream
7 ounces caramels

◆

In a food processor fitted with a metal blade, combine flour, oats, brown sugar, margarine, soda and salt and process until mixed. In a greased 9 x 9 pan, place 2/3 of the dough mixture and press evenly. Sprinkle 1/2 the chocolate chips over this and then 1/4 cup pecans. In a microwave-safe dish or over low heat on stove, melt the cream and caramels together. Pour over crust. Sprinkle remaining oat mixture, remaining chocolate chips and remaining pecans over caramel and place in a 350-degree oven for 20 to 35 minutes. Cool to room temperature before cutting. Makes 2 to 2 1/2 dozen.

PEANUT BUTTER CHOCOLATE BARS

2 cups dried oats
1/2 cup light brown sugar
1/8 cup light corn syrup
6 tablespoons margarine or butter, room temperature
1/8 cup peanut butter
6 ounces chocolate chips
1/2 cup peanut butter
1/3 cup peanuts

In a mixer fitted with a metal whip or a food processor fitted with plastic blade, combine oats, brown sugar, corn syrup, butter and 1/8 cup peanut butter. Spread and press into a greased 9 x 9 pan and bake at 350 degrees for 15 to 20 minutes. While cooking, mix together chocolate chips and remaining peanut butter. Remove pan from oven after cooking and immediately drop peanut chocolate mixtures by tiny spoonfuls over all cookie. Let melt for 3 to 5 minutes and spread gently to swirl and cover. Peanuts can be crushed or not. Sprinkle over chocolate when still warm. Pressing gently in with a spatula while cooling might be necessary to assure peanuts are intact. Slice into squares when cooled. Leaving the peanuts whole when serving an assortment of desserts will let the peanut lovers know which one to pick. If doubling the recipe, bake in two 9 x 9 pans. Makes 2 to 3 dozen.

Tip of the Trade:

Substitute peanuts or Macadamias for pecans or white chocolate chips for chocolate chips in Chocolate Caramel Squares.

When measuring out corn syrup in Peanut Butter Chocolate Bars, oil the measuring cup first for easy removal. This works with honey or syrup too.

Tip of the Trade:

When cutting pans of bar cookies, use a thin sharp knife. Wet the knife in warm water before slicing and wipe clean between each cut. The cookie bar should be room temperature for best results. Use a small, thin metal spatula to remove bars from pan. Picking up two to four at a time and then separating works best. Always remove the treats from the pan far in advance. This will help with time and mess when preparing serving trays.

All bar cookies can be stored tightly sealed in freezer or refrigerator. Treats are easily placed on serving trays while frozen. They will thaw, single layer, in about 10 minutes. Garnish trays with a small bunch of grapes, strawberries or a tiny bouquet of fresh flowers.

SHORTBREAD

A recipe from the collection of my friend, Nancy Denton, Kennesaw

2 sticks margarine, room temperature
2 1/2 cups plain all-purpose flour
3/4 cup sugar
Confectioners powdered sugar

In a food processor fitted with a metal blade, combine margarine, flour and sugar and process until dough forms. Grease a lipped baking sheet or 9 x 13 pan for thicker shortbread and press dough evenly into desired pan. Place in a 350-degree oven and bake for 15 to 25 minutes. Dough should be slightly brown along edges. Sprinkle with powdered sugar out of a sifter immediately after cooking. Cutting is necessary immediately after removing from oven. A pizza cutter works well with knife finishing edges or cookie cutter for desired shapes. Cool before removing cut shortbread from pan. Makes 3 to 4 dozen.

Variations to 1234 Cake:

Add 1/4 cup favorite liqueur to milk and vanilla.
Add up to 4 teaspoons of your favorite extracts to milk in addition to vanilla.

1234 CAKE

A Pound Cake Recipe

1 cup butter or margarine, room temperature
2 cups sugar
4 eggs
3 cups plain all-purpose flour
1 teaspoon baking powder
1/2 teaspoon salt
1 cup milk
1 teaspoon vanilla

In a mixer fitted with a metal whip, combine butter and sugar and whip until light in color and creamy. Add eggs one at a time while mixing and mix between each one. Combine flour, baking powder and salt. Combine milk and vanilla. Lower the speed of the mixer. Alternate adding flour and milk a little at a time. Start with flour and end with flour. Greasing and flouring of pan is absolutely necessary before baking. The only exception to this rule is if using cupcake pans and liners where only greasing is necessary for easy peeling. Tubed pound cake and Bundt pans bake at 350 degrees for 60 to 80 minutes. Three- or two-layer cakes bake at 350 degrees for 25 to 35 minutes and cupcakes bake at 350 degrees for 15 to 20 minutes. (Makes 24 cupcakes.) Stick a knife in the middle of cake and if it comes out clean, cake is done. This is the most basic pound cake recipe. Cool at least 10 minutes, loosen edges with a knife and then remove from pan.

CREAM CHEESE POUND CAKE

A family recipe from the collection of Mrs. Elizabeth Elrod, Marietta

3 sticks butter, no substitutions, room temperature
3 cups sugar
1 (8-ounce) package cream cheese, room temperature
6 eggs
3 cups plain all-purpose flour, sifted 3 times
1/4 teaspoon salt
1 1/2 teaspoons vanilla

Cut parchment or waxed paper for bottom of large 10-inch tube cake pan. Grease pan and paper with butter and sprinkle with a little sugar. In a mixer fitted with a metal whip or with a hand mixer, cream butter and sugar. Cut cream cheese into six equal portions. Add eggs one at a time with a portion of cream cheese, beating well between each addition. Add flour, salt and vanilla and finish beating. Pour into prepared pan and bake at 325 degrees for 90 minutes.

Tip of the Trade:

Before Teflon was made available on most cooking and baking pans, other methods were used to keep food from sticking. For tubed cake pans, a piece of waxed paper was cut for the very bottom of pan and then greased and floured with the sides. This helps with the top and corners not sticking and coming apart. It is not a bad idea even with Teflon pans. When cutting out, cut several at a time so that there are extras to have easily for the next time you bake.

If you are making cupcakes and have one place empty, fill it halfway with water so that your pan will be better preserved.

For Storing:

After cleaning pans, place paper towels in bottom of the pan so that a drop of water will not cause rusting during storage.

Tip of the Trade:

Before icing or frosting a cake, brush cake of all crumbs. The cake should be cold or room temperature. Most usually placed top side up and pan side down on a level surface. Cake can be placed on the stand, or on a piece of cardboard for easy transporting. Working from the top edges to the sides, start icing the cake. Remaining icing can be placed on top and leave in swirls, if desired. If a smooth texture is wanted, the decorating blade can be dipped in water to obtain the smoothness desired.

Tip of the Trade:

When baking any cake, the oven rack needs to be in the center of the oven. When baking a layered cake, be sure that the pans are set at least 2 inches apart on the oven rack to ensure the heat can circulate between the pans. If using two racks, do not sit one pan directly above the other. If oven cooks unevenly, wait at least 15 minutes before opening the oven door to change or turn pans around to keep the cake from falling.

BUTTER CREAM DECORATORS ICING

4 cups confectioners powdered sugar
1/2 cup shortening
1/3 cup water
1/8 teaspoon salt
1 teaspoon extract, any flavor
Food coloring paste, if desired

In a mixer fitted with a metal whip, combine confectioners sugar, shortening, water, salt and extract. Mix well. Add color, if desired. The coloring that can be bought from most cake decorating supply stores that comes in paste form works well with this icing. Ice cakes, cupcakes bakery style. Having the cake chilled before icing will help to set the icing. Keep cake crumbs away from icing by keeping knife on icing at all times while smoothing out. Most techniques call for a thin base layer of icing before applying the outer layer. Move from top edges of cake to sides. Use wet decorating blade or flat knife to smooth out icing immediately. Icing will harden on cake as it sits, so icing must be done at once. Wonderful fitted through decorator pastry tubes with tips for decorating. Cake decorating books can help with techniques. Will need two recipes for a three-layer cake.

CHOCOLATE LAYER CAKE

1 cup sugar
2 cups plain all-purpose flour
2 teaspoons baking soda
1/2 teaspoon salt
4 tablespoons unsweetened cocoa powder
1 cup cold water
1 cup mayonnaise, real, not low-fat
3 tablespoons blackberry jam or other dark jam or jelly
1 teaspoon vanilla extract

Mix all dry ingredients together in a mixer fitted with a metal whip. Turn mixer off, add all other ingredients and again mix well. Pour into greased and floured three-layer pans. Drop a couple of times on counter to remove bubbles. Bake in a 350-degree oven for 20 to 25 minutes. Knife inserted into middle of cake should come out clean. Cool to room temperature before removing from pan. Ice with desired icing. Seven minute icing or chocolate frosting both work well. Makes delicious cupcakes. (Bake cupcakes at 350 degrees for 8 to 10 minutes.) When serving, keep the ingredients to yourself until after the guests have been dazzled.

CHOCOLATE POUND CAKE

*A recipe from the collection of Mrs. Elizabeth Elrod, Marietta,
from the family recipes of Mrs. Jane McDowell Snipes*

1 cup butter or margarine, room temperature
1/2 cup shortening
3 cups sugar
5 eggs
3 cups plain all-purpose flour
1/2 teaspoon baking powder
1/4 teaspoon salt
3/4 cup unsweetened powdered cocoa
1 1/4 cups whole milk
1 teaspoon vanilla

In a mixer fitted with a metal whip, combine butter, shortening and sugar and cream until whipped and light in color. Add eggs one at a time while beating or beat between each one. Mix together flour, baking powder, salt and cocoa. Mix together milk and vanilla. Lower the speed of the mixer. Add alternately in small amounts the flour and milk to the batter while mixing starting with flour and ending with flour. Pour into a greased and floured 9- to 10-inch tube pound cake pan. Bake for 45 to 55 minutes at 350 degrees. A knife inserted in the middle should be clean when removed to ensure complete cooking.

Serving Tip:

Beautiful ribbon is available at decorating stores, craft stores and specialty gift stores. It is always beautiful garnishing any food.

At times with catering a special function, such as a Christening or Wedding Party, a ribbon was actually hot glued in a scallop around the cut glass cake stand. The hot glue simply peels off during washing. Often the same ribbon would be wrapped around the cake right on the frosting.

To continue on the theme, a loose bow on the punch bowl, the corsage, the gift, the invitation, the front door wreath can also be simply and tastefully done.

Tip of the Trade:

When adding eggs to the creamed butter and sugar, do not worry if the mixture looks curdled. When the flour is added, it will correct the problem.

◆

Tip of the Trade:

When icing a layered cake, dollop a little icing on a level surface to keep the cake in place, The surface can be the cake platter or a piece of cardboard the same size of the cake round. Place the cake top side down and pan side up for best evenness. Ice just on the top of the first layer, keeping in mind the levelness needed for the second layer. When stacked, ice the sides from the top edges and then the top. Swirls can be made or the cake knife can be dipped in water for a smooth texture.

Tip of the Trade:

Coconut Cakes are for holidays like Easter, Thanksgiving, and Christmas. They are for extra special occasions. This recipe is perfect and will please anyone with whom you choose to honor. Decorate with a few pastel colored fresh flowers for the spring or holly sprigs around winter holidays. They should be placed at the front and bottom rim of cake.

COCONUT CAKE

1/2 cup butter or margarine, room temperature
1/2 cup shortening
1 (8-ounce) package cream cheese, room temperature
3 cups sugar
6 eggs, separated
3 cups plain all-purpose flour
1/4 teaspoon baking soda
1/4 teaspoon salt
3/4 cup buttermilk
2/3 cup flaked coconut
1 teaspoon vanilla
1 teaspoon coconut flavoring or other extract
1/8 teaspoon cream of tartar

In a mixer fitted with a metal whip, cream butter, shortening, cream cheese and sugar. Add egg yolks one at a time or beat after adding each yolk. Combine flour, soda and salt. Lower the speed of the mixer. Add alternately and slowly to mixer the flour mixture and buttermilk, starting with flour and ending with flour. Add coconut, vanilla and coconut flavoring. Beat egg whites with cream of tartar until stiff but not dry. Fold into batter. Pour batter into three greased and floured 9-inch-layer cake pans. Bake at 325 degrees for 18 to 25 minutes. Knife inserted into center should come out clean. Cool 15 minutes at room temperature before removing from pan. Frost with Pecan Frosting.

PECAN FROSTING

1 (4-ounce) package cream cheese, room temperature
1/2 cup butter or margarine, room temperature
1 (32-ounce) package confectioners powdered sugar
1 teaspoon lemon juice or vanilla
1 cup coconut
1/2 cup chopped pecans

◆

Beat together cream cheese, butter, powdered sugar and lemon juice in a mixer fitted with a metal whip. Set aside 1/8 cup pecans and 1/3 cup coconut. Add the remaining coconut and pecans to frosting. Ice between the layers, on the top and sides of cake. Press remaining coconut to sides of cake and sprinkle remaining pecans on top of cake.

"Take the Cake"

This old Southern saying came from a custom of the cake walk dance contests. These walk dances were sometimes the sole entertainment for gatherings around the South. The winner of the contest got to "Take the Cake."

FUDGE SUNDAE CAKE

A recipe from the collection of my mother, Mimi Howard

1 cup plain all-purpose flour
3/4 cup sugar
2 tablespoons powdered unsweetened cocoa
2 teaspoons baking powder
1/4 teaspoon salt
1/2 cup milk
2 tablespoons oil
1 teaspoon vanilla
1 cup chopped nuts
1 cup brown sugar
1/4 cup powdered unsweetened cocoa
1 3/4 cup hot tap water

In an ungreased square 9 x 9 x 2 pan, stir together flour, sugar, 2 tablespoons cocoa, baking powder and salt. Mix in milk, oil and vanilla. Mix until smooth. Stir in nuts. Spread evenly over pan. Sprinkle cake evenly with 1 cup brown sugar and 1/4 cup unsweetened cocoa and do not mix in. Pour hot water over and again, do not mix in. Place in a 350-degree oven and cook for 30 to 40 minutes until edges are slightly removed from edge of pan and knife inserted into middle comes out clean. Serve warm. A wonderful cake for children to make on their own. Makes 18 to 24 servings.

Variations to Hot Fudge Sundae Cake

- Hot Fudge Marshmallow Sundae Cake by omitting nuts and adding 1 cup miniature marshmallows.
-Hot Fudge Coconut Sundae Cake by omitting nuts and adding 1/2 cup shredded coconut and 1/2 cup chopped almonds.
-Hot Fudge Butterscotch Sundae Cake by omitting nuts and adding 1 cup butterscotch morsels, decreasing brown sugar to 1/2 cup and 1/4 cup cocoa to 2 tablespoons at the end.
-Hot Fudge Raisin Sundae Cake by omitting nuts and adding 1 cup raisins.
-Hot Fudge Peanut Sundae Cake by omitting nuts and stirring in 1/2 cup peanut butter and 1/2 cup chopped peanuts.

Tip of the Trade:

The bottom of the Fudge Sundae Cake is like hot fudge sauce when served warm, right out of oven. If left to cool, it is still good and slices a little cleaner.

CAKE MIX CAKE

A recipe from the collection of my grandmother, Mary Jo Underwood Carpenter

1 (18.5-ounce) box yellow cake mix
3/4 cup vegetable or corn oil
4 eggs
1 cup white carbonated soda beverage, (lemon-lime)

Mix together cake mix with oil, eggs and soda and mix well by hand with a whisk or mixer fitted with a metal whip. Pour into three greased and floured 8- to 9-inch cake pans. Bake at 350 degrees for 10 to 15 minutes or until slightly browned and knife inserted into middle comes out clean. Cool 10 minutes before turning out of pans. The cola in the cake hides the cake mix taste. Fill with Lemon Pineapple Cake Filling and serve with a flower garnish.

LEMON PINEAPPLE CAKE FILLING

3/4 cup sugar
3 tablespoons cornstarch
1/4 teaspoon salt
3/4 cup water
1 tablespoon butter or margarine
2 tablespoons grated lemon rind
1/3 cup lemon juice
1 (20-ounce) can crushed pineapple, drained well

Combine sugar, corn starch and salt in a medium saucepan. Gradually stir in water and bring to a boil over direct heat. Boil for 1 minute and remove from heat. The cornstarch should have thickened the sauce in this time. Add butter, lemon rind and gradually stir in lemon juice. Drain the pineapple very well by pressing with lid or pressing through sieve or colander. Add pineapple to sauce. Chill for 30 minutes or more. The sauce will thicken a little. Place cake bottom side up and ice between each layer. Add icing to the top and gently smooth a little glaze over sides. The cake layers will still show through the icing. Most of the sauce will be between and on top of cake. If the glaze is put between the layers while the cake and sauce are a little warm, it soaks up in the cake, which is quite tasty. It is impossible, however, to ice the sides with it warm, so chilling will still need to be done before icing the sides. Wipe platter clean before garnishing with fresh yellow flowers. Makes 12 to 16 servings.

CHOCOLATE CHIP RUM CAKE

A recipe from the collection inspired by Frances Howard

1 (18.5-ounce) package devil's food cake mix
1 (3.9-ounce) package instant chocolate pudding
1 cup sour cream
1/2 cup cooking oil or vegetable oil
1/8 cup very strong liquid coffee or expresso
1/2 cup dark rum
4 eggs
2 cups chocolate chips

In a mixer fitted with a metal whip, combine devil's food cake, pudding, sour cream and oil. Add liquid coffee and rum to batter with eggs. Beat until smooth. Add chocolate chips and pour into a greased and floured Bundt cake pan. Bake at 325 degrees for 70 to 85 minutes. Loosen from pan with a knife and turn out onto cake platter after 20 to 30 minutes of cooling. Very rich. Can be served alone or with Raspberry Purée and Whipped Cream. Makes 12 to 16 servings.

Tip of the Trade:

When a recipe calls for a pan to be greased and floured, it can be done easily with a commercial baking cooking spray with the oil and flour contained in an aerosol. Traditionally it means that the pan must be oiled with shortening, which I use, butter or oil and then with flour. This is done easily by pouring about 1/4 cup of the same type flour that is used in the recipe in the pan and patting or jiggling until it is covered. The extra flour can be discarded. These two steps are very important in making cakes. As important as following the directions and measuring as closely as possible.

Tip of the Trade:

This rum cake has been known to stick to the pan at times. If this happens, scoop the cake from the pan and form back into a cake. It is moist enough to do this. Place another cake platter on top and invert again. The bottom is now the top. Garnish with fresh flowers around the bottom base. This cake is outstanding. Guests will be fighting over the last crumb.

Tip of the Trade:

The key ingredient to a good cake recipe is a cook's secret. People are usually not too stingy with their recipes, it's finding out the secret to the recipe that is the trick. In this carrot cake recipe, the secret is the 2 cups of grated carrots and the 2 cups of puréed carrots.

A cake should be cooled before trying to remove. When removing a cake from the pan, loosen the edges first with a dinner knife. The knife should be pressed against the pan, not the cake. Place a plate or platter on top of the cake and then invert. Jiggle slightly until the cake is felt dropping from the pan. Slowly remove the pan. If the cake is upside down, place the desired plate or platter on top of the cake and invert again.

Serving Tip:

This carrot cake looks especially beautiful baked in square cake pans. It gives any cake an unique look and can be found in most cooking supply stores. A flower garnish is really not needed for this cake.

MOIST CARROT CAKE

A recipe from the collection of my sister, Patricia Howard

4 eggs
1 1/2 cups vegetable oil
2 cups sugar
2 cups plain all-purpose flour
2 teaspoons baking soda
2 teaspoons baking powder
1 teaspoon salt
3 teaspoons ground cinnamon
2 cup carrots, grated
2 cup carrots, puréed
1 cup pecans, finely chopped
1 teaspoon vanilla

In a mixer fitted with a metal whip, combine eggs, oil and sugar and beat well. Measure out flour and then add soda, baking powder, salt and cinnamon. Sift flour mixture in a regular sifter. Add flour mixture to eggs. Mix well. Hand stir carrots and pecans into batter. Pour into three greased and floured 8- to 9-inch cake pans and bake in a 325-degree oven for 25 to 30 minutes. Knife inserted into center should come out clean. Cool for 10 minutes before loosening and turning out from pan. Cool to room temperature before icing with Nutty Cheese Icing. Chill cake covered in refrigerator until ready to use. Plastic wrap can be held off icing with toothpicks stuck out from the cake to prevent wrap from touching icing.

NUTTY CHEESE ICING

2 (8-ounce) packages cream cheese, room temperature
1 cup margarine or butter, room temperature
1 1/2 pounds confectioners powdered sugar
4 teaspoons vanilla
2 cups pecans, finely chopped

In a mixer fitted with a metal whip, cream all ingredients together. Chill icing before placing on cake that has been cooled to room temperature. Makes icing for a three-layer 8- to 9-inch cake.

Serving Tip:

Serve this sweet, breadlike apple cake with a cup of coffee or tea at morning gatherings. It would work perfectly to keep on the kitchen cake stand for out-of-town guests to nibble on, or for parents to enjoy at a playgroup. Grandmother served this cake at all times of the day, but at night it was served with a side of vanilla ice cream.

GRANDMOTHER'S APPLE CAKE

A recipe from the collection of my paternal grandmother, Mary Strayhorn Howard

1 1/4 cups vegetable oil
2 cups sugar
2 eggs
2 teaspoons vanilla
3 cups plain all-purpose flour
1 teaspoon baking soda
1 teaspoon salt
1/2 teaspoon baking powder
3 cups apples, peeled, cored and chopped
1 cup pecans, chopped

In a mixer fitted with a metal whip, combine oil, sugar, eggs and vanilla. Mix together flour, soda, salt and baking powder and add to mixer. Mix well with wet ingredients. Add apples and pecans and mix through. Grease and flour a Bundt pan and pour batter in pan. (Batter is very thick and almost dough-like.) Bake at 350 degrees for 80 to 90 minutes.

Tip of the Trade:

There are more than 900 varieties of apples. More than 100 million bushels are grown in America each year. It is a popular fruit because it is good raw, cooked or dried. Apples spread from Southwest Asia to Europe in the form of a crabapple, from which the apple as we know it was cultivated. Any baking variety will work well in this recipe. Grandmother probably used apples straight from her tree during season when she lived on her Georgia farm. Whether picking your own or purchasing from the store, Apple Cake is a good wholesome cake recipe.

The batter of the cake is very thick. This is not unusual for cakes that contain fruit or nuts. A thicker batter will keep the fruit or nuts from sinking to the bottom.

ANGEL FOOD CAKE WITH LEMON FILLING

*A recipe collection from my husband's grandmother,
Mrs. Marie Barnes Rambo*

1 angel food cake
6 egg yolks, reserve whites
3/4 cup sugar
3/4 cup lemon juice
Grated lemon rind, from 1 lemon

1 envelope unflavored gelatin, 2 teaspoons
1/4 cup water, cold
6 egg whites, beaten
3/4 cup sugar

Purchase an angel food cake and slice horizontally into three sections. Most store-bought angel food cakes are larger at top than bottom. Use the largest section on the bottom layer of the cake and place brown side down. In top of a double boiler or medium saucepan, combine egg yolks, sugar, lemon juice and rind from 1 lemon. Heat over medium heat in double boiler and low to medium heat if using a saucepan. Stir constantly until it thickens and remove immediately from stove and cool to room temperature. In a small separate saucepan or a microwave safe cup, combine gelatin with cold water to dissolve. Heat until bubbly on stove or microwave and place in a mixer fitted with a metal whip. Cool slightly. Add egg whites and sugar to mixer and beat until egg whites are white and stiff. Fold cooled lemon curd in to egg white by hand. If not stiff enough to stand up between layers, chill until partially set. Spread about 1/4-inch between layers of angel food cake. The top layer should be brown side on top and iced completely. Decorate with lemon peel curls or serve with a garnish of sliced lemon or fresh berries.

Tip of the Trade:

*Contrary to most legends,
it is not true that
chocolate is an
aphrodisiac. Some researchers
believe the chemical
phenylethylamine, or PEA,
could put the chocolate
consumer into a
state which
might be mistaken for
being in love. However,
other foods contain as much or
more of this chemical,
(like salami or Cheddar cheese)
and no one would confess the same
effects when eating these.
Possibly, it is the delicious
taste that just makes
you feel good.*

Serving Tip:

*I display this beautiful Decadence on a buffet, but serve it
on fixed plates to guests at their seats. Raspberry Purée
can be placed on the plate, a slice of decadence on purée,
whipped cream over the top and a chocolate mint leaf and
raspberry garnish for the finishing touch.*

MINT CHOCOLATE DECADENCE

13 ounces bittersweet chocolate squares
10 ounces minted chocolate chips
1 cup butter or margarine
1/4 cup sugar
2 tablespoons plain all-purpose flour
6 eggs

In a double boiler, saucepan or in microwave, melt the bittersweet chocolate, chocolate chips and butter over very low heat in a saucepan, medium heat in a double boiler or medium heat in 3-minute intervals in microwave. In top of a double boiler, combine sugar, flour and eggs. Using a hand-held blender or mixer, place egg mixture over medium heat. Beat eggs constantly until frothy. Another method would be to warm egg mixture in a double boiler while stirring and transferring to a mixer fitted with a metal blade and mixing until doubled in size. Doubling of size should occur while beating when heated. Fold egg mixture into melted chocolate mixture and pour into a greased 8-inch springform pan. Place in a 325-degree oven for 25 to 35 minutes. Remove from oven, cool to room temperature and store covered in refrigerator for up to 2 days or in freezer covered tightly for up to 1 month. Slice and serve with Raspberry Purée or Crème Anglaise with fresh raspberries or strawberries and Whipped Cream. Garnish with fresh mint leaves. Makes 12 servings.

Tip of the Trade:

*To decorate the top of the
decadence, place finely chopped
chocolate or chocolate chips into a
heavy ziplock bag. Place bag in
microwave on medium heat, (50
percent power), for 5 minutes.
Pierce or cut a tiny whole in the
corner of the bag and drizzle the
chocolate on top of the cake in a
zigzag design. White or dark
chocolate can be used. This can be
done after fixing on plates, or on
the entire cake.*

◆

*It is a European trait
to serve sauce on the
bottom of the dessert when being
served on a fixed dessert plate.
It can be fancy by swirling
chocolate with a toothpick with
Crème Anglaise or with
heavy cream with
Raspberry Purée. I never had
the patience, but perhaps
it is your cup of tea.
The sauce is beautiful
on the bottom unless
the dessert is a little
messy. Then it looks
good hiding any flaws.
Whipped cream placed on top can
also hide any imperfections.*

Tip of the Trade:
After Dinner Coffee

*Coffee with Liqueured Chocolate
Mousse will enhance this
wonderful dessert. Have a small
bottle or tiny pitcher of the liqueur
to splash in the coffee with the
cream and sugars. It is
appropriate to pass coffee already
poured or serve directly to guests
at their seats. Coffee or dessert can
be offered in another room for a
cozier or more comfortable setting.
This will give time for the table to
be cleared by staff, if available.*

LIQUEURED CHOCOLATE MOUSSE

2 cups graham cracker crumbs
1/2 cup butter or margarine, room temperature
6 ounces semi-sweet chocolate chips
4 teaspoons unflavored gelatin, 2 packages
1/4 cup cold water
1/2 cup favorite liqueur
1 pint half and half
4 eggs, separated
1/3 cup sugar
1 cup heavy whipping cream

In a food processor fitted with a metal blade, combine cracker crumbs and butter and process until mixed through. Press crumbs into a greased 8-inch springform pan. In a double boiler, place chocolate and melt over medium low heat. Dissolve gelatin in cold water and then add to chocolate while melting. When melted, add the liqueur and remove from heat. In a medium saucepan, place half and half over medium high heat until slightly warm. Combine egg yolks and sugar and add to half and half, stirring constantly, over medium heat. As mixture thickens, remove immediately from heat. (Frothy top should disappear and metal spoon should coat when dipped. Overcooking can result in curdling of custard.) Combine melted chocolate and custard and set aside. In a mixer fitted with a metal whip, place egg whites and whip until soft peaks form. Fold egg whites into cooled chocolate mixture. In same mixer fitted with the same whip, place whipped cream and mix until thickened to very soft peaks. Overwhipping cream can cause the cream to separate, so watch for thickening. Fold whipped cream into chocolate and place in prepared springform pan. Cover and refrigerate for 8 to 24 hours. Serve with Crème Anglais as a sauce. The crust can be omitted from this dish and it can be served out of parfaits for a simply elegant ending to a sit-down dinner or luncheon. Makes 12 to 16 servings.

◆

AMARETTO CHEESECAKE

Tip of the Trade:

2 cups graham cracker crumbs
1/4 cup pecans
3/4 stick butter or margarine, room temperature
4 (8-ounce) packages cream cheese, room temperature
1/2 cup sour cream
1 cup ricotta cheese
1/2 cup light brown sugar
1/2 cup sugar
2 tablespoons plain all-purpose flour
4 eggs
1/2 cup Amaretto liqueur
1/2 cup pecans, chopped well
2 cups sour cream
1/2 cup sugar
1 teaspoon vanilla extract
Pecan halves for garnishing

Liqueurs are so wonderful to have around with baking desserts. Amaretto is an almond flavored liqueur. If the alcohol content is a concern, the alcohol will cook out during baking. If wanting to substitute liqueurs for extracts, which is great economically, especially compared to pure extracts, use in the same amount listed for the extract in the list of ingredients.

In a food processor fitted with a metal blade, combine graham crackers, 1/4 cup pecans and butter and process well for 3 to 4 seconds. Press crust in the bottom of a greased 9- to 10-inch spring form pan. In a mixer fitted with a metal whip, combine cream cheese, sour cream, ricotta cheese, light brown sugar, sugar, and flour and cream well. Add eggs one at a time while mixing or mix between adding. Add Amaretto liqueur and pecans and mix through. Pour into crust and place in a 375-degree oven for 10 minutes and lower temperature to 300 degrees for remaining 60 to 70 minutes. Meanwhile, combine sour cream, sugar and vanilla. Pour on top of cheesecake the last 5 minutes of cooking just to set the top. Let cool to room temperature before placing covered in refrigerator. Can leave in cheesecake pan until ready to serve. Freezing works, but can cause crumbling. Can store in refrigerator for up to 4 days covered tightly. When serving, garnish with pecan halves and serve with whipped topping. Makes 10 to 12 servings.

With pure vanilla extract, there is really no substitute. It is worth the little extra cost. Vanilla was first tasted by the Europeans when Mexico was invaded by the Spanish in the 16th century. The vanilla plant is a type of orchid which has to be pollinated by hand or by a bee native to Mexico. The vine grows on large tree trunks and produces beans similar in design to a string bean. The vanillin, the flavor component of vanilla, is taken from the bean while still green, then dried and chopped. After filtering, the sweeteners are added and the pure vanilla extract is the end product. Vanilla flavor is natural, however, not as strong. Imitation vanilla is what its name suggests.

CRANBERRY CHEESECAKE

1 1/2 cups graham cracker crumbs
6 tablespoons butter or margarine, room temperature
3 (8-ounce) packages cream cheese, room temperature
1/2 cup sugar
3 eggs
1/4 cup ricotta cheese
1/4 cup sour cream
2 tablespoons plain all-purpose flour
4-ounce package fresh cranberries (dried can be used)
1/3 cup diced dried fruit
1 1/3 cups apple juice
1/4 cup brown sugar
3 tablespoons orange marmalade

In a food processor fitted with a metal blade, combine crumbs and butter and process to a meal-like texture. Press into a bottom of a greased 6- to 8-inch springform pan. In a mixer fitted with a metal whip, combine cream cheese and sugar. Add eggs one at a time and beat between each one. Add ricotta, sour cream and flour. Mix well. In a medium saucepan, combine cranberries, diced fruit, and apple juice. Cook for 8 to 12 minutes until cranberries are soft. Remove from heat and add marmalade. Pour 2/3 cranberry mixture into cheesecake and mix well. Leave remaining 1/3 for garnishing. Cranberry relish or chutney can be substituted for this cranberry mixture, if desired. Pour batter into prepared springform pan and cook at 325 degrees for 55 to 65 minutes until set. Cool before covering and refrigerate until ready to use. Freezing works well up to 1 month. Garnish with whipped cream and extra cranberry relish. Makes 8 to 10 servings.

Tip of the Trade:

Cranberries grow in the swamplands of Cape Cod and New Jersey. They are native to the United States and were used as dye, a preservative for meats, and to draw poisons out of wounds by the Indians.

The popularity of cranberries present day is booming. They are enjoyed fresh on the holidays, traditionally being served with turkey as a relish or side dish. They can be eaten dried as a snack, like raisins, and enjoyed as a juice.

Cranberry Relish:

2 cups fresh cranberries
2 granny smith apples, peeled, cored and diced
2 tablespoons preserves
1 cup brown sugar
1 teaspoon orange rind, grated
1/2 cup liqueur
1/2 cup pecans or walnuts, chopped
1/4 cup golden raisins

Heat first 6 ingredients together in a saucepan for 20 minutes over medium heat. Add nuts and raisins. Pour into sterilized jars and seal. Give a boiling water bath for 10 minutes or store in refrigerator until ready to serve.

Place your favorite cake, pie or cookie in a hat box or decorative box rather than a bakery box when giving gifts from your kitchen. Tie with beautiful ribbon or tulle. Use invitation cards or note cards to write or print the recipe to share.

CHEESECAKE ROGÉT

A recipe from the collection of Laurie Chilton Phillips

Crust:
6 tablespoons butter, melted
1 1/2 cups crushed graham crackers
1/4 cup sugar
1 tablespoon cinnamon
1/4 cup ground toasted almonds
Filling:
3 ounces heavy cream
7 ounces chocolate chips, melted
1 tablespoon Amaretto liqueur
1 pound 10 ounces cream cheese, room temperature
1 cup sugar
3 eggs, room temperature
1 egg yolk
1 tablespoon vanilla
1/4 cup plus 2 tablespoons Amaretto liqueur
1/2 cup heavy cream, lightly whipped

For crust, line the bottom of an 8-inch springform pan with foil. Put bottom of pan in place and tighten the springform. Press foil overlap up on the outside of pan. Process graham crackers, sugar, cinnamon and almonds. Pour melted butter and process until ingredients are combined. Press in bottom of springform pan (not sides). Preheat oven to 325 degrees. Bring cream to boil. Whisk into chocolate until smooth. Stir in tablespoon Amaretto. Set aside. Beat cream cheese until light and fluffy. Gradually add sugar while beating. Beat in eggs and yolk one at a time, beating well after each addition. Stir in Amaretto and vanilla. Fold in whipped cream. Pour 2/3 of this mixture into a separate bowl and set aside. Add chocolate mixture to the 1/3 of cream cheese mixture. Stir until completely blended. Pour this mixture into the bottom of prepared springform pan. Very carefully pour remaining 2/3 of the cream cheese mixture on top of chocolate cream cheese mixture in pan. Place in oven. Bake at 325 degrees for 15 minutes. Reduce temperature to 300 and bake 1 hour and 20 minutes. After baking time, turn oven off, open oven door, and leave ajar for 2 hours with cake in oven. Remove cake and set on cooling rack until completely cooled. Cover and refrigerate for 8 hours. Keep refrigerated until ready to serve.

Laurie, a native of Cobb County, Georgia, has graciously shared her Cheesecake Rogét recipe. In an effort to make Roger, her husband, the perfect cheesecake, this recipe was created for the 1989 US Chef's open. Rogét is the "European translation" of Roger and was used to impress the judges. The recipe was the gold medal winner.
As many know, her desserts are quite famous in our community. Once you have served this beautiful and rich cake, you will know why she has a reputation for fine desserts and chocolate confections.
Use her famous recipe for a very special occasion.

Tip of the Trade:

To remove the Cheesecake Rogét from pan, run a knife around the edge of pan to loosen. Remove side of springform pan. Lift up cake with the foil lining to separate cake from bottom of pan.

For an elegant presentation, pour chocolate glaze over top of cake, score into slices and top each slice with a Chocolate Truffle.

Basic Pie Dough:
Two 9- to 10-inch Crusts

2 cups all-purpose flour
1 teaspoon salt
1/3 cup shortening
1/3 cup chilled butter
5 tablespoons water

Sift then measure out flour and salt. Resift and place in food processor fitted with pastry blade. Pulsing processor, cut in shortening and then butter. Pulsing processor quickly, add water slowly by tablespoons and lightly blend until all ingredients are held together. When ball forms, stop. Keep chilled and covered until ready to roll. When rolling dough, roll to the size needed. Stretched dough will shrink during baking.

Tip of the Trade:

This Kentucky Pie tastes like a chocolate chip cookie in a pie shell. It is a dessert every age will enjoy, making it perfect for family gatherings.

The American Pie

Pies are a treat across America. They do not belong to just one region or area. There's a lot of competition among pie makers. This fact is shown through county and state fairs, where exhibitors of jams, preserves, pickles and pies compete for that cherished blue ribbon.
Even though the competition is strong between cooks, they usually are very giving with their treasures and their recipes. Bring your family home with a special homemade pie and share your secrets with others.

KENTUCKY PIE

A recipe from the collection of Linda Abel McDill, Gadsden, Alabama

1 (9-inch) prepared deep dish pie crust, uncooked
1/2 cup butter or margarine, melted
1 cup sugar
1/2 cup self-rising flour
2 eggs, slightly beaten
1 cup pecans, chopped
1 (6-ounce) package semi-sweet chocolate chips

Melt butter in microwave or on stove and let cool back to room temperature. In a mixer fitted with a metal whip or by hand, combine cooled butter and sugar and mix well. Add flour and eggs. Beat until creamy. By hand, fold in pecans and chocolate chips. Spread in uncooked pie shell and bake at 325 degrees for 50 to 60 minutes. Bake on a cookie sheet or on foil due to any bubbling over. Serve with a scoop of chocolate chip ice cream or whipped topping for a truly perfect dessert treat. Makes a beautiful tart by using a 2-inch-deep and 10-inch-wide tart pan greased and lined with a pie crust. Makes 6 to 8 servings.

FAMOUS CHOCOLATE PIE

A recipe from the collection of Jimmy Alexander, Marietta

1/2 cup butter or margarine
1 cup self-rising flour
1 cup nuts, chopped fine, walnuts or pecans
1 (8-ounce) package cream cheese
1 cup confectioners powdered sugar
1 teaspoon vanilla
1 cup whipped topping
2 (3.9-ounce) packages instant chocolate pudding
3 cups whole milk
1 teaspoon vanilla

In a food processor fitted with a metal blade or in a mixer fitted with a pastry whip, combine butter, self-rising flour and nuts. (If using a food processor fitted with metal blade, nuts need not be chopped. They will be chopped during processing.) Dough can be pressed right into 9-inch pie plate. Patch where needed and scallop edges with fingers. Bake for 20 to 25 minutes at 350 degrees. In a food processor fitted with a plastic or metal blade or a mixer fitted with a metal blade, combine cream cheese, powdered sugar, vanilla and whipped topping and cream well. After pie crust has cooled to room temperature, pour in cream cheese mixture. In a mixer fitted with a metal whip or by hand with a bowl or whisk, combine pudding, milk and vanilla and beat until thick. Pour over cream cheese filling. Top with extra whipped topping. Chill until ready to serve. If storing for a day, leave off whipped topping so pie can be covered with plastic wrap in refrigerator. When ready to serve, add extra whipped cream. This pie is very gooey and might work better on buffet rather than a fixed plate dessert. Makes 6 to 8 servings.

> *It has been said that good pie makers must have warm hearts because they rarely cook for themselves and cold hands because crusts must be kept chilled at all times while preparing.*

Tip of the Trade:

When making the crust for the Famous Chocolate Pie, the amount of oil in the nuts affects the outcome of the crust. Pecans and Walnuts contain the most oil and will make the crust less crumbly. Almonds are tasty with the pie, however, contain less oil, making the crust a little crumbly. The crust will work with either nut and any variety is fine. The crust is pressed rather than having to roll out, which helps in preparation.

Use 2 packages of pudding as directed rather than 1 large package. The ounces may vary and cause pie to be runny.

◆

To roll out a pastry successfully, lightly flour the surface and the rolling pin. Dough should be in a ball. Flatten a bit with the rolling pin and roll lightly from the center out to the edge. The rolling pin should be lifted as it nears the edge. The circle should reach 1-inch past the pie plate. The pastry should never be more than 1/8-inch thick. The pastry can be rolled up onto the rolling pin, lifting over the center of the pie plate and unroll. Loosely fit the pastry into the pan. Edges then can be scalloped with fingers, keeping very uniform. The right index finger should be placed on the inside rim of the pastry, with left index finger and thumb on the outside. Press together, working around the rim to form the scallop or flute. If baking before filling, the crust needs to be pricked twice to keep from rising. The crust also can be lined with waxed paper or aluminum foil, filled with dried beans and baked to keep crust from puffing. Also, the top crust needs to be pricked if the pie has the second crust. If a second crust is used, the scalloped edge should be done with both crusts together by gently pressing them over edge and fluting them with fingers as above.

BUTTERMILK PIE

1 3/4 cups sugar
1/2 cup butter or margarine, room temperature
1/4 cup plain all-purpose flour
2 eggs
1 cup buttermilk
1 teaspoon vanilla or lemon extract
1/4 teaspoon nutmeg
1 (9-inch) pie shell, deep dish or two shallow 8-inch shells

Cream together butter and sugar in a mixer fitted with a metal whip. Add flour and eggs and mix well. Add buttermilk and extract. Pour into unbaked pie shell and bake for 45 to 55 minutes at 350 degrees. Bring to room temperature before slicing. Can be stored covered in refrigerator for up to 2 days. Makes a thick pie. Can divide between two smaller crusts, if desired. Cooking time will vary if this is done. The Southern gourmet can serve this with a side of raspberry sauce for a delectable treat. Makes 6 to 8 servings.

OLD FASHIONED CHESS PIE

A recipe from the collection of Jane Smith, Marietta

1 1/2 cups sugar
1 tablespoon plus 1 teaspoon cornmeal
1/2 cup butter, melted
1 tablespoon vinegar
1/2 teaspoon vanilla extract
3 eggs, beaten
1 (8-inch) unbaked pastry shell

In a mixer fitted with a metal whip, cream sugar, cornmeal, butter, vinegar and vanilla. Stir in eggs well. Pour batter into crust and bake at 350 degrees for 50 to 55 minutes. Serve with Raspberry Purée, if desired. Makes 6 servings.

◆

LOW-FAT LEMON PIE

A recipe from the collection of my client and friend,
Mrs. Mary Ellen Trippe, Marietta

3 egg yolks or 1 whole egg and 1 yolk
1 (1-ounce) can fat-free condensed milk
1/2 cup fresh lemon juice
1 reduced fat graham cracker pie crust,
**   prepared and uncooked**
Nonfat whipped topping

In a mixer fitted with a metal whip or with a hand-held mixer fitted with metal whips, beat egg yolks until light. Add condensed milk and lemon juice and mix well. Pour into crust. Bake at 325 degrees for 30 minutes. Cool completely and refrigerate until ready to use for up to 1 day. Top with nonfat whipped topping and serve chilled. If meringue topping is preferred, reserve egg whites when separating yolks. Whip egg whites with 1/2 teaspoon cream of tartar and 1/4 cup sugar until soft peaks form. Remove pie after baking at 325 for 20 minutes, add meringue and return to oven for an additional 10 minutes. Cool and chill before serving. (One slice of pie contains 254 calories with 47 calories from fat.) Makes 8 servings.

Tip of the Trade:

Pastry making is an art in itself. It is one that needs to be mastered. Practice, practice, practice is the only way to learn. Take each disaster as a learning experience. The one goodness of pies is their crust, and a homemade crust will surely please the ones around you. Keep trying until you have a tender and flaky recipe that works for you. If you are lacking in patience and time, frozen sheet pastries work pretty well.

Tip of the Trade:

When placing meringue on any pie, make sure the meringue covers the filling and seals the edge of the crust (to prevent weeping and shrinking of the meringue).

Lemon desserts are wonderful after a heavy meal. Try to display desserts where guests can see them before or during the celebration. They can look forward to the last course and save room for the special homemade treat.

Tip of the Trade:

There are advantages to cooking in a 9- to 10-inch clear-glass pie plate. The crust can be seen through the glass to help judge when it is done. Crusts bake best in heavy pans because they hold heat and penetrate heat the best, which makes a crispy crust. The flaky aspect of crust is obtained by keeping the dough chilled until ready to bake.

Classic French Pastry:

2 cups all-purpose flour
3/4 teaspoon salt
7 tablespoons butter, chilled
1/4 cup shortening, chilled
6 to 8 tablespoons ice water

*Sift the flour and salt
together. Place in a mixer
fitted with a pastry handle.
Cut the butter and shortening
into the flour, mixing slowly until
it resembles a very coarse
meal. Add the water
a little at a time until a
dough starts to form.
Divide the dough in half
and roll out one crust
on a lightly floured surface
with a lightly floured
roller. Place in the pie
pan, trim and scallop.
The second portion can
be rolled out for the top crust if
needed, or sealed
tightly and refrigerated or
frozen until ready to use.
I have found it much easier
to roll it out immediately
and make a second pie or
place the second crust in a
disposable aluminum pie pan,
sealing and freezing for
another time.*

ALMOND AND BRANDY TART WITH FRESH FRUIT

1 (9-inch) pie crust
1 (7-ounce) tube almond paste
2/3 cup sugar
1/4 cup butter or margarine, room temperature
4 eggs
1/4 cup almonds
4 teaspoons brandy
1 teaspoon vanilla
1 teaspoon almond extract
3/4 pound fresh berries
2 kiwi fruits, peeled
3 tablespoons light colored jelly, heated

Place pie crust in a greased deep 8- to 9-inch pie plate or a greased 8- to 10-inch tart pan. This is beautiful making individual tarts or pies. Press crust down into desired pan and scallop top. In a food processor fitted with a metal blade, combine all ingredients, with the exception of the fresh berries, kiwis and jelly, and process until smooth. Pour into prepared uncooked crust and place in a 350-degree oven for 30 to 50 minutes, depending on size. Remove from oven and cool to room temperature. No more than 3 to 4 hours before serving, garnish entire top with berries, sliced kiwis and strawberries and brush with a light colored jelly to show glaze look, if desired. A beautiful presentation or perfect pick-up desserts. Makes 6 to 8 servings or 4 dozen mini-muffin tin desserts.

If making individual tarts, use Teflon or non-stick muffin pans or tart pans. The crust does not need to come to the top of the pan, nor does it need to be scalloped. Simply cut into size needed with a cookie cutter, press down into the greased pan and fill crust 3/4 full.

APPLE PIE WITH SPIKED WHIPPED CREAM

1 pound package commercial pie crust sheets
8 Granny Smith apples, peeled
1 cup sugar
1 teaspoon cinnamon
4 tablespoons plain all-purpose flour
1/2 cup pecans, chopped
1 tablespoon liqueur
4 tablespoons butter or margarine

1 cup heavy whipping cream
1/4 cup brown sugar
1/2 cup sour cream
2 tablespoons liqueur

Tip of the Trade:

*Any type baking apple can be used when making apple pies.
I prefer the tartness of the Granny Smith with the sweet of the pastry.
The Classic French Pastry will work well if a homemade crust is wanted.*

This pie can be made and cooked in advance and stored in refrigerator or even room temperature. It can also be reheated in oven if wanting to serve it warm. I have to admit, however, there is nothing quite like it coming right out of the oven. The aroma and taste go hand in hand.

Serve warm with vanilla ice cream, if not the spiked whipped cream.

Pie crusts should come in two sheets. Place first sheet into the bottom of a deep dish pie plate. Peel and slice Granny Smith apples from the core and place in bowl. Sprinkle apples with sugar, cinnamon, flour, pecans and liqueur. Toss gently to mix. Place in crust and dot with butter. Place second crust on top and scallop edges together. Sprinkle top of crust with a little sugar (about 2 tablespoons). Place immediately into a 350-degree oven and bake for 25 to 35 minutes. Top should be golden brown. Meanwhile, place whipping cream and brown sugar in a mixer fitted with a metal whip. Whip on medium speed until thickened. Watch carefully, if whipped too long the cream will separate. Fold in sour cream and liqueur. Use the same liqueur used in pie. Chill whipped cream until ready to serve. Pie can be reheated in oven for 5 to 10 minutes or served room temperature. Cooked pie can be stored for 3 days cooked in the refrigerator or frozen for up to a month. Cover well during storage, being careful not to crush crust. Spiked whipped cream would work well on pumpkin pies or cheesecake. Makes 6 to 8 servings.

Tip of the Trade:

*Before we lose the fine art
of our ancestors, the skills,
the techniques and traditions
of making homemade desserts,
each cook needs to gain
a deeper knowledge of the
methods of making them.
We now have mixers, food
processors, kitchen utensils
and equipment that make
cooking so much easier than
our ancestors, which most
take for granted. The time
and effort that can be devoted
to such a simple task will
be most likely more pleasurable
and less work than
anticipated. By making
just one dessert for your
family, you will be giving
a fond and sweet memory
for the ones you love.*

FRUIT COBBLER

A recipe from the collection of Todd A. Rambo

1 1/4 cups apples or peaches, peeled and chopped
3 tablespoons brown sugar
1/2 teaspoon ground cinnamon
1/2 cup butter or margarine
3/4 cup sugar
3/4 cup self-rising flour
3/4 cup milk

Set oven at 350 degrees. Set apples or peaches in a bowl and sprinkle with brown sugar and cinnamon. Toss and set aside for 10 minutes. Grease a 1-quart baking dish/serving dish and fill with butter. Place dish in a 350-degree oven for 5 to 8 minutes until very bubbly. Meanwhile, combine sugar, flour and milk together and whisk by hand or with a mixer. Remove dish with butter and immediately pour in batter. Drop fruit and its juices over batter and continue baking for 20 to 25 minutes until golden brown. Serve warm with whipped topping, ice cream or Creme Anglaise. This recipe can be doubled and multiplied very easily. Keep baking dish no more than 4 inches deep for easier cooking without burning for very large portions. Using canned fruit is optional. Makes 4 servings.

Tip of the Trade:

*When making desserts, keep
regular margarine and butter on
hand rather than any low-fat,
whipped, liquid or reduced fat
margarines. The recipe outcome
could be altered to the point of
disaster if not using real butter or
regular margarine.*

APPLE PAN DOWDY

*A recipe from the collection of my husband's grandmother,
Mrs. Marie Barnes Rambo*

6 apples, peeled and cored
1/2 cup light brown sugar
3/4 cup sugar
1/2 cup butter or margarine, room temperature
1 cup plain all-purpose flour

♦

Peel and core apples and slice paper thin. Place apples in a greased 9-inch deep dish pie plate or baking dish with brown sugar and let juices begin to develop. In a food processor fitted with a metal blade or a mixer fitted with a metal whip, combine sugar, butter and flour. This mixture will be very crumbly. With clean hands, press dough firmly on top of apples and place in a 320-degree oven for 50 to 60 minutes. Serve with ice cream or whipped topping. Very easy to make. Makes 6 to 8 servings.

Tip of the Trade:

Dessert comes from the French word desservir, which means to remove dishes from the table. This allows the room needed for the final course, dessert.

Serving Tip:

These three old Southern recipes are scoop from the bowl desserts and are best served from a buffet or family style from the table rather than by fixed plate.

BANANA PUDDING

1 recipe Boiled Custard
4 to 5 bananas, freshly yellowed
5 ounces vanilla wafers
1 pint whipping cream
1/3 cup sugar

Use a trifle dish or beautiful serving dish to prepare this old Southern dessert. This needs to be made at least 4 hours before serving and up to 24 hours. Make one recipe of boiled custard. In serving dish, place 2 to 3 cups boiled custard. Slice one to two bananas and lay on top of custard. Lay 1/4 package vanilla wafers around edges and on top. Repeat this process two to three times. Leave at least 12 vanilla wafers to garnish top of whipped cream. In a mixer fitted with a metal whip, place whipping cream and sugar. Beat on medium speed while watching. When thick but not stiff, pour on top of dessert and garnish with extra wafers. This is a dessert that is better served on a dessert buffet rather than fixed plates, unless preparing in individual dishes. Makes 12 to 16 servings.

Tip of the Trade:

There are many men who claim Banana Pudding is their favorite dessert or rather, favorite food altogether. It is a very special Southern dessert and should be served to family and friends, sprinkled with love.

Remember, bananas can be frozen, wrapped tightly, or refrigerated in their skins. Their skin will turn brown, but the banana will be unharmed. Frozen bananas slice very well.
Bananas can be ripened quickly in a brown paper bag at room temperature, if needed. Adding a ripened apple to the bag will speed up the process even more.

♦

Tip of the Trade:

For busy lives, a 6-ounce package vanilla pudding can be substituted for custard and frozen dessert topping for whipped cream.

Traditional trifle bowls are perfect, but any glass bowl can be used. One that is smaller at top than bottom works well. Trifles can be made 6 to 24 hours in advance and refrigerated until ready to serve.

Tip of the Trade:

Shortcakes have been part of the South for many generations and are simply a stacked dessert, large or small. Individual shortcakes are perfect for the ladies luncheon or a sit-down dinner and can be made by baking cake in cupcake pans. Large shortcakes are the traditional desserts for Sunday lunches or celebrations and can be made by baking cakes in layered pans.

A chocolate raspberry shortcake can be made by substituting a chocolate pound cake for cake and raspberries for strawberries in the recipe.

STRAWBERRY TRIFLE

1/2 pound cake, chocolate pound cake or angel food cake
1 recipe Boiled Custard, 2 recipes Creamy Lemon Custard, or 2 recipes Chocolate Ganache
1 pound fresh strawberries or other favorite berry
1 tablespoon fruited liqueur
1/4 cup sugar
1 to 2 recipes Whipped Cream

Place 1/3 sliced pound cake in bottom of dish. Pour 1/3 custard. Trim and slice strawberries with juices and sprinkle with liqueur and sugar. Let sit until juices form. Place 1/3 of strawberries with juices along the edge and top of custard. Place 1/3 whipped cream and continue on for two more layers, ending with whipped cream. Top with chocolate shavings and strawberry garnishes. Refrigerate until ready to serve.

STRAWBERRY SHORTCAKE

1 recipe pound cake batter, 1234 Cake
2 pounds strawberries
1/3 cup sugar
2 tablespoons fruited liqueur
1 1/2 to 2 recipes Whipped Cream

Bake the pound cake in three greased and floured 9- to 10-inch cake pans. Cool cake completely. (If rushed, buy an already made pound cake at the store or perhaps half the recipe with a frozen loaf pound cake.) Trimming of the top of the cake will be necessary to have completely flat. Discard extra trimmed pieces. Save five to eight strawberries for garnishing. Trim and slice remaining strawberries and mix gently with sugar and liqueur. Let strawberries sit for at least 15 minutes so that juices will make. Place one cake layer on platter. Ladle 1/3 of strawberries with juice on top. Place second cake layer on top. Place 1/3 strawberries on second cake layer. Place third layer on top and cover with remaining strawberries and juice. Ice the sides

♦

with whipped cream leaving the top center of cake with strawberries showing. Slice the strawberries saved for garnishing neatly and decorate the top. Leave one strawberry whole for the top center. If whipped cream is left, save for the side or for coffee. Makes 16 servings.

NAPOLEONS

1 pound package frozen filo sheets
3/4 cup butter or margarine, melted
1/2 cup white sugar
1/2 cup pecans, crushed to a meal
2 recipes Crème Anglaise, Chocolate Ganache
  or Lemon Curd
1 1/2 pound strawberries
1 tablespoon fruited liqueur
3 tablespoons sugar
1 recipe Whipped Cream

Filo pastry dries out very quickly. After opening the package, keep a towel over pastry. Unfold and pull out two sheets, laying out flat. It's best to start with two that are not flawed. Cover the rest with the towel. Brush the top of the two sheets with butter, sprinkle with 1 tablespoon sugar and 1 tablespoon pecans. Place two sheets on top. Brush with butter, sprinkle with 1 tablespoon sugar and pecans. Repeat, using all six pastry sheets. Cut the sheet into 12 rectangles. Place waxed paper or aluminum foil on a baking sheet and grease with vegetable spray. Place pastry squares on prepared pan. Repeat process again with 6 more filo sheets. Bake in a 325-degree oven for 12 to 15 minutes. The pastries should be golden brown. Check after 10 minutes of cooking, they will burn easily. When cooled, peel off paper. These can be stored in a sealed container in layers of two with waxed paper placed between layers. The pastry can be frozen for up to 1 month, if desired. To create the dessert, place one pastry on a plate, spoon 1/4 to 1/3 cup Crème Anglaise over pastry. Mix sliced strawberries with liqueur and sugar and let sit 10 minutes, and up to 4 hours. Top with a pastry, spoon strawberries over pastry, dollop with whipped cream and garnish with a strawberry. These must be assembled right before serving. Makes 12 servings.

Tip of the Trade:

A store-baked pound cake can be purchased and sliced into three sections to make Strawberry Shortcake, if desired.

Tip of the Trade:

When I make the Napoleon pastries, I always make extras due to their breakage. The filo dough will not keep well after opening the package, so I usually make as much as I can with one package. There never has been a time when the entire package can be used. Expect waste of almost one-half from drying and cracking of dough. When assembling, the broken pastries always can be used for the bottom of the dessert with the more presentable ones being placed at the top. The custard drizzles off the pastry. It does not stay perfectly together. Puddings can be substituted for custard, if desired. The ingredients can be spread among 16 to 18 desserts if more pastries are made. Additional melted butter, sugar and pecan meal might need to be added to ingredient list for pastries, and additional strawberries for assembling if making more than twelve. This is one of my best. A perfect luncheon or dinner dessert.

♦

*Zabaglione also can be made
with Marsala wine if desired.
Any nutty liqueur can be
substituted, however it
has to have some kind
of liqueur (or Marsala) in
it. Serving a Biscotti cookie,
pound or sponge cake with
the fruit and sauce is very
pleasing. Have the liqueur
available for splashing in coffee
for an extra special treat.*

ZABAGLIONE

4 eggs
3/4 cup sugar
1/2 cup pecan, hazelnut or almond liqueur
1/2 pint whipping cream, whipped

In a mixer, combine eggs and sugar. With the metal whip, beat well for 2 minutes. Place egg mixture into a double boiler or even sit mixer bowl on top of a medium saucepan filled with water to rig your own double boiler. Whisk or mix with hand-mixer until mixture is hot to touch, light and frothy. Remove from heat and continue mixing. Cool and fold in whipped cream. If storing before serving, cool custard to room temperature, refrigerate covered for up to 2 days and fold in whipping cream just before serving. Serve this Italian custard chilled with fresh fruit. Makes 8 to 12 servings.

*Crème Anglaise is a rich and
thicker custard than the Boiled
Custard on the following page. It
is commonly used in French
dessert cooking. Traditionally, it
is put through a fine sieve to make
a smooth and delicate sauce,
however, I find nothing wrong
with not using a sieve. If custard
is not desired smoothness, blend
with a hand blender.*

CRÈME ANGLAISE

1 1/2 cups half and half or cream
4 egg yolks
1/4 cup sugar
1 teaspoon vanilla

In a medium saucepan, place half and half. Set over medium heat and warm but do not boil. Combine egg yolks and sugar. When half and half is steamy and warm to the touch, add egg and whisk constantly at this point. Custard will thicken to the eye and to the touch. Frothy top will disappear and a metal spoon will coat well when dipped. Remove from heat as soon as you feel it is thickened. Plunging bottom of pot into icy cold sink water will stop cooking immediately. Watch for curdling and burning while cooking. Vanilla can be added as it is removed from heat. A rich sauce to be served with fruits, cobblers, Liqueured Chocolate Mousse, Napoleons, cakes or as a dessert sauce.

♦

BOILED CUSTARD

6 cups whole milk
7 eggs
2 tablespoons plain all-purpose flour
1/2 cup sugar
2 teaspoons vanilla extract

Place milk in a large pot over medium heat and heat until steam rises and warm to the touch. Beat together eggs, flour and sugar. Placing in a mixer with a metal whip is preferable. Fill kitchen sink with 3-inches cold water and ice cubes. When milk is warm, add egg mixture. Lower heat a little and stir and whisk constantly at this point. You will notice frothy topping. The disappearing of this frothy topping, a slight notice of thickening and the thin coating noticed on the dipping of a clean metal spoon, a temperature of 170 degrees, are all signs to remove from heat. If you think it's thickened, then it is. Overcooking can lead to curdling, and not stirring constantly can lead to burning. When you feel it is thickened, remove from heat and place in iced sink water. Add vanilla. Custard always can be reheated to master thickness if you remove it too soon. It cannot be fixed when curdling has taken place. Sometimes, the bottom of the pot will thicken and curdle slightly. Use a hand blender to smooth out or pour through a sieve. Refrigeration will continue thickening your custard. Cover and refrigerate for up to 3 days. Custard can be used on cakes, in trifles, in homemade ice cream and puddings, or as sauce or by itself. It is a wonderful Southern dessert. Do not be scared to try at least twice, once for learning and another for mastering. Makes approximately 2 quarts.

Tip of the Trade:

Custard is one of the dishes a cook must learn from trial and error. It is done by eye, taste and smell. If you cook it too much, it's too thick, and too little makes it too thin. Only a cook willing to try knows the right consistency. It is a delicious combination of true, basic ingredients: milk, eggs, sugar and vanilla. In some recipes, you will find whole eggs, and in others, just the yolks. Either way is delicious. The milk and vanilla quantities will change from cook to cook, but the mastered outcome is a treat of the South.

Serving Tip:

It would not be uncommon to show up at a Southern neighbor's door, perhaps a new, sick or mourning neighbor, with a Mason jar full of boiled custard.

*The variety of sauces given on
these few pages can help you host
a Build-Your-Own-Sundae party
for a gathering. Different sauces
can be offered with large
scoops of vanilla ice cream.
The ice cream can be scooped
and placed in individual
serving containers and placed in
the freezer before guests arrive
for easy serving.
Almond Orange
Caramel Sauce, Hot Fudge
Sauce, Praline Pecan Sauce,
and Lots of Whipped Cream
or Topping.
Additionally, individual bowls
filled with candies, nuts and
toppings can be offered. Place
berries in compotes and sprinkle
with sugar or a little
liqueur. Serve pitchers of
lemonade and bottled soft drinks or
assorted coffees.
It is a wonderful way to
gather friends, children
or families on a
budget and busy schedule.*

LEMON CURD

1/2 cup butter or margarine
2 lemons
5 egg yolks
3/4 cup sugar

In a medium saucepan, place butter over low heat and melt. Measure out lemon juice and zest from 2 lemons to equal 1/3 cup. Add to butter with eggs and sugar. Stir constantly with a whisk over low to medium low heat until thickened. Remove from heat and cool to room temperature before storing covered in refrigerator. Serve with Napoleon Pastries, Pound Cake or with fresh fruit. Makes 1 1/2 to 2 cups.

CREAMY LEMON CUSTARD

1/2 cup butter or margarine
1/3 cup lemon juice
4 egg yolks
3/4 cup sugar
1 tablespoon lemon rind, grated
1 1/4 cups whipping cream

In a medium saucepan, melt butter over low heat. Add lemon juice, egg yolks, sugar and rind and cook over medium heat, stirring with a whisk constantly. When thickened, remove from heat and add whipping cream. Cool to room temperature before storing covered in refrigerator. Serve with pound cake or angel food cake and fresh berries. For an extra light topping, whip the whipped cream before folding into cooled curd. Makes 2 1/2 cups.

MOCHA FUDGE SAUCE

2 cups sugar
4 tablespoons unsweetened powdered cocoa
1 cup whipping cream
5 tablespoons corn syrup
2 tablespoons butter
1/4 cup instant-coffee granules

In a medium saucepan, combine all ingredients over medium low heat and bring to a soft boil. Stir occasionally. Sauce needs only to be smooth and sugar and coffee granules need to be dissolved. Serve warm or room temperature. Can be stored in refrigerator for up to 1 week before serving. Reheating can be done in microwave or on stove. Serve with cake or ice cream. Makes 1 3/4 cup.

Old Fashioned Floats:

Fill a long float glass or ice cream glass with 1 to 2 scoops of vanilla ice cream. Pour a regular soft drink to top. Garnish with whipped topping and serve with a cherry on top with a straw and long spoon.

One quart of ice cream will serve six to eight guests a single individual serving.

PRALINE PECAN SAUCE

1 cup pecan halves, toasted
1/3 cup light corn syrup
1/3 cup dark corn syrup or light corn syrup
3 tablespoons butter or margarine
1/4 teaspoon vanilla extract

In a large skillet, combine the pecan halves and corn syrups over high heat until it reaches a soft boil. Remove from heat and add butter and vanilla. Cool to room temperature before storing covered in refrigerator for up to 5 days. Can be reheated in microwave or on stove top. Serve with vanilla ice cream, cheesecake or pound cake as an ending to a spicy or summer menu. Makes 2 cups.

Tip of the Trade:

Pecans are the traditional nut for pralines, but any nut can be used. Try toasted hazlenuts or almonds.

GANACHE AND STRAWBERRY CREPES

1 recipe Basic Crêpes
1 recipe Chocolate Ganache
1 pound strawberries or
raspberries
Shaved chocolate

Place chocolate ganache in middle
portion lengthwise in crêpe and
roll up. Trim and slice berries and
place in a bowl with 2 tablespoons
of sugar for 5 to 10 minutes or up
to 1 hour. Pour strawberries over
top middle of crêpe and garnish
with shaved chocolate.
Makes 6 to 8 crêpes.

Tip of the Trade:

Almond Caramel Sauce or one of
the sauces on page 225, are
wonderful sauces to share with
friends as a gift from your kitchen.
Try canning one of them for best
storage results. Attach the recipe
on the jar with ribbon tied around
the rim. Adding a basket of ice
cream servers, spoons, straws,
napkins or dishes, would only add
a special touch. Perhaps give with
a pound cake for birthday wishes or
the holidays. It will bring smiles
to your loved ones. A true
celebration of giving.

CHOCOLATE GANACHE

1 pint heavy whipping cream
3 tablespoons unsweetened powdered cocoa
1/4 cup confectioners powdered sugar

In a mixer fitted with a metal whip, combine all ingredients. Start mixer out slowly to prevent unnecessary splattering. As Ganache starts to thicken, adjust to higher speed as desired and remove when thickened to soft peaks. Cream will separate, keep an eye on mixer so not to overbeat cream. Serve as a trifle filling, with fresh berries, with angel food cake or meringues. Use in Ganache and Strawberry Crêpes or Napoleons. Makes 3 cups.

ALMOND CARAMEL SAUCE

2 cups brown sugar
1/2 cup orange juice concentrate
1/2 cup whipping cream
4 tablespoons butter or margarine
1 teaspoon orange peel, grated
1 teaspoon lemon peel, grated
1/2 teaspoon almond extract
1 cup sour cream
1/2 cup almonds, toasted

In a medium saucepan, combine brown sugar, orange juice concentrate, whipping cream, butter, orange and lemon peels and heat over medium heat to a soft simmer for 6 to 8 minutes. Remove from heat and add sour cream. Almonds can be sprinkled in the sauce or on top of sauce. Can be served warm or room temperature. Store in refrigerator covered for up to 5 days and reheat in microwave or stove for desired warmness. The brown sugar gives the sauce the caramel color without having to rely on excellent cooking skills. Makes 1/2 quart.

RASPBERRY PURÉE

2 (10-ounce) cartons frozen raspberry in syrup
1/8 cup fruited or berry liqueur

In a food processor fitted with a metal blade, place raspberries and syrup and process until smooth. Pour raspberry through a sieve using a spoon to scrape along sides to help sauce through holes. Liqueur can be used as a thinner, or rinse in sieve to make sure no sauce is wasted. Scrape bottom of sieve and store sauce in freezer for up to 1 month or refrigerator for up to 5 days. Frozen strawberries in syrup or blackberries in syrup can be made the same way. Powdered sugar makes a perfect sweetener, if needed. Frozen rhubarb or peaches can be made the same way, but sieve is not needed with fruits that do not contain seeds. A sauce to be served with most any dessert. Great with chocolate or lemon desserts. Makes 2/3 cup.

WHIPPED CREAM

1 pint heavy whipping cream
1/3 cup sugar

In a mixer fitted with a metal whip or with a hand blender, combine heavy whipping cream and sugar. Beat on low speed at first to avoid unnecessary splattering. Gradually move speed higher. As whipped cream starts to thicken, keep a close eye to avoid overbeating and separating cream. Store cream covered in refrigerator for up to 3 days. Use on all desserts or as a coffee or hot chocolate topper.

Tip of the Trade:

Raspberry Purée is a catering recipe I use over and over in my business. It is quite easy if a food processor and sieve are available in your kitchen inventory. The color served or displayed with desserts is fabulous.

Tip of the Trade:

One pint of whipping cream will daintily dollop 18 to 24 desserts. It will heavily cover 12 to 18 desserts.

Whipped Cream will enhance any dessert. It only takes a few minutes to whip and stores very well. So many people are afraid to make such an easy side dish.

If serving on coffee, just dollop whipped cream and sprinkle the top with a little ground cinnamon or chocolate. Guests will go crazy over this special touch. Great at cocktail buffets, passing to guests or served on the side with cream and sugar at dinner parties. Perfect with hot chocolate or hot fruit cider. Best served in mugs.

ACKNOWLEDGEMENTS

♦ I have had the pleasure of working with many wonderful people who have assisted me with my book. With the encouragement of these family and friends, I have been able to pursue my dream.

♦ A sincere note of thanks to my family. My parents, Ross and Mimi Howard, and in-laws, Ed and Sue Rambo. To my husband, Sam, my daughters and to my extended family for their support. A special thank you to my teaching hands, Margaret Carpenter, Mary Jo Carpenter and the late Mary Howard and Lily Mae Carpenter. To my family members who trusted me with their treasured recipes, Frances Howard, Trisha Howard, Betsy Rambo, Todd Rambo and a special thank you to Margaret and Meredith Rambo for sharing Grandmother Rambo's recipes with me.

♦ My deepest gratitude to Nancy Edwards for your advice and time and to Maryanne Elliott, my lifelong friend, for your countless hours and expertise.

♦ My appreciation to Richard Anderson at Starr Toof for your professional manner, years of patience and advisement.

♦ Thank you Otis Brumby, Martha Giddens, Sam Hensley, Pouncey Graphic Arts, D & S Litho, Ross Reynolds and Neely Young for your suggestions.

♦ A special thank you to my clients and friends who graciously shared their recipes, time and talents: Jimmy Alexander, Wendy Childs, Melda Collins, Nancy Denton, Spud Dobbs, Angela DuPre, Patsy Dupree, Carolyn Doxey, Elizabeth Elrod, Loretta Gilmer, Joan Greene, Melanie Henrickson, Robin Ivey, Madeline Knox, Eleanor Knox, Dianne Matthews, Colleen Moore, Ginny Northcutt, Linda McDill, Jenny Nucholls, Laurie Phillips, Anne and Hall Rigdon, Jane Smith, Mary Ellen Trippe, Shelby Weeks, Melissa Worley and Betsy Young.

♦ My appreciation to my friend, Anne Rigdon, for your words of inspiration and for the outstanding watercolor illustrations painted for this book. A native of Cobb County, Anne studies art and is being discovered in her community with her portraits and still-life paintings, while staying devoted to her husband and three children.

♦ Thank you Frank Ryan, the wine specialist who suggested wines for each main course menu. Frank is a fine wine manager and a lifelong enthusiast of food and wine. He lives with his wife, Melinda and daughter, Molly.

♦ To my wonderful friend, Sandra Stephens, I can't thank you enough for making me laugh and cry at the same time when I read your Foreword. Sandra, a former newspaper columnist for the Marietta Daily Journal, lives in Cobb County with her husband and enjoys her time with their two children.

♦ Warmest thanks to my college friend Laurie, who designed the cover. Laurie is taking time off from her graphic design career to enjoy staying home with her two children and husband. She takes on freelance work at her Florida home.

♦ My appreciation to Bill Davis of William R. Davis Photography. Bill is receiving wonderful recognition with his portraits of children and individuals around the Atlanta area.

♦ Special thanks to my friend Kaye Cagle of Cagle Consulting/Marketing and Writing communications. Her back cover copy and suggestions were valuable contributions to this project.

♦ I can't thank Martha Collins, Marietta Daily Journal, and Scott Penley, First United Methodist Church enough for all the red ink marks. They took on editing and proofing the book in their free time.

MEASUREMENTS AND CONVERSIONS

TABLE OF SIMPLIFIED MEASURES

Dash equals less than 1/8 teaspoon (t.)
1 cup equals 1/2 pint (pt.)
2 cups equal 1 pint (pt.)
2 pints (4 cups) equal 1 quart (qt.)
4 liquid quarts equal one gallon (gl.)
8 solid quarts equal one peck (pk.)
4 pecks equal 1 bushel (bu.)
16 ounces (oz.) equal 1 pound (lb.)
4 tablespoons equal 1/4 cup (c.)

5 1/3 tablespoons equal 1/3 cup
8 tablespoons equal 1/2 cup
10 2/3 tablespoons equal 2/3 cup
12 tablespoons equal 3/4 cup
14 tablespoons equal 7/8 cup
16 tablespoons equal 1 cup
3 teaspoons equal 1 tablespoon (T.)
16 tablespoons equal 1 cup

WEIGHTS AND MEASURES

3 teaspoons equal 1 tablespoon
4 tablespoons equal 1/4 cup
16 tablespoons equal 1 cup
1/2 cup equal 1 gill
4 gills equal 1 pint
2 cups equal 1 pint

4 cups equal 1 quart
2 pints equal 1 quart
4 quarts equal 1 gallon
8 quarts equal 1 peck
4 pecks equal 1 bushel
16 ounces equal 1 pound

METRIC CONVERSION

1 teaspoon equals 5 c.c.
1 tablespoon equals 15 c.c.
1 ounce equals 30 milliliters
1 cup equals 1/4 liter, approximately
1 quart equals about 1 liter

SUBSTITUTIONS

1 cup sour milk or buttermilk is equal to 1 cup milk with 1 tablespoon vinegar or lemon juice added and stirred.

1 cup sweet milk is equal to 1 cup sour milk or buttermilk with 1/2 teaspoon baking soda added and stirred.

1 cup whole milk is equal to 1/2 cup canned evaporated milk with 1/2 cup water added.

1 cup cake flour can be substituted with 2 tablespoons flour taken from 1 cup plain all-purpose flour adding 2 tablespoons cream of tartar or 2 tablespoons cornstarch.

1 cup self-rising flour can be made by 1 cup plain all-purpose flour with 1/2 teaspoon salt and 1/2 tablespoon baking powder added.

1 teaspoon baking powder can be made by 1/4 teaspoon baking soda plus 1/2 teaspoon cream of tartar.

1 1/4 cup brown sugar is equal to 1 cup regular granulated sugar.

1 cup honey can be substituted for 1 cup sugar with 1/4 cup juice added.

1 ounce unsweetened chocolate or 1 square unsweetened chocolate can be substituted with 3 tablespoons unsweetened powder cocoa with 1 tablespoon oil or 1 tablespoon melted butter or margarine added.

HEALTHY SUBSTITUTIONS

Use skim or 1% milk in substitution of whole or 2% milk.

Use chilled evaporated skim milk, whipped, in place of whipping cream.

Using cheeses equal or less than 5 grams of fat per ounce.

Use 2 egg whites or 1/4 cup egg substitute in place of 1 egg.

Use 1/2 cup whole wheat and 1/2 cup white flour to equal 1 cup white flour.

Use 2/3 cup white flour and 1/3 cup oat bran in place of 1 cup white flour.

Reduce salt by one half and add at the end of cooking, right before serving or eliminate completely.

Use light vegetable oil or oil low in saturated fat when using oil.

Use pasta not made with egg yolks.

Use whole wheat pastas, grains and rice when preparing dishes.

Always remove all skin when preparing poultry, and use white meat portions only.

Use only ground white meat when purchasing ground turkey or chicken.

Drain cooked ground meats completely, and even rinse before using in dishes.

Trim all fat off of red meats or porks before cooking and select only lean meats when purchasing.

BIBLIOGRAPHY

Southern Food, At Home, on the Road, in History, John Egerton, Borzoi Book, Alfred A. Knopf, Inc, 1987.

LaRousse Gastronomique, The Encyclopedia of Food, Wine and Cookery, Proper Montagne, Crown Publishers, Inc., New York, NY, 1961.

Ladies Home Journal Cookbook, Edited by Carol Truax, Doubleday and Company, Inc., Garden City, New York , Curtis Publishing Company, 1960.

The Secrets of the Seed, Vegetables, Fruits and Nuts, Barbara Friedlander, Grosset and Dunlap Publishers, New York, 1974.

The Good Housekeeping Cook Book, Rinehart and Company, Inc., New York, Toronto, 1942.

The Heritage of Southern Cooking, Camille Glenn, Workman Publishing Company, Inc., New York, 1986.

Harrowsmith's Sourcebook for Cooks, Kitchen Wisdon, Pamela Cross, Camden House Publishing, Telemedia Publishing, Inc., 1991.

Entertaining, Martha Stewart, Clarkson N. Potter, Inc., New York, Crown Publishers, 1982.

The Secret Life of Food, A Feast of Food and Drink History, Folklore and Fact, Martin Elkort, Jeremy P. Tarcher, Los Angeles, 1991.

Southern Living, The Canning and Preserving Cookbook, Oxmoor House Inc., 1972.

Emily Posts Etiquette, 15th edition, Elizabeth L. Post, Harper and Collins Books, New York, 1992.

Miss Manners, Guide for the Turn of the Millennium, Judith Martin, Pharos Books, Scripps Howard Company, New York, 1989.

The First Hundred Years, A Short History of Cobb County, In Georgia, Sarah Blackwell Gober Temple, Walter W. Brown Publishing Company, Atlanta, 1935 and 1962.

Cobb County, At the Heart of Change, Longstreet Press, Atlanta, Georgia, (In cooperation with Cobb Chamber of Commerce), 1991.

Rumford Common Sense Cook Book, Lily Haxworth Wallace, , Department of Home Economics of Rumford Company, Rumford, RI.

Southern Cooking, S.R. Dull, Grosset and Dunlap Publishers, New York, 1928.

Time Began In A Garden, Emilie Barnes, Harvest House Publishers, Eugene, Oregon, 1995.

The Food Lover's Tiptionary, Sharon Tyler Herbst, William Morrow and Company, New York, 1994.

Cook and Love It, A Collection of Favorite Recipes and Entertaining Ideas, The Mother's Club, The Lovett School 1976, Stein Printing Company, Atlanta, Georgia

INDEX

V